Cormac McCarthy

Manchester University Press

CONTEMPORARY AMERICAN AND CANADIAN WRITERS

Series editors
Nahem Yousaf and Sharon Monteith

Also available

Crossing borders and queering citizenship: Civic reading practice in contemporary American and Canadian writing ZALFA FEGHALI

The quiet contemporary American novel RACHEL SYKES

Sara Paretsky: Detective fiction as trauma literature CYNTHIA S. HAMILTON

Making home: Orphanhood, kinship, and cultural memory in contemporary American novels MARIA HOLMGREN TROY, ELIZABETH KELLA, HELENA WAHLSTROM

Thomas Pynchon SIMON MALPAS AND ANDREW TAYLOR

Jonathan Lethem JAMES PEACOCK

Mark Z Danielewski EDITED BY JOE BRAY AND ALISON GIBBONS

Louise Erdrich DAVID STIRRUP

Passing into the present: contemporary American fiction of racial and gender passing SINÉAD MOYNIHAN

Paul Auster MARK BROWN

Douglas Coupland ANDREW TATE

Philip Roth DAVID BRAUNER

Cormac McCarthy

A complexity theory of literature

Lydia R. Cooper

MANCHESTER UNIVERSITY PRESS

Copyright © Lydia R. Cooper 2021

The right of Lydia R. Cooper to be identified as the author of this work has been asserted by them in accordance with the Copyright, Designs and Patents Act 1988.

Published by Manchester University Press
Oxford Road, Manchester M13 9PL
www.manchesteruniversitypress.co.uk

British Library Cataloguing-in-Publication Data is available

ISBN 978 1 5261 4858 2 hardback
ISBN 978 1 5261 7205 1 paperback

First published by Manchester University Press in hardback 2021

This edition published 2023

The publisher has no responsibility for the persistence or accuracy of URLs for any external or third-party internet websites referred to in this book, and does not guarantee that any content on such websites is, or will remain, accurate or appropriate.

Typeset by Servis Filmsetting Ltd, Stockport, Cheshire

Contents

Series editors' foreword   vi
Acknowledgments   viii
List of abbreviations   xi

Introduction   1
1 Cars, trucks, and horses: man in the age of the machine   33
2 War and the wanderer: the rise of empire in *Blood
   Meridian*   69
3 Professionals: late capitalism and the illegal drug trade in
   No Country for Old Men and *The Counselor*   100
4 Prophets: imagining the end of the Anthropocene in *The
   Road*   132
5 Pilgrims: nomadism and the making and unmaking of the
   world in the Border Trilogy   158
6 Death and the poet: *Suttree* and art that sustains   190
Epilogue   213

Bibliography   217
Index   231

Series editors' foreword

This innovative series reflects the breadth and diversity of writing over the last thirty years, and provides critical evaluations of established, emerging and critically neglected writers – mixing the canonical with the unexpected. It explores notions of the contemporary and analyses current and developing modes of representation with a focus on individual writers and their work. The series seeks to reflect both the growing body of academic research in the field, and the increasing prevalence of contemporary American and Canadian fiction on programmes of study in institutions of higher education around the world. Central to the series is a concern that each book should argue a stimulating thesis, rather than provide an introductory survey, and that each contemporary writer will be examined across the trajectory of their literary production. A variety of critical tools and literary and interdisciplinary approaches are encouraged to illuminate the ways in which a particular writer contributes to, and helps readers rethink, the North American literary and cultural landscape in a global context.

Central to debates about the field of contemporary fiction is its role in interrogating ideas of national exceptionalism and transnationalism. This series matches the multivocality of contemporary writing with wide-ranging and detailed analysis. Contributors examine the drama of the nation from the perspectives of writers who are members of established and new immigrant groups, writers who consider themselves on the nation's margins as well as those who chronicle middle America. National labels are the subject of vociferous debate and including American and Canadian writers in the same series is not to flatten the differences between them but to acknowledge that literary traditions and tensions are cross-cultural and that North American writers often explore and expose precisely these tensions. The series recognises that situating a writer in a cultural context involves a multiplicity of influences, social and geo-political, artistic and theoretical, and that contemporary fiction defies easy categorisation. For example, it examines writers who invigorate the genres in which they have made their mark alongside writers whose aesthetic goal is to subvert the idea of genre altogether. The challenge of defining the roles of writers and assessing their reception by reading communities is central to the aims of the series.

Overall, *Contemporary American and Canadian Writers* aims to begin to represent something of the diversity of contemporary writing and seeks to engage students and scholars in stimulating debates about the contemporary and about fiction.

Nahem Yousaf
Sharon Monteith

Acknowledgments

This book's making is a story that fills me with gratitude beyond measure. It would not have been possible without the wisdom, advice, and collegiality of Katie Salzmann, lead archivist for the Wittliff Collections, and the generosity of the William J. Hill Visiting Researcher Travel Grant, which provided invaluable support during my time researching in the Cormac McCarthy Papers and the Woolmer Collection of Cormac McCarthy in the Southwestern Writers Collection. During my time at the Wittliff Collections in the Alkek Library, Sherri Turner-Herrmann was an excellent help and support and an all-around pleasure to spend my days with. (She has the best recipes, too.)

Dianne C. Luce's incredible body of scholarship on McCarthy has enriched my thinking and understanding since I first discovered McCarthy. But in the making of this book, particularly, Dianne offered advice, support, and insight with such generosity of spirit that I find myself struggling to articulate my gratitude. Dianne was gracious in answering my many (many!) questions and she shared her experience of the different collections of letters, McCarthy's royalty schedules, and her own personal insights, warnings, and recommendations along the bumpy path this book took. I aspire to be half the researcher, scholar, mentor, and human that Dianne is. (Mistakes in any of these categories, it goes without saying, are mine alone.)

In terms of generosity, what can I say about Steven Frye and Stacey Peebles? Both of them were gracious beyond all reckoning; both have offered so much of their time and help to me over the years. I would not have been able to write this book without them—and indeed, I would not have attained tenure and promotion without them. (If they wanted any additional firstborn offspring, I'd have to give them some, though I think we're all happier if I settle for thanking them in my acknowledgments, insufficient as that is.) Stacey and Steve are the very embodiment of collegiality, and I hope to model their many kindnesses. Lee Clark Mitchell's research and his gracious support of this project in its many stages are also gifts for which I will forever be grateful. In the world of scholars who know and love McCarthy, one man must always and forever be thanked: Rick Wallach introduced me to McCarthy scholarship and to the weird and wonderful fellowship of Cormackians. Thank you, Rick, from the bottom of my heart.

At Creighton University, Bridget Keegan, dean of the College of Arts and Sciences, Tracy Leavelle, then-associate dean of the College of Arts and Sciences and now inaugural director of the Kingfisher Institute, and Tom Murray, then university provost, granted me a generous sabbatical in which I was able to do the bulk of the research for this book. Despite my intention to perfect my day drinking during sabbatical, I found the joys of living hermit-like in archives too profound to be resisted and ended up being excessively productive.

In addition to institution support, my Creighton community is peerless. Barb Bittner offered her keen insight and unfailing good humor when I pestered her for help editing grant proposals, book chapters, and everything in between. She is a saint and a hero. My colleagues Matthew Reznicek and Jeffrey Hause helped this book's ideas take flight through countless conversations. They are the best and most brilliant of colleagues and dearest of friends, and I am so fortunate to know them. My work-in-progress group of superstar colleagues, Matthew Reznicek, Adam Sundberg, Surbhi Malik, and Brooke Kowalke, saved my sanity and strengthened my work with their keen insights.

Finally, I want to thank Sharon Monteith and Nahem Yousaf for their incredible work as series editors. Paul Clarke was everything a person could hope for in working with an editor. I would also like to thank Fiona Little for her meticulous work with me during the copy-editing stage. Any remaining mistakes are my own, of course.

Material from Chapter 1 first appeared in 'Barracuda: Cars and Trucks in Cormac McCarthy's Fiction,' published in *Southwestern American Literature*, vol. 41, iss. 2 (Spring 2016), 7–18. Part of Chapter 3 appeared in 'Diamonds, Drugs, and the Digital Age: Global Capitalism in Cormac McCarthy's *The Counselor*,' published in *Critique: Studies in Contemporary Fiction*, vol. 38, iss. 2 (January 2018), 1–14. Material from Chapter 4 first appeared in 'Eating at the Empire Table: Cormac McCarthy's *The Road* and the Anglo-Irish Gothic,' published in *Modern Fiction Studies*, vol. 63, iss. 3 (September 2017), 547–570.

Abbreviations

APH	*All the Pretty Horses*
BM	*Blood Meridian*
Co	*The Counselor*
COP	*Cities of the Plain*
Cr	*The Crossing*
KJV	King James Version of the Bible
NCOM	*No Country for Old Men*
S	*Suttree*
TGS	*The Gardener's Son*
TOK	*The Orchard Keeper*
TR	*The Road*
TS	*The Stonemason: A Play in Five Acts*
TSL	*The Sunset Limited: A Novel in Dramatic Form*

Introduction

Chaos was the set of ideas persuading all these scientists that they were members of a shared enterprise. Physicist or biologist or mathematician, they believed that simple, deterministic systems could breed complexity; that systems too complex for traditional mathematics could yet obey simple laws; and that, whatever their particular field, their task was to understand complexity itself.

(James Gleick, *Chaos: Making a New Science*)

I know that one life can change all life. The smallest warp in the fabric can tilt all creation to run anew. Choice is everywhere and destiny is only a word we give to history.

(Cormac McCarthy, *Whales and Men*)[1]

In a 2007 article for the *Guardian*, George Monbiot says, 'A few weeks ago I read what I believe is the most important environmental book ever written.' He did not mean that he had read Rachel Carson's *Silent Spring* for the twenty-first century. Instead, Monbiot had read a novel—Cormac McCarthy's 2006 Pulitzer Prize-winning *The Road*. For Monbiot, the crisis facing the planet is not just the exigencies of climate change, but rather the incapacity of human imaginations to grapple effectively with so large and so potentially dire a catastrophe. 'Last week we learned that climate change could eliminate half the world's species,' Monbiot writes. 'But everyone is watching and waiting for everyone else to move.'[2] And public media, rather than organizing or energizing collective imaginations toward solutions, are 'hopelessly biased towards the consumer economy and against the biosphere.' Against such a bulwark of human apathy, self-interest, and the pressures of a fossil fuel-driven global economy, McCarthy's post-apocalyptic novel confronts its readers with a vivid and prophetic world in which humanity has reached its event horizon. In the face of immanent annihilation, the collapse of a living planet, the novel asks its audience to examine not just the human cost of a world driven by consumption but the cost to the nonhuman world, and to our capacity for self-knowledge, for ethical choice, and for hope.

The Road is not unique among McCarthy's novels, screenplays, and dramas in its representation of the causes and consequences of geopolitical, economic, and environmental systems. McCarthy's works as a whole demonstrate how the complex structural and semiotic interplay of literary texts is uniquely capable of making chaotic and complex systems imaginable. Scholars and fans alike have long noted McCarthy's penchant for scientific inquiry as well as his predilection for posing complex philosophical problems in narrative form. In this book, I offer the first sustained analysis of McCarthy's literary engagement with complex systems, focusing on McCarthy's depiction of the role of economics and art on social inequality and ecodisaster—crises that call on all of us to imagine with clarity and force not only the causes and consequences of global economic and environmental policy, but also alternatives to systems that too often seem inevitable.

Before moving further into the study of complexity and literature, I want to examine McCarthy's authorial persona and make the argument for why his works offer such a compelling case study for complexity theory as depicted in and applied to the study of literary texts. The public's image of McCarthy is heavily influenced by a now-famous interview that appeared in the *New York Times* in 1992 when Richard B. Woodward tracked down a wildly talented novelist who, until that year, had not sold more than 4,000 copies of a single published book.[3] McCarthy had won the William Faulkner prize for his first novel, a Rockefeller grant, an American Academy of Arts and Letters Travel fellowship, two Guggenheim Fellowships, a Lyndhurst Foundation grant, and a MacArthur Fellowship, though. Until 1992 McCarthy's career path had been supported almost entirely by grants, fellowships, and the recognition of certain literati.[4]

In addition to crafting a career characterized by literary and critical recognition rather than broad-based popularity, McCarthy had cultivated an image of himself as an iconoclast, a wandering bard more at home with car mechanics than with storytellers, more comfortable with rattlesnakes than with publicity shoots. He spent the early decades of his career in relatively impoverished migration from Knoxville to Chicago, from New Orleans to Asheville, back to Knoxville, and then, by various stages, to Tucson, El Paso, and Santa Fe. By 1992 he had been divorced twice, and Woodward figures that poverty played a role in both. McCarthy, for his part, seemed stoical about his impecunious path. 'Three moves is as good as a fire,' Woodward recalls him saying 'in praise of homelessness.'[5] This is not to say that McCarthy subscribes to a romanticized image of a 'starving artist.' His correspondence with editors and agents shows a persistent, soberminded interest in increasing book sales, selling manuscripts and scripts, and making a living as an author.[6] However, McCarthy never intended to become a *commercial* artist, a distinction that he seemed to hold onto even after the dizzyingly swift change in fortune that struck with the publication of the *New York Times* bestseller and National Book Award winning *All the Pretty Horses* in 1992.

In 1999, after McCarthy's eighth novel, *Cities of the Plain*, was published, the literary critic Steven Shaviro asserted that McCarthy is 'our greatest living author.'[7] He would not be the only one to reckon so. By 2007 McCarthy leaped to the forefront of American literary luminaries, becoming one of the best-known living authors and bagging such high publicity honors as a Pulitzer, an Oscar-winning film version of a novel, and an interview with Oprah Winfrey. No longer a little-known author with a cult-like following, by the time of his interview with Winfrey, McCarthy could boast of multiple *New York Times* bestsellers along with a coveted Oprah's Book Club selection. Toward the end of their televised interview, Winfrey questions McCarthy about this fame and popularity. 'Do you care if now millions of people are reading your books,' she asks him, 'versus when there were only a few thousand reading your books?' McCarthy laughs softly, shrugging off the question. 'I really don't,' he says. 'I mean, you would like for people who'll appreciate the book to read it,' but adds, 'It's okay; there's nothing wrong with it.'[8]

McCarthy comes across in that sit-down interview recorded at the Sante Fe Institute as tentative, perhaps shy. He admits to Winfrey that such a public, filmed interview is 'a first' for him, but as Stacey Peebles points out, this interview offers a different perspective on the reclusive image of the author that Woodward painted a decade and a half earlier.[9] McCarthy's reluctance to participate in publicity spectacles that are expected to create 'buzz' may reflect more than a Salinger-esque caricature of disdain for publicity and fandom. After all, as he told Winfrey, there is nothing *wrong* with fame. Instead, it is a 'head problem' that McCarthy identifies as the root of his reluctance to participate in such media marketing strategies. 'I don't think it's good for your head,' he tells Winfrey, and suggests, slyly, that she 'work [her] side of the street,' as he works his.[10]

McCarthy suggests here that the methodological requirements of skilled artistic construction require a certain exclusivity of function. He indicates that he perceives artistic creation, like any career (talk show host? automobile mechanic?), to be a vocation requiring specialist focus. For McCarthy, publicity is not *writing*. And the mental energy required to accomplish such high-visibility marketing strategies may damage his capacity to do well in his chosen career. He comes across as an author open to the economic possibilities of literary stardom but uncomfortable with what he considers the dissipation of his energy into non-specialist fields, such as online and social media marketing campaigns. For an author born in 1933, one could write off this reluctance as a factor of age. But his resistance to public-facing marketing strategies has remained consistent throughout his career.

A letter that McCarthy sent to the Lyndhurst Foundation's Deaderick (Rick) Montague, date-stamped October 6, 1986, offers a glimpse into his refusal to participate in public-facing commercial events. Montague had invited McCarthy to speak on a panel at the Southern Literary Conference in Chattanooga, a request posed on behalf of the foundation's committee members. McCarthy's response begins, 'You've got to get me out of this. I feel bad already.' In an uncharacteristically emotive rush, McCarthy says he 'would do anything in or out of reason' to support the foundation, but that he *cannot* present on a panel: 'I simply cant [sic],' he says. 'I've been trying to write this letter for three days. I dont think I've ever been able to make myself understand about this but I dont *want* to be a public figure.' His interest in pursuing a career as a literary author extends to a desire to produce literary texts and to make a living from doing so, but it does not extend to certain characteristics of being a commercial or public figure that he finds so off-putting, including speaking in public about his own work.[11]

If the work of becoming a 'public figure' is anathema to McCarthy's vocational commitment to writing, so too are other forms of labor. In her interview with McCarthy, Winfrey pushes him to answer why, in his many lean years, he refused to seek a well-paying gig as anything but a writer, and his answer is just as clear-minded, just as obdurate. Winfrey suggests that he has 'worked at not working' ('not working' as in a nine-to five career job of some sort). McCarthy replies, 'Absolutely. It's the number one priority.' Here we begin to see McCarthy's philosophy of work emerging. This conception of meticulous, artistic creation as antithetical to modern-day labor pervades his corpus, creating a recurring critique of a culture that has created what Hannah Arendt calls *Animal laborans*, those who labor to survive, paycheck to paycheck, without the sense of *meaningful* contribution to their world. This perspective undergirds not only McCarthy's own early decades of navigating cheap motels and a gig economy of small advances and literary grants, but also the fictional worlds of his characters who search for meaning in an industrialized consumer economy that destroys what it needs to survive and deteriorates humans' capacity to live reflectively and to find meaning in their work. As one of his characters puts it, 'We [humans] were put into a garden and we turned it into a detention center.'[12]

If the capacity to take such a high-minded view of writing seems uniquely suited to the career of an author who landed a deal with William Faulkner's editor and who gained status through access to luminaries who, for the most part also happened to be white American men, that's because it is.[13] In a piece studying the impact of the MacArthur 'Genius' Grant on David Foster Wallace's career, Alexander Rocca argues that 'the MacArthur Foundation was the most visible representative [in the 1990s] of a radically new development in twentieth-century literature: the emergence of an institutional philanthropy' that became the dominant model of literary 'patronage.' Rocca terms this patronage of the arts 'trickle-down aesthetics.'[14] Where the MacArthur Foundation's grants were meant, by their financial generosity, to liberate artists from the 'tyranny' of institutions and institutional expectations, many, like Wallace, found creativity stifled instead by the unnatural alienation of being 'liberated' from institutional affiliation. Of significant contributions to American literature in the late twentieth and early twenty-first centuries, Wallace's emotionally fragile, middle-class morality-strangled intellectual elites seem the farthest thing from McCarthy's laconic, often violent, unreflective working-class laborers. Yet both authors' careers were lifted from relative obscurity through the big-name patronage of the MacArthur Foundation, and by other prestigious literary grants. These awards create a sort of 'winner takes all' dynamic, and, not surprisingly, white men have tended to dominate recipient lists since the emergence of the 'trickle-down aesthetics' patronage model.[15] McCarthy, in this latter regard, fits the MacArthur bill as neatly as Wallace.

In another respect, McCarthy's career path took a distinct turn from Wallace's: by the end of his years sustained by his MacArthur money, McCarthy was spending most of his time at the Santa Fe Institute, an 'independent research center exploring the frontiers of complex systems science.'[16] The interdisciplinary and communal experience of his years at the institute has clearly affected the content of his works, but more importantly, the geographic conjunction of an otherwise single-minded literary author with string theorists, economists, and physicists highlights one of the most important topics in literary studies today: the interactions of scientific, sociological, and economic factors in artistic creation and dissemination, and the role of artistic creations in shaping and restructuring how the reading public perceives the complex effects of economic structures on art, as well as—and more importantly— on ecosystems and human societies.

Economics and the role of literary arts may not seem an obvious pairing. One can certainly imagine a man who sold fewer than 2,000 copies of a book that Harold Bloom would one day call 'a canonical imaginative achievement' agreeing with that assessment.[17]

But as Rocca's analysis of 'trickle-down aesthetics' suggests, artistic creation and dissemination are never accomplished in a political vacuum. By the same token, McCarthy, a white male author of a certain generation, does not offer apolitical visions of the role and value of artistic creation. As so many have noted, his works rarely offer nuanced portrayals of ethnic minorities (with the possible exception of Black American working-class life in *The Stonemason*) or gender or sexual minorities: even *women* characters are few and far between.[18] McCarthy's unwillingness, perhaps inability, to offer rich, literary depictions of human experience outside his own demographic is worth noting, but the converse is worth noting as well: McCarthy *does* imbricate straight, white masculine identity and experience within discussions of ethical failures, power, and privilege in the United States. His fiction consistently represents and critiques, sometimes brutally, the interrelated structures of race, class, region, and gender on forms of labor, types of work, social privilege, and economic precarity in the United States—albeit through the lens of white working-class men.

As a rough overview, McCarthy's works demonstrate a deep fascination with the economic implications of exclusionary, specialist, and meticulous work—that is, of *craftsmanship*—in market-capitalist economies that rely on the mass consumption of cheaply produced goods. For example, McCarthy explained that he wrote a play called *The Stonemason* (produced in 1997) precisely because he wanted to explore the vanishing career of stonemasonry—the 'oldest trade there is'—because of the invention of hydraulic cement.[19] The erosion of craftsmanship in the interests of war, mass production, and mechanization haunts McCarthy's fiction. Like many other economists, philosophers, and artists, McCarthy depicts capitalism not as a system external to humans, but rather as an entirely human construction, understood as an expression of a strain of aggression and acquisitive violence that is linked to political, hegemonic power identified primarily with white, male persons through US history. Craftsmanship, by contrast, requires a repudiation of the behaviors that privilege such expressions of power.

What is more interesting, however, is that his depiction of economic structures highlights their interrelation with ecosystems, forms of production, legislation, national identity, and psychology.

To be sure, McCarthy has always had an autodidact's approach to fields not obviously related to the writing of fiction. His collaboration with scholars in a variety of fields in Santa Fe has only expanded and clarified his interests, particularly in evolutionary economics—the study of the 'relationship between animal behavior and marketlike forces'—and in complexity theory more broadly. Research in complexity economics, a non-orthodox although now generally accepted sub-field of evolutionary economics, draws on an artificial stock market modeling program at the Santa Fe Institute.[20]

Even before his tenure at the Santa Fe Institute, McCarthy's works have incorporated notions of complexity as it has been understood in physics, economics, and biological sciences. Throughout his career, his fictional worlds have consistently applied aesthetic and narrative strategies for depicting the interrelated and often irrational and alienating movements of global market capitalism, of a planet on the brink of environmental disaster, and of species—human, wolf, whale, and more—whose need to live in societies is endangered by their own inability to cope with the increasing rate of changes to their ecosystems. What he adds to these already complex notions is the capacity of literary fiction to, first, vivify such complex ideas in readers' imaginations, and, second, to represent pressure points in these fragile systems, such as the implication of certain identities (white, male) in the center of these crises. In short, McCarthy applies principles of complexity, particularly complexity in economic and ecological systems, to stories that illuminate in brutal, brilliant prose death, love, and our need to critically examine how we value the world around us. Studying these two intersecting attributes (economics and literary aesthetics) in McCarthy's works not only demonstrates the achievements of a significant American author, but also directs attention to the possibilities of literary criticism as a methodological engagement with complexity through narrative.

Narrative as a complex system

What does it mean to consider literature in the context of complex systems? And how might I justify my claim that literature is itself a complex system? One field of complexity theory in which McCarthy has engaged in cooperative research at the Santa Fe Institute is the study of the evolution of human language. Evolutionary linguistics offers a way to explore the most fundamental principles guiding human evolution: the method by which human beings communicate, build society, understand mathematical and scientific phenomena—basically, how humans created their world. In a nonfiction essay published in the popular science magazine *Nautilus*, McCarthy explores the workings of the subconscious and its evolutionarily complex relationship with language. The problem of the unconscious, he suggests, is that while it understands language, it surely precedes it or at least operates independently of it, because the unconscious often operates through symbols—as in the case of the German organic chemist August Kekulé, whose dream of a snake enabled him to solve the problem of the benzene molecule (it is shaped like a ring). McCarthy's essay provoked heated debate, mainly because it seems to repudiate Noam Chomsky's argument that language systems are hardwired in human brains. However, McCarthy's claim that language is a tool that developed later in the evolution of the species is hardly a revolutionary claim, and actually reiterates Chomsky's theory of a universal grammar, which gained prominence in the 1960s, and which suggests that language, even if it developed later in humans' evolution, is nevertheless a shared characteristic of the species as it evolves.[21]

The notion of the universality of grammatical languages came on the heels of a trend in narrative theory to find universalities in story and symbol. Carl Jung's theory of archetypes and the collective unconscious bled into narratology in the early twentieth century, notably through Russian formalists such as Vladimir Propp, whose *Theory and History of Folkore* (first appearing as *Morphology of the Folktale* in Russian in 1928 and translated into English in 1958) proposes that narrative, too, follows archetypes and adapts to human population migration and shifts in language and culture. The popular comparative mythology scholar Joseph Campbell, author of *The Hero with a Thousand Faces* (1949), applied Propp's work in folklore to myth structures, arriving at much the same conclusions about the universality of narratological archetypes. Archetypal images and narrative patterns that seem so deeply ingrained that they transcend vast cultural, geographic, and temporal gulfs suggest that the human unconscious *needs* forms of communication that provide for an understanding beyond, or perhaps beneath, the conveyance of information. Human minds seek meaningfulness. And the story we tell ourselves about our lives weaves our own small threads into some greater tapestry. If this all seems a bit dated, McCarthy followed up his essay on the Kekulé problem with a clarification, explaining that linguists at the Santa Fe Institute are indeed pursuing (among, one assumes, any number of projects) research on the concept of an Ur- or proto-language—an even older linguistic theory. 'We believe that language is based on an idea,' he writes. 'The idea of representation.'[22] Despite criticism that such a proto-language, if it existed, could never be proven scientifically, given vast linguistic shifts over humans' evolutionary history, a yearning persists to identify what lies beneath the human yen for story, or the universality of archetypal images.[23]

McCarthy demonstrates a persistent fascination with preliterate or unconscious apprehensions of abstract concepts that the conscious mind encodes in archetypal images and narratological tropes. As an example, images of fire—of a person striking a fire, carrying fire, or forging stories of meaningfulness while gathered around a fire—recur through his works. Images of fire draw characters into connection with primordial fears or yearning for meaningfulness, and in so doing draw readers into Platonic associations with narrative's search for truth in varied forms. Thus, in *The Orchard Keeper* (1965), the youthful protagonist and his half-feral friends are 'troglodytes gathered in some firelit cave,' listening to myths and legend from old 'Uncle Athur' (150).[24] Fire lights the dark, literally and metaphorically, all the way from the wastelands of *Blood Meridian* (1985), where a man kindles fire on a darkened plain, to dream visions of a father carrying fire in a horn and lighting the way for an aging sheriff in *No Country for Old Men* (2005). At the end of human existence, *The Road*'s dying father tells his son that the boy must carry the fire into the world beyond. When the boy says that he does not know how to, or even where the fire is, the man responds, 'It's inside you. It was always there' (234). Stories are the conscious mind's way of spelling out that near-instinctual, unconscious *knowledge* of what fire means, from Promethean cosmology tales to the twenty-first century and beyond.

Claiming that the unconscious mind is capable of grasping deep or elemental knowledge of a thing, however, does little to explain *how* narrative communicates between the unconscious mind's revelations and the conscious mind's engagement with the external world. It is one thing for the mind to solve the problem of how valence electrons in benzene molecules bond ('the electrons bond in a ring-shape!') and another entirely to have a dream of a snake eating its tale and *make that connection*. How does the single, primordial image of eternity—a ring—find an applicable analogy to a particular molecular structure, rather than, say, through musical language becoming Wagnerian epics (*Der Ring des Nibelungen*), or through the visual rhetoric of marketing campaigns, a form of birth control (the 'NuvaRing®')?[25] The idea here is that languages (mathematical, musical, literary) may help our brains sort out bafflingly complex problems. *Narrative* language provides a particularly useful tool for expressing the most abstract and complicated questions that drive us—questions such as whether our lives are meaningful, or what our value is.

Narrative language employs the unconscious mind's capacity to grasp archetypal tropes and images and directs the conscious mind's analytic capacity toward particular applications of those tropes or images in order to solve irreducibly complex problems or to grasp irreducibly abstract notions. Literary analysis, then, can take on the project of unpicking the signs and deeper structures of a text to get at that Kekuléan insight. To be clear, this argument does not presuppose that archetypes in narrative suggest the existence of a singular metanarrative, Campbell's infamous monomyth. Campbell identified common mythic tropes across (certain) human cultures.[26] However, he over-extended his argument, attributing those commonalities to 'spontaneous productions of the psyche' rather than, as seems more likely, traditions that travel through mimetic repetition. Languages universally function according to grammatical processes that have many common characteristics. Language can similarly be employed in narratives that connect both speaker and audience to larger human concerns: loneliness and familial obligation, courage and fear of pain, fear of death, fear of the unknown, and so forth. Recognizing the universality of *method* suggests a commonality in the way human brains operate, but such methods are not necessarily predicated on a commonality external to the brain's processes. Each human experience of the world is contingent on unique constellations of factors, but humans' tools for communicating that experience—a range of emotions and linguistic methods—share commonalities across the species.[27]

The Kekuléan problem and McCarthy's exploration of the origin of human language suggest that, while archetypal images may be (near-) universal, the narratives that employ, decode, or explain them are constructs meant to translate the inexpressible into the expressible—to identify order within chaos, perhaps, or to trouble supposedly simple notions by examining their narratological complexity. Narrative may make simple notions messy as frequently as it makes messy notions graspable. Language is a representational sign system, but the polysemeity of narrative exceeds any simplistic notion that it can be 'uncoded' in some mathematically predictive way. As a complex system, narrative encodes archetypal images in contextually contingent structures that apply any number of various context cues and morphological transpositions, and which render any number of interpretive claims about those images in readers who exist in various and divergent political realities.

In calling narrative a complex system, I am drawing on the increasingly popular study of complex systems in the natural and social sciences today. Complexity studies find their origin in the late twentieth century's emerging interest in the study of chaotic behavior within ordered systems and order within chaotic systems. James Gleick's *Chaos* (2008) explains that complexity science's precursor, chaos theory, emerged as 'the century's third great revolution in the physical sciences.' Chaos describes those processes in nature that seem to violate Newtonian principles; in a universe ruled by entropy, it asks, 'how does order arise?' Yet arise it does. 'The simplest systems are now seen to create extraordinarily difficult problems of predictability,' Gleick says. 'Yet order arises spontaneously in those systems—chaos and order together.' The study of chaos examines the apparent order that emerges in complex systems, that is, systems characterized by the interaction of different parts such that isolating any given part of the system deteriorates or dismantles the system's identity or capacity to function. Even apparently simple and easily understood phenomena are often observable or understandable *only* because they are studied in isolation; but their function or behavior depends largely on the function or behavior of other phenomena. Explaining what can be quite simply observed about the system, then, requires complexity. Birds flocking, children's behavior on a school playground, and weather are examples of complex systems whose behaviors are not determined by isolatable parts but by the complex interactions of all constituent parts of that system—from pathogens to genetics to gravity. Yet observable, mathematically measurable behaviors arise from such complex systems.[28]

Complexity science draws attention to the interplay between complexity and simplicity. Murray Gell-Mann, one of the founders of the Santa Fe Institute and a personal friend of McCarthy's, writes that complexity theory attempts to answer the question of why there appears to be such a gap between the rigid precision of particle theory—as 'all electrons are rigorously interchangeable' with 'no individuality'—and the systems that they form: 'particular objects such as our planet Earth' and, through biological evolution, condors, jaguars, human civilization and language systems, each characterized by wildly divergent and irreplicable individuality. In order to bridge this gap, Gell-Mann explains that complexity science distinguishes the regular from the random.[29] The study of emergent patterns within randomness reveals the adaptation of complex systems to various influences in order to function, to replicate.

Textual patterns and organizational principles shape interpretation, and complexity theory can offer analogous language and methods for describing the ways in which literary texts produce multitudinous interpretations through regularities in pattern and pattern deviations. To be clear, this book's project is not a return to New Criticism; twenty-first-century critics are well versed in the much-deserved critique leveled at that particular methodology. By the 1960s the once-revolutionary proposal of the New Critics— that narrative language functions in more complex ways than the study of language itself can account for—became a battleground between two camps. The first group sought to double down on New

Criticism by narrowing the study of a text to its structural semiotics, almost as one might scrutinize a diamond under a magnifying glass, studying cuts, facets, and flaws—presuming the diamond itself the only artifact of value, divorced from its provenance. In this first camp, structuralism gave way to post-structuralism and deconstruction, a methodology so limited in scope it often slid into self-parody. The other camp approached the text as a material object to be interpreted in terms of its political, economic, and historical contexts.[30] In this camp, a rising awareness of the ethical implications of arguments for 'literariness' predicated on texts that *could* be read without contexts—that is, texts that looked familiar to predominantly white, predominantly middle-class academicians—led to calls to interrogate power, race, gender, and class structures underlying texts' production. Audre Lorde's *Sister Outsider* (1984) famously asserts that the failures of academic feminism to name and account for differences in the experiences of artists and scholars based on their respective and intersecting racial, gendered, sexual, class, and national identities led to failures of interpretation. Aesthetic criticism that presumes a work of art can be interpreted objectively ignores how profoundly difference affects interpretation.[31] In *Excitable Speech* (1997), Judith Butler reiterates Lorde's call to reflect on underlying power structures within the language of texts themselves, warning that '[i]f language can sustain the body, it can also threaten its existence.'[32] The power to erase identities or diminish the agency of bodies in the real world is not separable from the power of the text to elide those subjectivities. A text studied in isolation and praised for its clarity just might be clear only to a certain handful of people whose identities are seen and valorized in that text—to the brutal exclusion, derision, or subjugation of others. This second approach subjects texts to rigorous critique of implicit and explicit negotiations of power, privilege, and speaking authority. It bore the additional benefit of broadening the field of literary studies by applying its skill sets to the study of cultural artifacts rather than only texts deemed 'literary'; popular culture texts, advertisements, and political stump speeches often interpellate identities more immediately than literary texts, after all. It had the deficit, at times, of depressing the study of aesthetic aspects of the text, to the point that such criticism sometimes managed to suck the idea of aesthetic pleasure or the notion of literariness out of reading altogether. Although the energies of both camps were marked with a near-religious fervor during the hysterically appellated 'theory wars' of the 1970s to 1990s, Catherine Gallagher sees a new generation of literary scholars 'capable of moving fluidly among available models of subjectivity and "literariness."'[33] At the forefront of this movement, Elaine Scarry, in *On Beauty and Being Just* (1999), allies calls for political interrogations of texts with a hunger for the aesthetic. She reminds readers of the 'radical decentering we undergo in the presence of the beautiful.'[34] Even the most 'identity politics'-oriented critical theory can take a combinatorial approach. For instance, in *Methodology of the Oppressed* (2000), Chela Sandoval proposes a theory of processes, procedures, and technologies capable of 'decolonizing the imagination.' Her methodology employs Roland Barthes's semiological deep reading of texts, a Marxist and postmodern 'chiastic' analysis of power structures encoded in texts, and both lateral and vertical analysis of the 'sovereignty' of texts and their contexts.[35] Certainly, scholars today are more apt to recognize the need to analyze the real-world implications of a text's content and context through a variety of methodological lenses without losing the benefits of 'deep' reading.

More recently, critics have begun to call for a method of literary analysis that opens itself to the multitudinous concerns of political context while re-centering the pleasures of close reading. For example, in 2017 Lee Clark Mitchell called for a return to 'slow reading,' and Timothy Aubry (2018) argues that necessary political criticism must also take into account texts' 'aesthetic pleasures.' Mitchell's *Mere Reading: The Poetics of Wonder in Modern American Novels* outlines an approach to reading that is the antithesis to the 'speed reading' quackery of the 1980s and 1990s, one that re-centers the praxis of close reading. Such a methodology does not have to be divorced from real-world concerns, he asserts: 'We are more likely to notice and become suitably engaged' with the political implications raised by a text precisely because slow, thorough close readers 'are schooled in noticing.'[36] Aubry similarly argues that there is 'considerably more common ground' between formalists and 'politically oriented scholars who succeeded them' than we may assume. Specifically, he defines 'aesthetic criticism' as that form of literary study which focuses on the sensory pleasures of the text as much as its content—the syntactic, phonetic, and metaphoric attributes that contribute to our sense of pleasure in reading; as such, he uses 'aesthetic criticism' more or less synonymously with the methods of formalism. Yet those methods, he says, are not irreconcilable with the demands of political criticism; they often drive those concerns. Aubry inverts Fredric Jameson's assertion that literature deserves study because it can 'offer symbolic resolutions to real-world contradictions' by suggesting instead that, because literature can offer complex insights into complex realities, it becomes politically relevant. While he overturns the hierarchical assumptions that Jameson makes about the purpose and goal of literary scholarship, Aubry is careful to say that he is not asserting in its place a different hierarchy, but rather an enmeshed view of the function and purpose of literature, in which the critic is 'aware of the multiple, *distinct* components that typically constitute a given act of interpretation.'[37]

As Aubry and Mitchell demonstrate, it is not only possible to unite the pleasures of aesthetically focused examinations of a text with the rigors of complex, politically minded interrogations of texts and contexts: it is necessary. I take as a starting point the assertion that literature is both political and aesthetically realized. Building on Mitchell's and Aubry's arguments, I apply stylistic analyses to McCarthy's representations of the implications of market capitalism on social inequalities and anthropocentric scientific models that fail to account for the human cost of 'progress.' More importantly, such an approach illustrates a larger need to establish the merits of an intersectional, layered, and critical approach to context as well as text in studying all literature.

In the field of literary scholarship today, too often impassioned calls for returns to close reading are applied to white authors, often white male authors; impassioned calls to interrogate representations of power, privilege, and voice are more often applied to Black, Indigenous, and other racial-, ethnic-, gender-, and sexual-minority authors' work. No author or text can exist in a vacuum; no text can be studied and understood well when read in isolation from context, as impoverished applications of New Criticism would assert. By contrast, an approach to texts that reads them as complex systems assumes the irreducible complexity of the intersections of identity, power, privilege, and temporality on the text as well as on the reader's interpretation of that text. While the methods of reading literature as a complex system may not be new, the assumptions underlying such an approach bear noting: literature is political; literature is aesthetically realized.

By applying a complexity-informed methodological approach to the study of economic systems, climate disaster, and an ethics of care for human and nonhuman subjects in McCarthy's works, I gesture more broadly to the need for literary analysis to help us frame meaningfulness in a culture that too often reduces the natural world, art, and life itself to use value on a global marketplace or, by contrast, seeks to isolate artistic creations from messy political realities. In its methods, then, this book builds on recent interest in reclaiming the possibilities of close reading while recognizing the necessary interventions offered by economic and political critique in literary studies.

It is not surprising that the works of an author who spends his days at the Santa Fe Institute make for a particularly interesting case study for the application of this approach. Topics such as capitalism and climate change are systems too complex for our minds to fully grasp. Narratives can provide scaffolding to such mental exercises, embedding archetypal images in complex applications capable of concretizing abstractions or complexifying simplistic assumptions. McCarthy's writing foregrounds a particularly 'Kekuléan' literary style, using patterned syntax and narratological tropes, archaic vocabulary, and archetypal imagery to create ordered arguments within chaotic and irreducibly complex literary landscapes. McCarthy interweaves simplistic semiotics and complex stylistics to make explicit and immediate the crises facing us: the consequences of US economic imperialism; ecological disaster; and the need for a non-anthropocentric ethics of care for human and nonhuman others. From an examination of biblical versus Homeric syntactic structures in *Blood Meridian* in Chapter 2 to the chiastic narratological structures in *Suttree* in Chapter 6, this book makes the argument that McCarthy's prose stylistically reiterates its claims about the need to recognize the fragility of increasingly destabilized ecosystems and the nonmaterial value of human and nonhuman others.

McCarthy on economics and art

The first attribute of McCarthy's works I will examine is their representation of economic systems and those systems' valuation of human and nonhuman subjects; the second, their representation of the role of narrative in shaping our engagement with complex systems. McCarthy's fascination with economics and, more specifically, the ramifications of post-Fordist capitalism in the United States has been frequently noted, but less frequently given sustained attention. In one of the seminal early collections of scholarship on McCarthy, Rick Wallach's *Myth, Legend, Dust* (2000), Christine Chollier points out that 'the issue of economics has hardly ever been addressed in McCarthy studies.' Her essay, which undertakes the task of addressing that lack, laid the groundwork for later scholarship. Chollier argues that McCarthy's works are skeptical of market economies, or perhaps more accurately, skeptical of the capacity of decadent Western societies to have achieved any form of civilized, functional market economy, yet she nevertheless concludes that McCarthy's fiction argues for the naturally civilizing effect of market capitalism on human societies. Chollier even claims that John Grady Cole, perhaps the closest thing to a heroic protagonist McCarthy's readers will find, 'stands for a form of capitalist exchange.'[38]

Dave Holloway's *The Late Modernism of Cormac McCarthy* (2002) is to date the only book-length study that has as its central focus McCarthy's representations of late capitalism. In contrast to Chollier, Holloway claims that McCarthy's fiction functions like a series of 'experiments' that test the limits of postmodernity, destabilizing the reactionary politics implicit and explicit in such critique.[39] While Holloway is the only scholar to devote an entire book to McCarthy's engagement with the aesthetic movements critiquing and reacting to late capitalism, many more recent scholars recognize the centrality of critiques of capitalism to McCarthy's works and focus more directly on the economic philosophy at play in them. Michael Tavel Clarke, building on Holloway's work, makes the compelling claim that neoliberal policies underlie an intensified, deterministic fatalism, or at least a keen awareness of the diminished agency of the laborer class, in Western nations that translates into a 'new naturalism,' exemplified by authors such as McCarthy.[40] Clarke's work is the most ambitious claim about the role of neoliberalism in shaping McCarthy's philosophical framework, but Clarke has little time for more than a cursory rush through McCarthy's fiction to exemplify his claim.

Since Holloway's study, many critics, like Clarke, have paid more attention to an emerging economic philosophy in McCarthy's corpus in shorter scholarly works that focus on one single text or a particular thread of economic philosophy teased out across multiple works. Representative analyses include Stephen Tatum's examination of the sociopolitical and economic ramifications of the brutality of the border country in *No Country for Old Men*; Raymond Malewitz's examination of the commodification of people and systems in McCarthy's fiction (in a number of articles); and Susan Kollin's reading of *The Road* as a study of the causes and human parameters of ecodisaster. These three and other recent scholars have tended to identify a more persistent strain of critique in McCarthy's work—namely, a fundamental critique of late capitalist consumption. In an insightful critique of Chollier's argument, John Mark Robison claims that McCarthy's works do not suggest any efficacy in attempts to 'civilize' human interaction. Instead, 'the introduction of currency [in *Blood Meridian*],' he says, reveals 'not ... the exorcising of violence from the marketplace but rather a subtler encoding of it.'[41] Published in 2017, Robison's piece represents a shift in scholarship, from Chollier's reading of *All the Pretty Horses* as advocating a modified form of capitalism to positions that read individual McCarthy texts as inimical to capitalism.

Far from finding pro-social or democratizing forms of capitalism in his works, scholars are beginning to identify an excoriation of neoliberalism and its effect on the human laboring-class subject. For example, Jonathan and Rick Elmore offer a compelling exploration of neoliberalism as a new anthropology in *No Country for Old Men*. They contend neoliberalism becomes a form of 'anthropology' because it extends the doctrine of economic competition to 'every aspect of individual action'—personified by the novel's coin-tossing hitman, Anton Chigurh.[42] Casey Jergenson offers perhaps the clearest explanation of *The Road*'s use of the post-apocalyptic genre to draw a metaphorical line between the 'cannibalistic present and the capitalistic past' in a stunning indictment of neoliberalism's capacious appetite for 'human capital.'[43] Other similar approaches to McCarthy's critique of neoliberalism include Jordan Dominy's 'Cannibalism, Consumerism, and Profanation: Cormac McCarthy's *The Road* and the End of Capitalism' (2015), which covers similar thematic territory to Jergenson's article, and Dan Sinykin's 'Evening in America: *Blood Meridian* and the Origins and Ends of Imperial Capitalism' (2016), whose title nicely captures the article's focus. A scholarly concurrence is emerging: McCarthy's works critique neoliberal systems in which humans are valued as capital and which represents a dire threat to humanity and the natural world.

All that may be true, but *work* is treated with opposite and equal force in McCarthy's corpus. Jay Ellis provides the most extensive description of the value of manual labor: 'one of the few things of insistent value' in McCarthy's fiction, he says, 'is work.'[44] James William Christie, in his analysis of work in *Blood Meridian*, argues that the brutal world vision of that novel actually effaces the dancing Judge in favor of the image of 'the irreducible, originary horizon [on which is] the worker digging the fence post holes.'[45] There seem to be two oppositional forces at play in McCarthy's work, according to most scholars. On the one hand, while there is some debate about the valuation of market capitalism in his works overall, scholars concur that there is nevertheless a persistent critique of industrialization, globalization, and neoliberalism. Yet manual labor—work done with meticulous, professionalized care—is granted an innate dignity.

In *Cormac McCarthy's Philosophy* (2017), Ty Hawkins, following Holloway and Malewitz, argues that McCarthy's fiction 'pushes back at modernization and its shadow of nihilistic, post-modern self-referentiality.' He also argues persuasively that Arendt is the philosopher whose theories about work and human meaningfulness most closely reflect McCarthy's own.[46] Arendt's *The Human Condition* spells out this distinction between *labor* as part of the dehumanizing values of capitalist excess, and *work* as a human condition that allows us to engage meaningfully in efforts that sustain our lives. Arendt identifies the alienation of modern human society not only from labor, as a Marxist critique would have it, but from earth and nature—a concept she describes through her opening image of the first satellite sent into orbit, representing modern humanity's yearning to escape earth. Humans want to flee, she argues, only because of the philosophical shift in the Western, developed world that began to see the purpose of labor as an end in itself: humanity working in order to work (labor), rather than working to sustain life and those pursuits that provide a sense of greater meaningfulness (such as aesthetic pleasure).

For this book, I use the term 'labor' as synonymous with actions meant to ensure survival in and of a market-capitalist society, and 'work' for actions undertaken to create—to produce something valuable for more than its utilitarian function (i.e., an ornate rifle in *Blood Meridian* or a perfectly constructed stone arch in *The Stonemason*). Work put to the latter purpose, the creation of an object requiring skill and dedication, is synonymous in McCarthy's fiction with craftsmanship, a notion reflecting Aristotelian *techne*, a knowledgeable making or doing that constructs beautiful or well-made artifacts (which can range from poetry to rifles) that contributes to a greater sense of meaning or aesthetic value. Labor, by contrast, reduces the laborer to performance at the 'job,' a series of replicated tasks reflecting a division of labor to ensure the proper function of a mass society.[47] Laborers, in which category I place *No Country*'s Anton Chigurh (see Chapter 4), may demonstrate professional skill and knowledge in their subject area (in his case, murder) that suggests a kind of *techne* (he creatively murders someone with a cattle gun), but this labor is performed under the aegis of an economic empire's interests, or in the interests of a global marketplace (in Chigurh's case, the illegal drug trade), and the laborer is reduced to his function in that marketplace (he is a hitman who reduces competition to increase profit margins).

My citing of Arendt to offer functional definitions of labor, work, and art in McCarthy's corpus makes it immediately apparent that he is a profoundly philosophical writer. But I do not intend to examine the many philosophical considerations that burst forth from McCarthy's polymathic pages.[48] Instead, I want to examine one very particular, yet resonant, problem posed in his works: the problem of the human condition in a post-industrialized, globalized society, an alienation from acts of creation that provide meaningful, thoughtful reflection on human nature beyond the world of work. This book therefore offers a sustained examination of, first, McCarthy's philosophy of economics: a trenchant critique of post-industrialized, global capitalism that results in an alienation from forms of work and acts of creation that provide meaningful reflection on human nature; and, second, his philosophy of art: a philosophy in which craftsmanship is a sacred orientation toward human and nonhuman others that requires the practice of ecological sustainability and a mastery of the work of one's hands, represented by characters who are nomadic wanderers and who exhibit a capacity for skilled labor.

A brief explanation may be needed for my use of the adjective 'sacred' to describe the ethics of craftsmanship and sustainability in McCarthy's works. McCarthy's critique of economic systems and his presentation of alternative value systems are forged through image and allusion, much of which is rendered in the idiom of the sacred. McCarthy's play *The Stonemason* offers perhaps the clearest articulation of a philosophy of work and art, and that articulation is formed through—the pun seems unavoidable—the concrete image of stone masonry. Ben Telfair, the grandson of the eponymous stonemason, describes the craft of 'true masonry' as finding the natural join of stonework. 'The keystone that locks the arch is pressed in place by the thumb of God,' he says. The 'true gospel' of stone masonry, therefore, is the belief that 'we [masons] invent nothing but what God has put to hand' (10). In describing the craft as human hands fitting together what God has provided, or even physically manifesting the work of God, Ben accomplishes two key tasks. First, he explains that 'true' masons 'invent nothing': they create no artifact beyond arranging pre-existing materials. True masons, in other words, are environmentally low-impact and adaptive to natural resources rather than inventing new, cheaper, economically smart materials, like concrete. Second, Ben associates the idea of the sacred with the image of human hands, and with the handiwork of artisans. 'God' has 'pressed in place' the keystone—not in the sense that God supplants the human laborer, but that the physics that explain the function of a keystone in holding stones suspended in the form of an arch determines the work of the mason. Ben extends this concept at the end of the play when he imagines his grandfather's hands '[s]haped in the image of God. To make the world. To make it again and again ... in the very maelstrom of its undoing' (133).

Sacred, world-making language describing craftsmanship appears throughout McCarthy's corpus and is examined in depth in Chapter 5. Here, I will briefly explain how these three categories—'god/the sacred,' 'craftsmanship/art,' and nomadism—are interconnected and are 'world-making.' 'God' is the most dubiously useful category, as the sacred is not a stable notion in McCarthy's fiction. However, sacred language consistently represents that work or craft that is meaningful and that which drives the human urge to 'make.' In its turn, craftsmanship reflects a particular *type* of creation, a making that reflects and is part of the natural system of the maker and not apart from it. The language used to hallow nomads, figures of sacred significance and equally creative energy in McCarthy's work, suggests the importance placed on an ethics of this integrated, adaptive life. For example, Ben's language describing his grandfather's hands echoes in the language used by the New Mexican housewife Betty when she considers Billy Parham's hands at the conclusion of *Cities of the Plain*. On Billy's '[g]narled, rope-scarred' hands is a 'map enough for men to read,' upon which she finds 'God's plenty of signs and wonders to make a landscape. To make a world' (291). To pull apart the three threads of this theme, 'God's hands' are a maker's hands; the maker is, first, in Ben's grandfather's case, a particular type of craftsman, and second, in Billy's case, a nomad.

In other words, 'God,' in McCarthy's lexicon, does not necessarily reflect a concrete, Catholic, or even monotheistic notion of deity so much as the *idea* of the Maker as creative force. In *The Crossing*, an old priest tells Billy that God is a man bent at his work, '[w]eaving the world' (149). In McCarthy's unpublished screenplay *Whales and Men*, Kelly McAmon's God is 'so large that there's no place to even stand outside of him to say that he's not so. [... God] includes everything and everybody so that there's nothing left over outside of it with which to compare it.'[49] Second, craftsmanship is uniquely tied to the adaptive nomadism of people who leave their ecosystems un-ruined. Craftsmanship—manual labor, the work of one's hands informed by thoughtfulness, as in the elder Telfair's masonry—requires a recognition of that natural order, the physical properties of the world alongside an ecologically balanced perspective that 'invents nothing' and leaves no permanent mark or stain upon that order (*TS* 10). The craftsman, working within that sacred order, reflects a divine mastery of the world: an ability to create but a refusal to destroy. This attitude toward the natural world is characteristic of people groups that adapt their sustenance and the work that they do to the exigencies of their bioregional time and place, communities that are frequently identified as nomadic in land-rooted, property-owning Western viewpoints.[50]

For McCarthy, the critical connection between economics and art lies in this orientation toward sustainability and ecological balance. For example, when Ben imagines his grandfather's stone-masonry, he imagines it as a fundamentally creative act, one that 'make[s] the world ... in the very maelstrom of its undoing' (*TS* 133). Western capitalism birthed industrial revolutions, the expansion of capital across national boundaries, and increasingly unsustainable consumption of natural resources and human labor. Counter to the driving forces of capitalism, craftsmanship requires time, thoughtfulness, and an ecologically sustainable relationship to natural resources. This last quality is intensified by McCarthy's connecting it to nomadic lives. For McCarthy, perhaps no struggle is more imperative in these early decades of the twenty-first century than the struggle against the vast inequality and over-consumption of late capitalism; and no figure better represents the heart of that struggle than nomads and craftsmen—those who 'make' in the very maelstrom of the world's undoing.

Two movements: chapter by chapter

This book is divided into two movements: a critique of the world as it is (economics) and a call for a vision of the world as it should be (art and nomadism). The first movement studies McCarthy's evolving critique of US economic imperialism, beginning with, in

Chapter 1, an overview of mechanization and industrialization, the manifestations of the early twentieth century's rapidly changing industrial landscape, first in his early Appalachian works and then, in brief, through McCarthy's later works. Chapters 2 through 4 examine the rise of a military-industrial economy and the turn toward global capitalism, beginning with westward expansion during the era of Manifest Destiny in *Blood Meridian* in Chapter 2; jumping to the late twentieth and early twenty-first centuries' global economies as depicted through the black market drug trade along the US–Mexico border in *No Country for Old Men* and *The Counselor* in Chapter 3; and finally, turning a retrospective gaze on the United States' consumer economy in the post-Anthropocene wasteland of *The Road* in Chapter 4.

This book's second movement shifts away from examining the critique of property ownership, consumer-based economies, and militarism characteristic of consumer capitalism in the US and turns instead toward images of a nomadic ethics, a worldview characterized by adaptation and care for human and nonhuman others. Chapter 5 examines images of suffering bodies in the Border Trilogy and proposes the need for a non-anthropocentric, embodied ethics of care. Chapter 6 examines that embodied ethics of care in the context of late modernism's overpopulation through a dual thematic focus on suicide and artistic creation as responses to late modernism's excesses and alienation.

In addition to dividing the content of the book into two movements, the analysis follows a sort of Kekuléan strategy. First, I identify how McCarthy uses a simplistic semiotics to indicate complex problems. Second, I examine the complex treatment of those problems through a deep structure reading of the texts. Chapter 1 provides the case study, a semiotic examination of how mechanization and industrialization are represented through images of transportation machines (trains, cars, trucks) and how those images code a complex web of interrelated notions of labor, masculinity, and nationalism. This chapter also provides a brief overview of these ideas throughout McCarthy's corpus, while Chapters 2 through 4 delve into deep structure analyses of economics in individual texts, from analyzing contrasting uses of Homeric and biblical stylistic modes in *Blood Meridian* in Chapter 2; to the *sicario* narrative embedded in *No Country* and an imagistic history of late capitalism in *The Counselor* in Chapter 3; and finally to *The Road*'s evocation of the Anglo-Irish gothic and its use of fractal images and fractured syntax to exemplify an anxiety about settler American complicity in the destruction of its human and nonhuman communities in Chapter 4. The second part of this book turns to examinations of complex systems—what McCarthy terms 'matrices' or webs of being. Chapter 5 examines the problem of pain, specifically why bodily pain is such a powerful act of unmaking in individuals and in complex systems. Chapter 6 explores chiastic narrative structures used to represent order arising from chaotic, evolving systems.

In his 1992 interview, Woodward says that McCarthy's 'prose restores the terror and grandeur of the physical world with a biblical gravity that can shatter a reader.' Denis Donoghue claims that McCarthy's fiction reminds us that 'creative force is not a force alternative to form but itself the particular form of its erupting into being.'[51] McCarthy's texts are exceptionally rich case studies for an approach that examines the interrelated contexts and methods of meaning. But good reading is more than just a form of craftsmanship in its own right; such readings are also exercises in imagining and interpreting complex systems.

When Mark Fisher claims in *Capitalist Realism* that the most dangerous aspect of capitalism today lies in its obviation of imagination, he suggests the importance of the work of artists who do that. Fisher argues that late capitalism 'subsumes and consumes all of previous history,' creating an impression of a system that is inevitable, that could never and will never be otherwise.[52] If late capitalism's claims of inevitability are to be challenged, if ecological disaster is to be imagined to the extent that it motivates concerted human *action*, we will need narratives that allow us to imagine these very things. And we will need to read those stories well. While the capacity of humankind to ever achieve the migratory, ecologically balanced ideal in McCarthy's fiction is perhaps not realistic, the aesthetic reverence with which those images are presented fires the imagination. No revolution can be achieved if it cannot be first imagined. McCarthy's critiques of global capitalism and images of a radical and embodied ethics of care as its alternative may be, in the end, one of his most significant contributions to the twenty-first century.

Notes

1 The first epigraph comes from James Gleick, *Chaos: Making a New Science*, 20th Anniversary Edition (Penguin Books, 2008), 307. The second is spoken by the character John Western in *Whales and Men*, cited from The Cormac McCarthy Papers, collection 91, box 91, folder 6, p. 129. As a brief note about citation of archival materials, I used each archive's available information where possible; in certain archives, materials are categorized by collection, box, and file numbers; other archives have only a single box for collected letters. In cases where the document being cited is from a paginated manuscript, I have also included the page number for the citation. In this case, the full manuscript of *Whales and Men* in file 6 of The Cormac McCarthy Papers, box 91, folder 6, is paginated.
2 George Monbiot, 'Civilization Ends with a Shutdown of Human Concern: Are We There Already?,' *Guardian*, Books: Opinion, October 29, 2007.
3 An editorial packet for *The Crossing* includes the following history of sales. *The Orchard Keeper*, published originally by Random House, sold 3,926 copies; reprinted by Vintage in 1993, it sold 20,105. *Outer Dark*, orig. Random House, 2,705 copies; Vintage (1993), 14,846. *Child of God*: orig. Random House, 2,415; Vintage (1993), 15,992. *Suttree*: orig. Random House, 2,705; Vintage (1992), 23,711. *Blood Meridian*: orig. Random House, 1,883; Vintage (1992), 39,287. *All the Pretty Horses*: orig. Knopf, 134,928; Vintage (1993), 213,862. This information is cited from The Woolmer Collection of Cormac McCarthy, collection 92, box 5, file 8. In a letter dated November 17, 1988, Howard Woolmer writes McCarthy: 'It's shocking that you've never received a royalty cheque. It's easy to see why Albert Erskine and Random House stick with you as they're well aware of your value even though the public doesn't seem to realize it yet.' While Erskine's records do show that McCarthy had received royalty checks of up to $1,000 in previous years, it is in any case true that McCarthy did not make enough in royalties to live on in any year prior to 1992. The Woolmer Collection of Cormac McCarthy, collection 92, box 5, file 7.
4 Robert Penn Warren, Ralph Ellison, and John Hersey nominated him for the Guggenheim Fellowship, for instance. The Albert Erskine Collection, box 29, unpaginated.
5 Richard B. Woodward, 'Cormac McCarthy's Venomous Fiction,' *New York Times*, April 19, 1992.

6 In the papers of McCarthy's editor at Random House, Albert Erskine, we find correspondence from McCarthy to Erskine reporting on the sales garnered from signed copies of his second novel, *Outer Dark* (1968), at Owl Books bookstore in Tennessee. McCarthy obdurately refuses to talk on panels or engage in such public readings now, but it is clear from his participation in this common marketing strategy, a book signing, as well as his subsequent careful attention to royalty statements, that from the beginning he intended to make a living as an author. A significant proportion of McCarthy's correspondence with Erskine deals with issues of royalty statements and advances, as well as queries about different grants and fellowships offering stipends to literary artists. The Albert Erskine Collection, box 29.
7 Steven Shaviro, '"The Very Life of the Darkness": A Reading of *Blood Meridian*,' *Perspectives on Cormac McCarthy*, rev. edn, eds. Edwin T. Arnold and Dianne C. Luce (University Press of Mississippi, 1999), 145–158: 146.
8 Oprah Winfrey, 'The Exclusive Interview Begins,' interview with Cormac McCarthy, *Oprah's Book Club*, July 2007.
9 Stacey Peebles, *Page, Stage, Screen: Cormac McCarthy and Performance* (University of Texas Press, 2017), 1.
10 Winfrey, 'The Exclusive Interview Begins.'
11 The Lyndhurst Foundation Records, #04723, box 15. I would like to thank Dianne C. Luce for drawing my attention to the Lyndhurst Foundation's collected correspondence with McCarthy.
12 Peter Gregory makes this assertion in McCarthy's unpublished screenplay, *Whales and Men* (58). The Cormac McCarthy Papers, collection 91, box 91, file 6, p. 58.
13 Not exclusively, of course: Ralph Ellison was an early supporter of McCarthy's work.
14 Alexander Rocca, '"I don't feel like a genius": David Foster Wallace, Trickle-Down Aesthetics, and the MacArthur Foundation,' *Arizona Quarterly*, vol. 73, iss. 1 (Spring 2017), 85–111: 86, 95.
15 Rocca, '"I don't feel like a genius,"' 97.
16 'Santa Fe Institute,' 2016, accessed August 22, 2018, www.santafe.edu/.
17 Harold Bloom, 'Introduction,' *Cormac McCarthy*, new edn, ed. Harold Bloom, Bloom's Literary Criticism (Chelsea House Publications, 2009), 1–8: 1.
18 Nell Sullivan, 'The Dead Girlfriend Motif in *Outer Dark* and *Child of God*,' *Myth, Legend, Dust: Critical Responses to Cormac McCarthy*, ed. Rick Wallach (Manchester University Press, 2000), 68–77: 68.

19 Woodward, 'Cormac McCarthy's Venomous Fiction.'
20 This modeling program is based on the principles of complexity theory and offers different models for non-intuitive (that is, non-representational agent-produced) market index movement. Complexity economics is not the only, or even the primary, field of mathematical complexity research at the Santa Fe Institute in which McCarthy has demonstrated a keen interest. McCarthy edited Lawrence M. Krauss's biography of Richard Feynman, whose methods have been used to study sub-atomic particle interaction. He has volunteered to edit many other mathematics and natural science books from various Santa Fe fellows, as well. David Kushner spends time in his profile of McCarthy describing his interactions with evolutionary economists through open conversations and specific research projects. See David Kushner, 'Cormac McCarthy's Apocalypse,' *Rolling Stone*, December 27, 2007.
21 Cormac McCarthy, 'The Kekulé Problem: Where Did Language Come From?,' *Nautilus*, March–April 2017.
22 Cormac McCarthy, 'Cormac McCarthy Returns to the Kekulé Problem: Answers to Questions and Questions that Cannot be Answered,' *Nautilus*, November 30, 2017. For a more detailed discussion of evidence for an Ur- or proto-language, see Murray Gell-Mann and Merritt Ruhlen's 'The Origin and Evolution of Word Order,' *Proceedings of the National Academy of Sciences of the United States of America*, vol. 108, iss. 42 (2011), 17290–17295. Gell-Mann was a friend of McCarthy's who worked closely with him on a number of projects and was likely influential in shaping McCarthy's views on the subject.
23 For a more thorough argument against the possibility of proving a proto-language, see Lyle Campbell and William J. Poser, *Language Classification: History and Method* (Cambridge University Press, 2008).
24 Because of the substantial references to McCarthy's texts in this book, I have chosen to use in-text citations rather than notes for his works to streamline the notes section. In in-text citations, titles of works are abbreviated where it is necessary to provide the title for disambiguation. A list of McCarthy's works and their abbreviations can be found at the beginning of the book.
25 In both examples, the ring is the thing itself—a ring-shaped object—and conjures and complicates ideas encoded in the history of rings, such as the 'eternity' represented by (heterosexual) sexual consummation in terms of procreation.
26 Campbell's formative work has many strengths, but he over-represents Euro-Western traditions, which leads to his facile description of a

singular 'monomyth.' Joseph Campbell, *The Hero with a Thousand Faces*, 3rd edition (New World Library, 2008), 2.
27 The fact that I share an experience of yearning for affection with humans I have never met in other cultures or times, for instance, does not indicate an external causational factor for that yearning, but does suggest that, as a human, I share certain brain structures that create the capacity for certain emotional experiences and expressions. A helpful analogy might be the eighty-eight keys on a standard piano keyboard, or a color wheel. An emotional index is shared across the species, but the particular arrangements of those emotions are, like musical compositions or paintings, unique.
28 Gleick, *Chaos*, 6, 7–8.
29 Murray Gell-Mann, *The Quark and the Jaguar: Adventures in the Simple and the Complex* (W. H. Freeman and Co., 1994), 8, 9, 54–55.
30 A helpful overview can be found in Catherine Gallagher, 'The History of Literary Criticism,' *Daedalus*, vol. 126, iss. 1 (Winter 1997), 133–153.
31 Audre Lorde, *Sister Outsider: Essays and Speeches* (Crossing Press, 2007), 112.
32 Judith Butler, *Excitable Speech: A Politics of the Performative* (Routledge, 1997), 5.
33 Gallagher, 'The History of Literary Criticism,' 150.
34 Elaine Scarry, *On Beauty and Being Just* (Princeton University Press, 1999), 112.
35 Chela Sandoval, *Methodology of the Oppressed*, Theory Out of Bounds, vol. 18 (University of Minnesota Press, 2000), 69, 86.
36 Lee Clark Mitchell, *Mere Reading: The Poetics of Wonder in Modern American Novels* (Bloomsbury Academic, 2017), 25; and Timothy Aubry, *Guilty Aesthetic Pleasures* (Harvard University Press, 2018).
37 Aubry, *Guilty Aesthetic Pleasures*, 1, 2, 11, 4, 5, 18, italics his.
38 Christine Chollier, '"I ain't come back rich, that's for sure," or the Questioning of Market Economies in Cormac McCarthy's Novels,' *Myth, Legend, Dust: Critical Responses to Cormac McCarthy*, ed. Rick Wallach (Manchester University Press, 2000), 171–177: 171, 176, 175.
39 David Holloway, *The Late Modernism of Cormac McCarthy* (Greenwood Press, 2002), 4.
40 Michael Tavel Clarke, 'The New Naturalism: Cormac McCarthy, Frank Norris, and the Question of Postmodernism,' *Studies in American Naturalism*, vol. 9, iss. 1 (2014), 52–78: 57.
41 John Mark Robison, 'The Authority of Currency in Cormac McCarthy's *Blood Meridian*,' *The Cormac McCarthy Journal*, vol. 15, iss. 1 (2017), 30–45: 31.

42 Jonathan and Rick Elmore, 'Human Become Coin: Neoliberalism, Anthropology, and Human Possibilities in *No Country for Old Men*,' *The Cormac McCarthy Journal*, vol. 14, iss. 2 (2016), 168–185: 171.
43 Casey Jergenson, '"In what direction did lost men veer?": Late Capitalism and Utopia in *The Road*,' *The Cormac McCarthy Journal*, vol. 14, iss. 1 (2016), 117–132: 127.
44 Jay Ellis, *No Place for Home: Spatial Constraint and Character Flight in the Novels of Cormac McCarthy* (Routledge, 2006), 59.
45 James William Christie, '"Days of begging, days of theft": The Philosophy of Work in *Blood Meridian*,' *The Cormac McCarthy Journal*, vol. 14, iss. 1 (2016), 55–77: 75. Christie's point reflects scholarly concurrence and is one I will extend in this book. However, this particular piece of evidence, the 'post hole digger' in *Blood Meridian*'s epilogue, does not clearly indicate manual labor producing *fence* posts, as Christie asserts. Given the novel's consistent interest in mechanization and war, the holes are more likely telegraph or telephone poles, representing the 'close' of the frontier. Christie's overly optimistic interpretation of this concluding image is problematic.
46 Ty Hawkins, *Cormac McCarthy's Philosophy*, American Literature Readings in the 21st Century (Palgrave Macmillan, 2017), 102. Michael Lynn Crews points out that Guy and Peter, in McCarthy's unpublished screenplay *Whales and Men*, discuss the 'banality of evil'—an explicit reference suggesting McCarthy's consumption of Arendt's seminal work. See Michael Lynn Crews, *Books Are Made out of Books: A Guide to Cormac McCarthy's Literary Influences* (University of Texas Press, 2017), 258.
47 Arendt defines 'labor' and 'work' this way: labor is 'the activity which corresponds to the biological process of the human body, whose spontaneous growth, metabolism, and eventual decay are bound to the vital necessities produced and fed into the life process by labor,' while work is 'the activity which corresponds to the unnaturalness of human existence, which is not imbedded in, and whose mortality is compensated by, the species' ever-recurring life cycle.' Labor is characterized by replication of actions and by a sense of necessity, which she likens to enslavement. Survival in a consumer-based economy requires the laborer to labor in order to be able to consume goods whose production requires more labor, and so forth. By contrast, the notion of work describes those human endeavors which may contribute to the human enterprise—to creating something that speaks to or represents human experience and as such may offer some semi-permanence, some relevance beyond the mere sustenance of a solitary human life. See

Hannah Arendt, *The Human Condition* (University of Chicago Press, 1958), 7.

48 Hawkins's book on McCarthy's philosophy, along with Brad Bannon and John Vanderheide's edited collection *Cormac McCarthy's Violent Destinies* (University of Tennessee Press, 2018) and Petra Mundik's masterful *A Bloody and Barbarous God: The Metaphysics of Cormac McCarthy* (University of New Mexico Press, 2016), already offer interested readers clear-eyed and in-depth overviews of the philosophical framework of McCarthy's fictional worlds.

49 The Cormac McCarthy Papers, collection 91, box 91, file 6, p. 45.

50 This distinction will be explained further in Chapter 5, but reflects the idea that 'nomadic' persons or groups are so characterized because of common traits of adaptability and sustainability; a nomadic group may be fairly stationary, but in its rejection of the notion of land *ownership* in favor of land *use*, it may be perceived as 'mobile'—as essentially removable—in a worldview that prioritizes land and resource ownership; Indigenous populations of Central and North America are typically used to reflect this idea in McCarthy's works.

51 Denis Donoghue, 'Teaching Literature: The Force of Form,' *New Literary History: A Journal of Theory and Interpretation*, vol. 30, iss. 1 (Winter 1999), 5–24: 21.

52 Mark Fisher, *Capitalist Realism: Is There No Alternative?* (Zero Books, 2009), 4.

1

Cars, trucks, and horses: man in the age of the machine

> It is our view that crisis and change in the Detroit region can be situated in the context of the reorganization of capitalism on a world scale that is the central theme of this book.
> (Robert J. S. Ross and Kent C. Trachte, *Global Capitalism: The New Leviathan*)

> Through all our history the self-made man was the exception not the rule. ... These are facts, but do men order their lives according to fact alone? ... Belief in the self-made man requires only an act of faith, and, as every Sunday School boy knows, faith is simply the substance of things hoped for, the evidence of things not seen.
> (Irvin G. Wyllie, *The Self-Made Man in America: The Myth of Rags to Riches*)[1]

Images of the toxic encroachment of the 'age of the machine' into pristine rural landscapes litter Cormac McCarthy's first novel, *The Orchard Keeper* (1965). The opening section finds a 'mangled fragment of fence' embedded in the flesh of a rotting tree, and the aging orchard keeper, Arthur Ownby, haunts a peach orchard now 'gray limb[ed]' and abandoned, abutted to a concrete insecticide pit which is being used as a crypt for a murdered body (3, 52). That crypt-pit provides one of the final, grotesque scenes in the novel, as Ownby, now in an assisted care home, imagines the 'green cadaver grin sealed in the murky waters of the peach pit, slimegreen skull with newts coiled in the eyesockets and a wig of moss' (224). The visceral horror and beauty of this image are the quintessential stuff of the American southern gothic tradition. Perhaps that is all it is. Some early reviewers of this debut novel certainly thought so. In a review in the *New York Times* on May 12, 1965, Orville Prescott claims, 'Some novelist [sic] can write with brilliance' about pastoral idylls lost to industrialization. 'Others,' he says, 'although they are highly gifted too, are sorely handicapped by their humble and excessive admiration for William Faulkner. Cormac McCarthy ... is one of these.'[2] However, a closer examination of the role of the 'age of the machine'—represented by the literal and metaphorical poison leaching into the pastoral landscape—reveals the complexity of McCarthy's eco-critical vision, as well as capturing his critique of the role of market capitalism and the myth of the 'self-made man' in American culture.

In her authoritative reading of McCarthy's earliest works, *Reading the World: Cormac McCarthy's Tennessee Period*, Dianne C. Luce pays attention to the signs and portents of an emerging 'ecocentric vision.' McCarthy's first four novels depict a gothic rural past threatened by the onslaught of the industrial and economic modernization of Appalachia in the 1930s through the 1950s. 'In its remembered healthiest state, before the opening of [*The Orchard Keeper*],' Luce explains, the titular peach orchard 'was an emblem of the fruitful collaboration between man and nature, specifically of the traditional, forest-dependent, pastoral culture of East Tennessee's mountain people.'[3] These early themes resurface in the Border Trilogy, where characters and places are haunted by memories of a wild or rural past and threatened by the tide of second-wave industrialization, modernization, and mechanized warfare. They recur in most of McCarthy's works, and are a central theme of his post-apocalyptic *The Road*.

Luce frames her analysis with Leo Marx's *The Machine in the Garden: Technology and the Pastoral Ideal in America*, originally published in 1964, to categorize McCarthy's novels as participating in what Marx calls the literary tradition of complex pastoralism, as opposed to sentimental pastoralism. The spinal column of the American literary canon is formed by this latter category, in which Herman Melville's, Nathaniel Hawthorne's, and Mark Twain's works fall. The defining image of this type of pastoral is the 'machine in the garden,' an image that poses stringent critiques of American national character. Specifically, Marx says, '[I]t is industrialization, represented by images of machine technology, that provides the counterforce in the American archetype of the pastoral design.'[4] That counterforce—the threat of and resistance to encroaching industrialization—adds complexity to thematic content in American literary pastorals.

In terms of McCarthy's use of the pastoral as cultural critique, Marx's most helpful insight is his description of the machine as the force of disruption and instability in the American psyche—and it is a force that is always gendered. In this complex pastoral tradition, the machine functions as 'a sudden, shocking intruder upon a fantasy of idyllic satisfaction.' That rupture of assumed innocence or safety is 'invariably ... associated with crude, masculine aggressiveness in contrast with the tender, feminine, and submissive attitudes traditionally attached to the landscape.'[5] That the pastoral is always a 'virginal' landscape is a given.[6] Why the machine's toxicity is *masculine* is less easily explained, for Marx, than the femininity of the land. In order to understand the reason for the machine's masculine characterization, it is necessary to turn to a broader examination of the role of industrialism in the US economy, and its relationship to the false premise of American economic philosophy: the myth of the self-made man.

Irvin G. Wyllie's *The Self-Made Man in America: The Myth of Rags to Riches*, originally published in 1954, provides a succinct narrative summary of that myth, its durability through the 1929 economic collapse, and its sticking power through sufficient data to turn any intelligent being away from belief in such a construct. But belief is not so easily lost. In the end, Wyllie concludes, the myth of the self-made man is not really about economic philosophy but is rather a quasi-religious system, the heart of which is a peculiarly American love of wealth. How 'success' is defined varies from person to person, he points out, but 'no one of these concepts enjoys such universal favor in America as that which equates success with making money.'[7] Wyllie's sociological assessment of wealth as the marker of 'making it' in America corresponds with economists' descriptions of the role of capital in Western nations. Ernest Mandel, for example, connects the driving force of capitalism to this fundamental belief that success can be defined best by an accumulation of wealth, particularly wealth as surplus profit (as opposed to less liquid forms of wealth, more common in hereditary land-based economies in old Europe). Technological advances are necessary processes through which capital surplus is increased. 'In capitalism, under the whip of competition and the constant quest for surplus-profits,' Mandel says, 'efforts are continually made to lower the costs of production and cheapen the value of commodities by means of technical improvements.'[8] The machine in McCarthy's works, then, represents not only the processes by which men become wealthy but also the voracious appetite for wealth that characterizes a society that correlates the value of a man to his capacity to generate and accumulate wealth.

In this regard, the complex pastoral imagery in McCarthy's works can be read as extended metaphors for that which is lost to human and nonhuman animal societies in the age of the machine, and the looming threat of industrialization brought by the 'whip of competition' that drives the production lines and the manufactured goods that feed the engines of the American consumer economy. Specifically, McCarthy's representations of the effects of the 'age of the machine' on human flourishing and the flourishing of the natural world are codified in a series of metaphors. Among the most obvious and most frequently occurring are contrasting, metaphoric depictions of engine-driven vehicles such as cars and trucks, and horses. That is, McCarthy's works code this critique of capitalism in familiar images of American industry against equally familiar images representing a pastoral or agrarian way of life: cars and trucks on the one side, and horses on the other.

This image-driven, largely implicit critique draws readers' attention to the suppression of alternative notions of 'success' or human flourishing under the hegemony of America's capitalist consumer economy. What possible alternative value system can survive, McCarthy's novels seem to ask, given American quasi-religious devotion to the myth of the self-made man? McCarthy imagines this question through attention to the gendered implications of industrialization of the late nineteenth through mid-twentieth centuries, and through those coded images poses this question: what happens to 'man' in an industrialized world? More importantly, what happens to *humanity* in an increasingly inhuman(e) world?

This chapter examines McCarthy's depictions of the 'machine in the garden' in his screenplay *The Gardener's Son* and in two early Appalachian novels, *The Orchard Keeper* and *Child of God*, and then traces its spore through the Border Trilogy, ending finally with a nod to the latter part of the twentieth century in *No Country for Old Men*, the contemporary world of *The Counselor*, and the apocalyptic future in *The Road*. First, a brief explanation for which texts are examined and which are not. In *The Gardener's Son*, set during Reconstruction and before the advent of the automobile, McCarthy levels his gaze on a critical era in American capitalism driven by the second industrial revolution and sets the stage, as it were, for his persistent critique of the myth of the self-made man. Next, his early Appalachian novels set up the function of complex pastoral imagery, with its threatening machine, which continues and expands in the Border Trilogy, recurs in *No Country*, and undergirds the central arguments of *The Counselor*, before arriving at a 'worst case' imagined future in *The Road*. *Blood Meridian* and *Outer Dark* are not represented in this discussion, as both are situated in engine-less worlds, although *Blood Meridian* focuses on the very economic question that emerges from this chapter: what is it that drives the violent dispossession inherent in American capitalism?[9] Because *Blood Meridian* traces the answer to that question back to the era of Manifest Destiny, the next chapter focuses on this novel in an historical examination of the theme of American capitalism in McCarthy's fiction forward from the mid-nineteenth century.

The primary historical context for this chapter is, first, the second industrial revolution; then the technological boom of the early twentieth century; the collapse and rebirth of the US's consumer-driven capitalist economy during the Great Depression and the Second World War; and finally the shift toward global capitalism in the 1980s. *The Gardener's Son*, based loosely on the true crime story of Robert McEvoy, who shot and killed a textile mill owner in Graniteville, South Carolina, in 1876, contends directly with the myth of the self-made man during the height of the second industrial revolution, shortly after the completion of the transcontinental railroad (1869) and shortly before the end of the Reconstruction Era's limited civil rights advances. *The Orchard Keeper* traces the collapse of rural, agrarian communities in East Tennessee during the boom era of the Tennessee Valley Authority and through Prohibition; *Child of God* reinforces its examination of rural collapse following the Second World War. The Border Trilogy spans the Second World War and the first decade following, with attention to the implications of nationalism and the military-industrial complex in the atomic age. *No Country for Old Men* revisits many of the themes of *The Orchard Keeper*, its nostalgia for a rural Texas homesteading past (instead of an eastern Tennessee rural past) undercut by brutal observations about the implications of market economics during the boom of the transnational marketplace in the 1980s. *The Counselor* picks up many of the same narrative threads from *No Country*, but transposes them to the first decades of the twenty-first century. And, finally, *The Road* offers a retrospective look at the end of human existence and the tenacity of the violence and aggression that, even at the end of civilization, dominate American masculinity.

Throughout each of these texts, the 'machine in the garden' and its implicit economic critique are represented by a sort of metaphoric shorthand in which trucks and cars and horses, critical forms of transportation in post-industrialized or industrialized societies on the one hand and rural or pre-industrial communities on the other, reflect larger themes about definitions of success, value, and meaningfulness. In McCarthy's metaphoric lexicon, this notion of innate value is described as a matter of *souls*; yet this is not, strictly speaking, a theological argument. Wild animals are consistently described as possessing souls, but when domesticated they lose access to the universal soul that grants them a profound communal connection with each other and a place in the matrix of the natural world. By implication, human beings' souls are damaged and fragile, quickened in the natural world but alienated, perhaps lost entirely, in the machine that cranks the engines of a market economy.[10]

Cars, trucks, complexity, and masculinity

Analysis of recurring motifs that speak to capitalist processes and environmental losses reflects the driving ideas of complexity economics. Complexity economics pushes against the pre-2008 dominant model, which reads market economies as systems with determinable 'optimal' functions and representable agents (market forces), and which accounts for irregularities by calculating in random stochastic processes (typically modeled on calculations of Brownian motion, random behaviors that are unpredictable yet measurable). Complexity theory applied to economics, however, reads markets as complex adaptive systems (CAS). It understands economic systems to be dynamic, with 'often abrupt transitions between some temporary order and volatile disorder.'[11] Rongqing Dai offers a more philosophical explanation: social collaboration is always a fraught contest between 'mutual reliance and mutual competition' for survival.[12] What may seem random irregularities in marketplaces in fact derive from the irreducibly complex interrelationship between 'social effects of production and distribution,' the 'relationship between production and natural resources plus environmental quality,' and inconsistencies between individual and systemic benefit.[13] Market capitalism would predict certain behaviors on the basis of economic benefit to the individual and to the society, presuming an 'equilibrium benchmark' as a balancing point between competing parties' needs.[14] Yet benefit can be real or nominal, as when an individual or group behave in accordance with something that they believe to be beneficial to themselves, but that, according to information they do not have or know or choose to believe, is detrimental to their interests. Economies reflect and affect dynamic social structures from political realities to environmental ones. Reading economies as complex adaptive systems moves away from the teleological language of 'benefit' and instead focuses on stasis and change.

Complexity economic models attempt to account for—without, necessarily, explaining or shaping—the interrelated complexities that affect markets. In fiction, the focus is not on transmitting models that account for markets' behaviors, but rather on exploring the complex interrelationships between social and political power, resources, productivity, and profit. In literary representations of complex adaptive economic systems, we would expect to find representations of dynamic change-and-stasis processes and the causes and ramifications of such processes on individuals, societies, and environmental systems. In McCarthy's fiction, cars and trucks stand as material referents for a market economy from the late nineteenth century through the present. They also represent more abstract notions of (white) masculine performance, national identity, and (patriarchal) power structures encoded within the US's market system, metonymically standing for many of the interrelated forces that produce and affect social and political power disparities, resource scarcity and surplus, profit sharing or isolation, and the implications of productivity on natural systems.

The significant role of cars, specifically, in McCarthy's fiction has often been noted, but noted in passing.[15] After McCarthy left the University of Tennessee without graduating, he and his first wife, the poet Lee Holleman, moved to Chicago, where for some time McCarthy worked 'reportedly as a salesman in an auto parts store.'[16] A *Knoxville News Sentinel* piece claims he was an auto mechanic as well.[17] McCarthy's interest in car mechanics extends to an enthusiasm for cars as luxury items—cars whose design is intended for more than just conveyance from place to place. McCarthy's second wife, Anne DeLisle, remembers McCarthy fixing up an old XK-120 Jaguar with no roof, which they drove on their honeymoon 'down through Geneva and all the way around through Italy and down the south coast of France to Barcelona, then to Ibiza.'[18] In correspondence with Guy Davenport, McCarthy mentions particular cars, usually sports cars, as points of interest. Once, he waxes poetical about a Corvette owned by a mutual acquaintance, 'Frank,' who describes driving that car as a 'sexual experience.'[19] Given McCarthy's interest in cars, it is not surprising that they appear in symbolic roles in his fiction. At times, even cars in insignificant roles are meaningful. For instance, on a manuscript page from an early draft of the novel *No Country for Old Men*, a page of dialogue between Llewellen Moss and the unnamed hitchhiking girl he picks up, McCarthy wrote 'The Barracuda' in the upper right corner, a space where he typically notes chapter heads or titles of manuscripts.[20] Although there is evidence that earlier drafts saw more of the sinister and mysterious black Plymouth Barracuda, the final version of the novel makes only three mentions of the vehicle, with two of those references being in the same scene (215, 236, 238). In that latter scene, the car has been abandoned after its cartel-affiliated driver has been shot. While processing the vehicle, Sheriff Ed Tom Bell questions with humorous understatement whether the Barracuda has anything to 'turn them tires with' (236). An enthusiastic police officer tells Bell that the car possesses the rare 440 'Super Commando' V8 engine (236–237). The almost pornographic delight demonstrated by the men clustered around the shot-out vehicle, which at this point is merely a crime scene, stands out in a narrative in which that vehicle plays no substantial role.

Describing the significance of the black Barracuda and Llewellen Moss's briefly acquired Ford pickup truck, Kenneth Lincoln suggests that the vehicular descriptions underscore that this novel is a 'man's world.'[21] On the surface, Lincoln's description makes sense; the detail associated with the vehicles is merely a thread in the hypermasculine tapestry of McCarthy's fictional worlds. Yet upon closer examination, Lincoln's comment raises a critical question. The notion that these fictional worlds belonging to 'men' is rife with interpretive challenges. It would not be a stretch to say that a central question in nearly all of McCarthy's works is what it takes to 'be a man,' and how survivable masculinity is in a post-industrialized, increasingly globalized world. The Barracuda that looms so invisibly over *No Country* represents the consistent function of cars and trucks as metaphoric externalizations of interior worlds, and representations of anxiety about masculinity, particularly white, working-class masculinity. Vehicles function as extensions of the hypermasculinity of the weapons fetishism of male-dominated genres such as spy thrillers or westerns, in which weapons serve as external evidence of internal fortitude and virility. In McCarthy's fiction, however, there is always an element of threat involved in depictions of masculine performance or proficiency, whether represented by weapons or vehicles. In these fictional worlds, masculinity is often expressed as an attempt to master the natural world, to exert force and dominance over it—at the expense of the flourishing life of others.

Why are cars such useful referents for the hegemonic masculinity on display in McCarthy's fiction? The Ford Motor Company's production model became one of the driving forces of capital that thrust the US into global markets in the early twentieth century and came to represent the ever-elusive 'American Dream.' Capitalism in the twenty-first century cannot be imagined without Henry Ford's mass-production model. In *Manhood in America* (originally published in 1996), Michael S. Kimmel describes the evolution of a particularly hegemonic form of masculinity in response to pressures from the American industrial revolution in the late nineteenth century. The alienation of labor in such a suddenly and heavily industrialized economy created a pervasive sense of emasculation: 'Manhood had meant autonomy and self-control,' Kimmel says, 'but now fewer and fewer American men owned their own shops, controlled their own labor, owned their own farms.' From 1870 to 1900, 'industrial output increased by 500 percent' in the US, and with industrialization and the consequent working-class boom, definitions of manhood shifted from internal (strong character, morality, and so forth) to external (definitions that comprise a set of traits and attitudes contrasted with 'femininity').[22] In other words, Kimmel suggests, '[m]asculinity was something that had to be constantly demonstrated' and defended against the ever-present threat of being thought too 'feminine,' and so alienated from the core of productivity and material wealth of American society.[23] That core of productivity is perhaps nowhere so concisely demonstrated as in the automotive industry boom following the second wave of industrialization. In his brief history of working-class masculine culture in the US, Stephen Meyer describes an emerging masculinization of working-class identity, which he calls 'shop floor culture,' around the turn of the twentieth century when US autoworkers 'used the new forms of masculine culture to resist the routinization, degradation, and monotony of disciplined work routines.'[24] That pushback seems to reflect a literary bent toward the use of cars and trucks as emblematic of the sociological dehumanization effected by that wave of industrialization and consequent urbanization.

The connection between cars, industrialization, and masculinity is not difficult to trace. Kimmel claims that globalization is 'always a gendered process.'[25] On the national level, male power is reinforced through a concentration of persons capable of embodying the requisite white, straight, cisgender masculinity in positions of economic and political power.[26] On the international level, nations which function as the global centers of economic and political power, such as the US, represent themselves through the proliferation of images of hegemonic masculinity performed counter to non-white, non-masculine images used to represent emerging economies. McCarthy's cars and trucks as referents for global hegemonic masculinities play with these gendered and racialized images of capitalist success. For instance, while in McCarthy's fiction American-made automobiles tend to represent idealized masculinity, foreign-made vehicles, which represent problematic images of masculinity, are European. No Hondas or Toyotas take up 'screen time.' It seems, then, that car and truck models and makes are not meant to reflect realistic American roads or highways but to comment instead on performances of domestic and national masculine identity. In general, Fords tend to represent the normative 'American' identity that is characterized by an assumed innate 'goodness,' or at least civic innocence. In *Cities of the Plain*, the stamina of a Ford pickup truck becomes the comparison point by which to illustrate male 'goodness': a character comments about the ranch foreman Mac McGovern that he is 'one of the good'ns,' so good that 'you'd wear out a Ford pickup finding a better' (235). In *No Country*, Chigurh steals a 'late model Ford sedan' after killing its civilian driver in order to blend in, appear civically innocent, and avoid capture, and Moss buys a Ford pickup truck to avoid detection (7, 210). By contrast, foreign-made automobiles often stand as phallic substitutes, a caricature of masculine performance, most memorably exemplified by Malkina's enthusiastic response to a Ferrari's windshield in *The Counselor*. Yet in none of these texts do vehicles grant the men who drive them the power or the masculine performance that they crave. It is perhaps inevitable, then, that a novel named for a space for vehicles, *The Road*, depicts a world in which cars and the men who make them are now defunct. Among the literally broken props of this landscape, a man explores a feminine masculinity in which nurture and violence contend for dominance.

It is not men or masculinity generally, but rather a particular type of hegemonic masculinity that is critiqued in McCarthy's fiction. Raewyn Connell and James Messerschmidt define 'hegemonic' masculinity as a type of masculinity dominated by certain traits and performances that reiterate social power and the concentration of power in certain masculine people. While these characteristic traits may classify some masculinities as 'hegemonic,' Connell and Messerschmidt note that not all masculinities are hegemonic and that even in hypermasculine societies, hegemonic masculinities may not be representative of a majority of male persons. Hegemony instead dominates *idealized* depictions of masculinity, often through the production of 'exemplars of masculinity' such as professional sports athletes or celebrities.[27]

This hegemonic masculinity is closely associated with wealth, that fundamental definition of American success. While it may be expressed through physical traits—strength, endurance, musculature, and athleticism—it is a practice of martial or muscular dominance in service of the doctrine of success. In part, the history of private property law in the nineteenth century suggests why American notions of capitalism and gender are so intertwined, given the coding of gender roles coinciding with legal rights of ownership and inheritance.[28] Peter Nolan's *Capitalism and Freedom* (2007) examines the competing possibilities of capitalism during the era of globalization, with the first being continued emphasis on the qualities of aggression and competition—'masculine qualities'—and the second an embrace of cooperation, love, and benevolence—what he terms 'feminine qualities.' Regardless of the risks inherent in an untroubled binary construction of two relative and contradictory trends in globalization, Nolan's tracing of the masculine-gendered language used to define market capitalism through Western history is telling. From the era of Adam Smith and early capitalist economic philosophy, competition and aggression are depicted as innate to capitalism, so that these traditionally masculine characteristics come to reflect the entire economic enterprise. Those values adopt an explicitly masculine coding during the popularity of social Darwinism applied to theories of capitalism from the early twentieth through the twenty-first centuries. Nolan cites Konrad Lorenz's explanation of the aggression required for effective accumulation of capital as a healthy channeling of the aggression coalesced in stronger-bodied human males relegated to 'warrior' roles in the evolutionary history of *Homo sapiens*. Then he tracks that male-coded language of the warrior-wealth manager to George W. Bush's rhetorical claims that martial masculinity is best suited to 'free' the world through capitalism.[29]

The myth is this: the masculine person, with aggressive competitiveness encoded in his DNA and embodied in his superior musculature, is best suited to achieving the American ideal of success, 'making' himself from poverty to financial mastery. The 'self-made man'—the (white) boy who rises from poverty to extraordinary wealth—is the embodiment of the American Dream, as potent a myth today as it was in Benjamin Franklin's guides to affluent manhood or during the age of the Carnegies and Rockefellers. But that mythology is a fragile one, as Wyllie's savage takedown of the myth-makers makes clear: '[S]ociologists, business historians, and others have piled up mountains of impressive statistical data to prove conclusively that a majority of our wealthy citizens do not now, and never did, come up from the ranks of the poor.' But those data are only *facts*. 'Belief in the self-made man requires only an act of faith,' he says, 'and, as every Sunday School boy knows, faith is simply the substance of things hoped for, the evidence of things not seen.'[30]

As Jack Halberstam makes clear, the fragility of hegemonic masculinity can be seen in cultural reproductions of idealized images of white, straight, cisgender masculine performance that rely heavily on 'props' to symbolize power, prestige, and male potency. As an example, Halberstam opens his book *Female Masculinity* (1998) with a description of James Bond in *Goldeneye*, a film which reveals that '[w]hen you take his toys away, Bond has very little propping up his performance of masculinity.'[31] It is to the notion of props as not only extensions but also participants in the construction of masculine identity that I now turn. By emphasizing the fragility of the 'prop'—cars and trucks which serve as metonyms for the 'all-American-ness' or the hegemonic masculinity of the male heroes—McCarthy's texts gesture toward the hollowness of the version of masculinity that Halberstam sees at play in the portrayal of James Bond.

The myth of the self-made man in *The Gardener's Son*

Set in South Carolina in 1876, during the second industrial revolution and Reconstruction, *The Gardener's Son* offers insight into McCarthy's critique of the myth of the self-made man as the masculine embodiment of the capitalist ideal. His papers contain exhaustive research into the event but also—perhaps more surprisingly—into the history of race and class in the push to diversify the southern economy through industrialization. In a letter to McCarthy, the film's director, Richard Pearce, notes that 'McLaurin's book *Paternalism + Protest*,' which McCarthy had recommended to him, includes information about 'the strike' mentioned in McEvoy's testimony.[32] Melton Alonzo McLaurin's *Paternalism and Protest* (1971) is a study of the suppression of unions in the South and the top-down generated ideology of a white working-class identity that was meant to pacify white, low-wage earners by reinforcing the idea that, even underpaid, they were a class distinct from (and higher than) Black workers, who were to be excluded from shop floors and contained in the agricultural sector.

Many other notes between Pearce and McCarthy provide evidence that McCarthy was particularly interested in the mill's tragic history as emblematic of the racial animus created by white industrialists in the South in order to maintain a low-wage white workforce and, thus, build an economy competitive with the industrialized north. McCarthy made a copy, for instance, of a lionizing eulogy of William Gregg and his Graniteville project, published in *The Journal of Southern History* in 1845. The eulogy's author admits that 'if necessary, slaves could be trained and used effectively as cotton mill operatives,' but Gregg's genius lay in his belief that using 'free' (in 1845) Black labor 'was undesirable and not necessary. ... For he [Gregg] was confident that as the advantages of the South became evident, capital, talent, and white labor ... would flow there and strengthen the "native."'[33] Since McCarthy's script opens with a eulogy offered for Gregg—and moreover one that suggests (less explicitly) the same ideology of white supremacy linked to laboring class industrialization—it is apparent that this document helped to shape the narrative's trajectory.

In early drafting, McCarthy played with different ideas for young McEvoy's motivation for murder, ranging from playing up his sympathies for unionization to emphasizing his vulnerability to the rhetoric of white working-class grievance.[34] In the final version, McEvoy is left as something of a mystery. But he is a mystery in the sense that McCarthy sketches him as a man with enough rage and grief to commit violence, yet illiterate and itinerate enough to be a slate on which other interlocutors can scrawl their own interpretations for that violence—a moving and disheartening commentary on white working-class rage in the American South. The industrialists are, by contrast, rather more transparent in the play, making explicit their motivations for sewing racial animus among the poor white mill workers. McCarthy's depiction of the mill's shareholders might lack dimension on the page, but their role certainly interested him enough: Stacey Peebles notes that the actor who plays 'one of the industry bosses that so enrage his protagonist' is McCarthy himself.[35]

It is important to pause and note the significance of the textile mill's specific textile: cotton. Technology is not replacing an agrarian or pastoral ideal. It is replacing a class of 'free' manual labor. On the one hand, the loss of the gardener's locus as the organizing principle of the orchard is central to the loss that haunts the story, but audience members note as well the racial hierarchy and barely suppressed racial tension simmering under the surface of the courtroom system, in which Black men are eligible for jury duty yet the lawyer for the defense fully understands that Black men do not have equal access to justice under the law in this Reconstruction-era southern town. The machines that revolutionized productivity in the textile industries of the American South supplanted enslaved humans in an already stained and morally diseased pastoral garden. Even prior to the 'machine,' the drama suggests, the need to accumulate surplus capital and to encode that capital within a small, hermetically sealed 'upper' class characterized US capitalism. The machine does not represent the advent of evil in the Edenic garden; it is a symptom of an evil already there.

As the drama opens, the mill's patriarch, William Gregg, has recently died. The Speaker, who narrates William Gregg's funeral, eulogizes the man, claiming that 'William Gregg was all his life an example of the virtue of hard work. ... By force of his own character, by the habits of energy and industry and perseverance, he acquired for himself a fair share of the world's wealth and some of its honors' (18). The Speaker's eulogy suggests that Gregg's legacy is a legitimization of the myth of the self-made man in American history. Several characters corroborate this idea, noting the economic benefits that the mill brought to this rural community. How his son came to be so corrupt, however, remains a matter of some debate. '[T]he blood runs thin,' the Timekeeper and play's narrator notes, ominously (2). Yet the narrative undercuts the audience's capacity to 'buy into' that social eugenics claim. The assumption that virtue is hereditary, and that it shows itself in the individual's material success, is suspect in this world beset by a crippling racial and economic hierarchy. Later in the play, Gregg's widow opines that '[p]urity of blood is a trust to those possessed of it' and mourns the 'ingratitude' of the working poor (73). As the play unfolds, the Speaker's hagiography of the elder Gregg becomes increasingly problematic.

James Gregg, the hypermasculine embodiment of capitalist 'winners' gone bad, first appears talking up the cotton mill to 'eight or nine' stockholders. When they pass a girl in the mill village, young Gregg winks at a stockholder (4); later he propositions the fourteen-year-old girl Martha McEvoy (25–27). Later, alluding to that predatory behavior, Robert McEvoy offers the only indication of his personal motivation for killing Gregg: that he *knows* James Gregg propositioned his sister and preyed on other women (83). Then, counter to James Gregg's representation of a spoiled scion of a lionized industrialist, *The Gardener's Son* presents its antagonist/protagonist: social outcast and one-legged murderer Robert McEvoy. McEvoy's violence is not motivated by greed or resentment against the wealth of the Gregg family. Instead, he lives a type of nomadic life that is counter-intuitive to the fundamental assumptions of value in a capitalist society in which the pinnacle of human success is the self-made man, the wealthy entrepreneur whose pluck, ingenuity, and work ethic bring him and his society into relative economic prosperity.

From the beginning, McEvoy is described as a man whose appetites are 'unaccountable': he does not value work in the mill, or betterment in material forms such as housing. He rides the rails illegally and wanders in caves where 'heathen' Indigenous people still live. To his sister, he admits his inability to understand the value system of the mill town: 'The good book says all men are brothers but it don't seem to cut no ice, does it?' he queries, reflecting on class disparities that are of more relevance than divine fraternity in social relationships between human beings (40). Captain Giles, the mill's 'time keeper' and floor manager, fires young McEvoy for his 'unaccountable' ways: 'them that choose to toil not neither do they spin has got to berth elsewhere' than the mill, he explains (32). The misquoted allusion to Jesus' words—'Consider the lilies of the field, how they grow; they toil not, neither do they spin'—underscores the gulf between Jesus' value system, in which humans are adjured to be no more anxious about food, clothing, or shelter than lilies in the field, and a value system in which crops are plucked and spun for clothing in vast mills that render wealth to the few and backbreaking labor to the many.[36]

In addition to illuminating the antihuman ethics of early industrial capitalism in the US, the drama also draws pointed attention to the implications of race during Reconstruction. Because he is poor (a literal carpetbagger), McEvoy is kept in cells with Black inmates. At this point in southern history, Jim Crow laws had not yet snapped into place to push back against the economic and legal inroads that Black southerners made following emancipation. The screenplay notes that there are Black lawyers on both the prosecution's and the defense's legal teams and nine Black and three white jurors (60). Nevertheless, McEvoy, placed by his society with Black men because of his economic status, refuses to eat with the Black men digging his mother's grave; he even yells a racial epithet at them when they extend kindness to him (49). His resentment finds an outlet in the form of racial animus. He is better than no one in his world, but he can at least hold onto the myth that, as a white man, he is better than *them*.

McEvoy's father, the gardener of the title, is a man both more circumspect and more humane than his broken son. During his son's trial, he visits with Whipper, the Black defense attorney, and tries to blame class for his son's conviction: 'If my boy were a Gregg he'd not even be tried,' he says. Whipper, however, responds by pointing out the other side of that coin—that class, in the South, is *always* trumped by race. Whipper says, 'If your son were black he'd not be tried' (67). Whipper explains to the older man that justice is the dream of a world that does not see its true nature: 'Everwhere I look I see men trying to set right the inequities God's left them with' (68). Whether it is God or some bone-deep human bent toward violence and oppression of others is irrelevant. No single character in this drama—with the exception of McEvoy's younger sister, Martha—can imagine a just or equitable world. Martha, who loses every person she cares for, is the only character who represents a capacity to love, an attribute that seems absent in other characters. While she loses her mother and, eventually, her older brother, perhaps her most poignant loss is her horse, Captain, whom she is forced to sell. In a heartbreaking scene, she recounts a time when she and her mother went back to Greenville after her father lost his job to the mill's evolving needs. In the larger town, she says, she saw her horse 'harnessed to a wagon in the street and he knowed me' (39). This young girl's sorrow is revisited at the end of the play; now an old woman, Martha returns to this great loss in the play's closing scene. 'I used to ride him [Captain] just everwheres and he'd foller me around like a dog,' she says (95). When she saw her horse harnessed to another's wagon in front of a store, she recalls, 'I just run across the street and throwed my arms around his neck and kissed him and I reckon everbody thought I was crazy standin there in the middle of the street huggin and kissin a old horse and just a bawlin to beat the band' (96). This one scene of grief, loss, and love is situated at the screenplay's conclusion, underscoring its importance. It is the only glimpse of some other way to be in a world defined by arbitrary and pernicious relative values for white lives and for Black, for poor lives and for rich. Martha's love for her horse is not further explored in *The Gardener's Son*, but characters who value other living things beyond their use value in a market society are a theme that recurs throughout McCarthy's corpus.[37]

The rise of the automobile in *The Orchard Keeper* and *Child of God*

The machine whose call echoes through *The Gardener's Son* is a train, but its haunting whistle portends a use of more advanced transportation technologies as emblematic of the self-made man and the capitalist success that makes him in McCarthy's novels. In *The Orchard Keeper*'s first scene, Kenneth Rattner, the antagonist of the narrative, enters a store, where he tries to convince the store's clerk that he is looking to purchase a jack for his car. He postures as he describes his vehicle: 'Why I got me a new Ford. Brand-new thirty-four, V-eight motor. Scare you jest to set in it' (9). The shopkeeper recognizes macho posturing and ignores him, and Rattner steals the car jack. In the following section of the narrative, the bootlegger Marion Sylder, who plays the narrative role of Rattner's dialogic opposite, pulls up to the Green Fly Inn in a strangely similar car: 'a glistening black Ford coupe' that is 'brand new' and has a powerful engine (13). Sylder's Ford coupe may be the transformative V8 Model 40. The narrative never explicitly claims that Rattner's performances of masculinity are failed performances—but he is a failed father and a villainous man whose violence is disproportionate and ineffective. Sylder, by contrast, eventually kills Rattner and provides a male role model for his son. The powerful Ford car, imagined by the former and possessed by the latter character, symbolically reiterates this dynamic.

However, possessing the Ford does not grant actual potency. Sylder is eventually betrayed by the machinery that makes him more of a man than Kenneth Rattner: his truck dies during a bootlegging run, and Sylder is chased on foot, caught, and sent to jail (210–211). *The Orchard Keeper*, set roughly from 1936 to 1940, draws a stark contrast between the industrialized men of the modern world (Rattner and Sylder) and the pre-industrialized Arthur Ownby and the romanticized youth, John Wesley Rattner, whose near-feral peregrinations are all on foot. The old man of the novel, Ownby, daydreams of bygone days in which people rode wagons as their primary mode of transportation, and is troubled at night by dreams of cars (59). He connects the sounds of car engines to the structures of society that threaten him, legal and illegal parties who may be in search of the body in the pit that he guards (Rattner's body, although Ownby does not know this). While Ownby is elderly and has reason to fear unknown parties approaching his property, it is worth noting that it is the sound of cars specifically that triggers his restless sleep. Ownby's antipathy toward cars and trucks of all sorts thus seems to be connected to an idea of a type of masculinity constructed within the context of an increasingly industrialized, anti-masculine, and anti-human world that McCarthy critiques.

In one of his few good dreams, Ownby recalls meeting the girl who would become his wife. In these long-gone days, he and the girl traveled in mule-pulled cart (21). While Ownby's dream-world is characterized by mule-power, rather than the horse-powered engines of Sylder's world, hound dogs—specifically Ownby's hound and John Wesley's pup—stand as symbolic representations of what humanity stands to lose in the rising tide of industrialism. *The Orchard Keeper* presents a particular history of Red Branch, Tennessee, focusing on its shift from a rural, Appalachian community to a developed, increasingly urbanized one during the years of the Tennessee Valley Authority (TVA), the development of atomic energy facilities at Oak Ridge, the Alcoa Aluminum plant, and the establishment of the Great Smoky Mountains National Park.[38] The two characters who most closely represent the pre-industrialized world are young John Wesley and Ownby. John Wesley's privileging of animal life represents his emotional and psychological connection to the natural world; he leaps into a river to rescue his hound dog, and when he catches a hawk and is offered a bounty for it, he realizes that commodification of the hawk violates his fundamental ethical principles, and he attempts to repay the bounty (124, 81). In both of these cases he orients himself toward animals in a way that suggests that he does not privilege human life over the hound dog (a non-anthropocentric expression of self-sacrificial love for another), and in the second he recognizes animal life as carrying an innate value not reducible to economic value—a being off of whose body the moral man does not profit. Here in his first novel, McCarthy begins to articulate a critique of the myth of the self-made man in American cultural history. Masculinity, when it is fused with the capitalist ideal of wealth as the fullest measure of manhood, is incompatible with a pre-industrial ideal of care for the natural world and fiscal integrity as the measure of a man.

Ownby is the vessel of the novel's image of that older sort of economic value system. In these early decades of the twentieth century through which the orchard's keeper lives, the 'expansion of machine culture, already introduced to East Tennessee in the industrial railroad logging era and continued with the advent of the TVA,' signals the end of the rural mountain community as Ownby knows it.[39] Not surprisingly, Ownby demonstrates a very different sort of masculinity from the other characters in the novel. Both Rattner and Sylder are violent men; Sylder is more proportionately violent (he kills only when he has been attacked first), and he also demonstrates a sense of adventure and risk with his bootlegging. Ownby does not take such risks, instead primarily hiding in trees and watching from distances. His is a feral, protective masculinity that is characterized more by nurture than by outright demonstrations of aggression. Ownby wanders the orchard, now fallow, and watches the makeshift crypt with his deformed hound dog, Scout. Like Martha's, his exhibition of love for an animal represents some other value system than the one practiced by the dominant social forces at play in the novel.

When the police find the 'X-marked' shot-out water tank near Sylder's crashed car with its burden of whiskey, they question John Wesley, who refuses to turn on Sylder. They then go to Ownby's house to question him. Ownby defends his home with a shotgun, the embodiment of Appalachian mountain folk who have seen the deforestation and loss of habitat from logging and the construction of the railroad and the increased dependence of mail-order and 'new-bought' material goods rather than subsistence living.[40] Sheriff Gifford and his deputy Legwater shoot out the windows of Ownby's home, representing a government that takes by violence what it cannot coerce more passively (185). Ownby flees his ancestral property, and the narrator observes that he and his dog are 'faint and pale shapes in the rain' (188). When Ownby shows up at a store to trade for food and supplies, he is arrested and sent to an assisted living facility. He is forced to leave Scout behind, and as they drive away, the old man looks back at the dog 'still standing there like some atavistic symbol or brute herald of all questions ever pressed upon humanity and beyond understanding' (205). In these haunting descriptions, it is the man's relationship with the dog, and some pre-civilized communion between them, that focalize the loss that Ownby represents. They are ghosts, remnants of a past time, and the scene closing around the pathetic image of a dog calls into question the humanity of those who have forced the old orchard keeper to abandon it.

Child of God doubles down on images that associate the rise of the automobile with human avarice and violence, and with the loss of pastoral wilderness, representing lost innocence and kinship communities. Like *The Gardener's Son*, *Child of God* is loosely based on true crime stories. In this case, its dubious protagonist, Lester Ballard, is an outcast from rural Sevier County who becomes a necrophile and serial killer. Unlike the single, relatively well-documented incident that inspired *The Gardener's Son*, there is not, as Luce points out, a single real-life event or person on which Ballard is based. Instead, historical analogs are James Blevins, the 'Lookout Mountain Voyeur,' and Ed Gein, the Wisconsin necrophile (and inspiration for *Psycho*), who seem to be composite inspirations for McCarthy's Appalachian misfit.[41]

In *Child of God*, unlike in *The Orchard Keeper*, no car is given a single identifying feature or named by make or model. For Ballard, cars represent the flat monolith of a society to which he has no access. It is no accident that Ballard finds couples engaging in sexual congress in cars, scenes that spawn his career of voyeurism and eventual necrophilia. Cars represent liminal locations for illicit affairs; they are 'safe' possessions of civilians, but the ones parked on Frog Mountain, in the wild, away from civilization, are where the part-feral Ballard comes into contact with an otherwise shut-off world. For example, Ballard's first voyeuristic adventure is by happenstance, when he stumbles on a car and, 'his ear to the quarterpanel,' discovers the inhabitants, a Black boy and a white girl, in a forbidden liaison (20).[42] Next, Ballard engages in his first rape of a corpse in a car, also by happenstance. Ballard comes 'down off Frog Mountain' and finds a 'car there with the motor chugging gently' (85). The car's inhabitants have asphyxiated while in flagrante delicto, and Ballard finally gets his chance to touch a woman's breast and to 'pour … into that waxen ear everything he'd ever thought of saying' (88). Ballard's behavior sets him apart from civilized society, but his desires for companionship, for sexual gratification, and to communicate with others mark him as fully human. To the civilized world, Ballard is a gothic monster who 'scuttle[s] with his ragged chattel down stone tunnels within the mountain' at night, but he is a hideous manifestation of the hidden selves of the visible world, the rapacious, violent, lonely, and yearning who, unlike Ballard, are able to mask their violent desires and pass as 'civilized' (154).

Ballard is also estranged from communion with the animal world. He carries his hunting rifle with him everywhere, and while he apparently *can* hunt, he is always depicted carrying small, easy game, such as a 'brace of squirrels' or other small prey (19). When he watches hawks whirling overhead, readers are told that Ballard 'did not know how hawks mated but he knew that all things fought,' and so he mistakes the graceful ballet of their mating ritual for a fight (169). Ballard then sees an old mountain man driving a cart pulled by a mule. Ballard, caught by the sight of a man practicing a way of life now on the brink of extinction in this mountain community, 'let his head drop between his knees and he began to cry' (170). For Ballard, there is none of the nostalgia that *The Orchard Keeper*'s Ownby evinces. He does not weep for what he has lost, but for what he has never had.

In his final attempt at escape, Ballard crawls into a cavern, trying to evade Fate (the aptly named sheriff). In that 'ancient ossuary,' he finds the skeletons of bison, elk, and jaguar (188). Indigenous jaguars are extinct in central and eastern Tennessee, but certain caves, such as Jaguar Cave, have paleontological records of the animals from 35,000 to 10,000 years ago, their bones found alongside fossils of other now-extinct animals such as the mastodon.[43] As he claws his way free of these fossil-haunted caves, the first thing Ballard sees on emerging is a domesticated cow (190). He then presents himself to the county hospital and says, 'I'm supposed to be here' (192). Having traveled through the geological and paleontological record of his geographic space, Ballard gives himself up to be locked in a cage and examined like a scientific specimen or a zoo animal. He is interred in the state hospital in Knoxville and kept in a cage until he dies (194). After death, Ballard is dissected, 'laid out on a slab and flayed, eviscerated,' his 'entrails ... hauled forth and delineated and the four young students who bent over him like those haruspices of old' (194). Ballard is literally excised from his community, but that excision is treated as though it encodes some prophetic insight into the human condition. The community that have failed to recognize their own natures in Ballard, instructed by the narrator to '[s]ee him' because Ballard is 'sustained by his fellow men,' will not be able to find in the remains what was not found in the living man (156).

After all, the opening scene indicates that Ballard's social transgressions are extreme forms of an ongoing violence already in motion. The novel opens with townspeople arriving like a 'caravan of carnival folk' in a truck followed by cars to auction off Ballard's ancestral property, literal machines erupting into the 'otherwise mute pastoral morning' (3, 4). The auctioneer entices the crowd by offering the logic of real-estate investment against venture capital: 'A dollar might not be worth but fifty cents a year from now. ... But real estate is goin up, up, up' (6). McCarthy draws an uncomfortable symbolic parallel between an economic system with a perpetual growth model, a system that will strip the poor and leave them even more vulnerable in favor of those with means being worth ever more, and Ballard's ever-increasing dehumanization and his use of the bodies of others. If the darkness that Ballard represents, a drive to take what is not offered, to horde what was once human, is sustained and 'borne up' by society, how can it be excised?

Not surprisingly, Ballard's remains are carted away on a trailer hitched to a jeep, a vehicle designed in the Second World War as a military all-terrain vehicle (196). As Luce points out, throughout McCarthy's Appalachian novels, '[t]he natural environment of Red Branch [Tennessee] is depicted in imagery stressing its repeated penetration by the paramilitary machine or, in a corollary image pattern, its enclosure or containment by the mechanical.'[44] Ballard is as much a victim of the machine as he is a human representation of the toxin it represents: he is violent, depraved, characterized by an inability to control his insatiable drives for sex and for collecting (mainly women's bodies). He is a caricature of toxic masculinity. Yet he is so extreme an example that he is repudiated by his community, expelled from the earth itself, and made a stranger in his own land.

Animals and virtue in the Border Trilogy

Ballard heralds the dark heart of the military industrial complex's bleeding into the rapidly industrialized mountain country of eastern Tennessee, while Arthur Ownby and John Wesley Rattner represent those who resist the incursion of such martial, wealth-driven value systems. Their affinity for the natural world characterizes their alternative priorities, for a subsistence-style life lived in close proximity to the 'wild.' Such affinity is consistent among the few 'good guy' protagonists in McCarthy's fiction, men whose virtues are obvious if not unproblematic. These men, not surprisingly, preferentially ride horses or walk, and John Grady Cole and Billy Parham of the Border Trilogy are McCarthy's fictional exemplars of this preferentiality for animals over machinery. Throughout the Trilogy, John Grady and Billy exhibit such overwhelming preference for horses and perambulation over machinery that relatively few vehicles appear at all, and those that do primarily exist in *Cities of the Plain*. In all three volumes, the Second World War lies at the heart, a silent horror that is never directly addressed. In this regard, the Border Trilogy reflects *The Orchard Keeper*'s largely implicit treatment of the military industrial complex's effects on the rural community.[45] While the Trilogy is discussed in greater length in Chapter 5, a brief overview here suggests its important thematic focus in McCarthy's corpus. *The Crossing* is chronologically the earliest of the three novels, opening in 1940 with its sixteen-year-old protagonist Billy Parham embarking on what seems initially like a simple quest: to capture a she-wolf who has been preying on his father's cattle. It ends, after violence, loss, three journeys into and back from Mexico, and the birth of a legend, with the first test atomic bomb explosion at the Trinity Site in July 1945.[46]

The Crossing is a novel about maps and the ways that men seize, claim, and profit from the violent acquisition of the bodies of human and nonhuman others. It is peppered with framed narratives, lengthy stories told by blind men and revolutionaries and travelers and shorter stories told to Billy by men and women he meets on his journeys. Douglas Wager, the artistic director of the Arena Stage, traveled by train from Washington, DC, to New York City with McCarthy in fall 1991—around the time McCarthy was drafting *The Crossing*—to accept a Kennedy Center award for *The Stonemason*. Wager recalls McCarthy talking about 'how narrative is basic to all human beings. ... our reality comes out of the narrative we create, not out of the experiences themselves.'[47]

The Crossing depicts wild animals (in this case, a gray wolf) as the embodied symbol of 'wilderness.' The wolf functions symbolically much as wild horses do in *All the Pretty Horses*; more extensive attention is given to 'wild' animals in Chapter 5, so treatment of this theme will be brief here. *The Crossing*'s opening action introduces a predatory wolf, but Billy soon un-tells his narrative about the nature of the wolf and replaces it with another story altogether. In this story, men prey on the wolf and do not know that they cannot afford to lose her. *The Crossing* is, perhaps, McCarthy's clearest articulation of what is at stake in the loss of the 'soul' of the wild: it is the loss of a story of another world, another reality, another system of value that is foreign entirely to the economic system that defines value in terms of wealth, and heroism in terms of violence. This theme is introduced through one of the only scenes that features a car. Billy manages to rope the injured wolf and lead her while mounted on his horse. They ride south, until a farmer driving a 'chugging' Model A startles the wolf and the horse, and nearly ends the episode (58). The farmer wants to know why Billy is trying to save the wolf, demanding, 'Have you always been crazy?' (59) This question signals the first time that Billy reckons with his McEvoy-like 'unaccountable' desires: his affinity for the natural world, and more specifically for the 'wild,' counter to his father's agrarian life.

All the Pretty Horses opens in the year following the Second World War, drawing attention to contrasts and similarities between an industrialized, post-war American economy in which small, privately owned operations are collapsing under the pressure of corporatized mass-production of cattle and the 'paradise' south of the border, where near-feudal fiefdoms persist. Yet both economies serve the wealthy. John Grady, failing to recognize the fundamental principles at play in each, is complicit in the world of taming and owning horses and cattle, and so he too is commodified, taken ownership of, and finally given back to the nation he came from. So committed to the world of horses and the dream of horses are they that John Grady and his cousin Rawlins ride south toward Mexico along and across roads, waiting for trucks to pass, and stop at a café that doubles as a sort of emergency automobile repair shop. The boys 'led the horses up through a midden of old truckdoors and transmissions and castoff motorparts' (32). However, the chivalric image they present—horseback in a world where pickup trucks are in their second and third generations—is only that: an image.

Once in Mexico, John Grady joins the ambitious horse-breeding project of Don Héctor, hacendado of the Hacienda de Nuestra Señora de la Purísima Concepcion. Héctor brings in a chestnut stallion from Kentucky via a '1941 International flatbed truck towing a homemade sheetmetal trailer' (125). After the stud horse arrives, John Grady and the hacendado select wild mares for their potential as future cattle horses, trying to find ones with 'cowsense' to breed with the stallion. As Héctor puts it, 'God had put horses on earth to work cattle and ... other than cattle there was no wealth proper to a man' (127). John Grady's passion for the stallion—'Le gusta?' the hacendado asks him, and John Grady responds, 'That's a hell of a horse'—is matched only by the boy's sudden infatuation with the hacendado's forbidden daughter, Alejandra (126). The horses, and the girl, are 'property' in the patriarchal world of mid-twentieth-century rural Mexico. Horses therefore represent a world that is not *separate* from industrialization; they represent the cost of such acquisitive, commodity-oriented value systems to living beings.

If women and horses can be commodified, so too can young men from America. John Grady's personal encounter with a truck occurs when he is taken to the Saltillo prison with Rawlins and Blevins. The boys are transported, in a similar fashion to the stallion, in a 'ton-and-a-half flatbed Ford truck' (172). In this instance, the boys are punished for John Grady's transgression with the prize possession of the man of the house, his daughter. Blevins, accused of horse theft, is taken away from the truck and executed, a 'small ragged figure' who possesses 'insufficient substance ... to be the object of men's wrath. There seemed nothing about him sufficient to fuel any enterprise at all' (177). In the economic mathematics of John Grady's imagined paradise, women, horses, and landless boys are all commodities, and their value lies solely in their capacity to increase the profits of the landowner. The dueña Alfonsa offers a chilling observation, that desiring to be ethical and being complicit in unethical systems too often coincide: 'Between the wish and the thing the world lies waiting' (238).

In other words, John Grady breaks wild horses, but that endeavor is presented as a heartbreaking, visceral metaphor for the young man's loss of his ancestral land and his eventual imprisonment first in a Mexican prison and then within the fenced-in boundaries of the US once he is repatriated. In the final scene, John Grady crosses the Pecos River at Iraan, Texas, and rides past the Yates Field pumpjacks, which are pumping '[l]ike great primitive birds welded up out of iron by hearsay in a land perhaps where such birds once had been' (301). Here, the machine is quite literally fused to the primitive plain. John Grady rides past these still-living relicts, watched by Native people 'solely because he would vanish' (301). He rides in a red desert, the word 'red' repeated six times in the final paragraph, along with the word 'coppering' (302). The emphasis on the color associated with blood suggests the life force of living beings, human and nonhuman—and how easily spilled it is in the acquisition of land, oil, wealth. A life is more fragile than land, oil, and money. Once lost, it is gone; it pales even from memory.

In the final novel in the Border Trilogy, *Cities of the Plain*, set in 1952, Mac McGovern's ranch is equipped with enough vehicles for the cowboys to drive around the border 'cities of the plain' (El Paso and Juarez) in the course of their duties and in pursuit of their off-duty pleasures. Mac owns a pickup truck that the hands use to transport horses, and while that truck's make and model are not named, Mac is later compared to the reliability and 'goodness' of a Ford, so it would make sense to assume he owns the all-American truck (29, 3). However, when Billy Parham and another ranch hand, Troy, drive it, an owl flies into the truck's front windshield and shatters it, a sudden and shocking reminder of the power of even the most fragile inhabitants of the natural world relative to the power of American industry (36). It is perhaps no surprise, then, that Billy rides his horse away from the ranch when he quits after John Grady's death, a man on horseback in mid-century America with a dog on his saddlebow (263). He is next seen as an aging, ambulatory pilgrim. As he wanders, the aging Billy finds 'kind' people throughout the American southwest, from Texas through central Arizona (289). The ability of a person to encounter kindness on the road is, in McCarthy's fiction, the single most unique and remarkable achievement. Billy's utter dispossession as a homeless, itinerate wanderer poses a stunning counter to the myth of the self-made man whose aggressive, violent and wealth-starved masculinity forged the industrialized world. Billy is defined by his *lack*: he is barren in terms of sexual and material acquisition. He is also the only one of McCarthy's protagonists to reach actual old age and to experience and demonstrate kindness toward others. Authentic goodness, in other words, is not conflated with vehicles; in McCarthy's fiction, it may be incompatible with them.

Cars and men in the present and future

No Country for Old Men, which opens in 1980, combines the patterns established in the novels that trace the rise of automobile culture with the patterns of the Border Trilogy. The connection between cars and trucks as accouterments to manhood has become strictly codified by this point in McCarthy's oeuvre. For instance, when Llewellen Moss, one of the primary protagonists, finds himself on the run and without a car, he legally purchases a '1978 Ford pickup with four wheel drive and a 460 engine' (210). He has the title notarized in a move that makes little sense until he explains to the girl he picks up that up until three weeks ago, he was a 'law abiding citizen' (210, 211). The truck marks him out as a citizen and a 'good-guy,' yet by this point in the narrative he has crossed the legal boundary line into the territory of outlaw. And so, when the girl asks Moss if he is 'queer,' he tells her that he is (228). On the surface, this statement is untrue, since she is clearly asking about his sexual orientation and he is a cisgender, straight man; but his response is a wry effort to express his 'wrongness,' which he does through emasculating himself, in terms of the homophobia coded into hypermasculinity in the US, telling her that he is 'queer' rather than admitting to her that he is embroiled in a drug deal. In addition to Moss's complex relationship with vehicles, the novel follows Anton Chigurh, the amoral hitman, who attempts to blend into civilian life by stealing a police car, then trading it for a 'late model Ford sedan' (7). His narrative ends abruptly when a civilian runs a stop sign and totals his car (261). It also follows the closest approximation of a 'good' guy in the novel, Sheriff Ed Tom Bell, who departs the narrative last, and departs it on horseback, riding after his wife, who, he tells his horse, is his 'heart' (300).

It may be simplistic to say that the capacity to love is innately connected to a preference for horses over cars in McCarthy's fiction, but it is nevertheless a connection that underscores the privileging of the animal over the machine. Blood—together with the life, death, and mystery it represents—is primal. Living creatures possess a value that transcends whatever value is associated with the manmade. Vehicles may indicate a type of manliness defined by the practice of power that characters wish to emulate, but vehicles are an inherently unstable prop to those masculine performances. Vehicles fail, while horses ride on.

The Counselor shares with *No Country* a geographic setting and many of the same central themes (a drug deal gone wrong, an ordinary man's greed precipitating his path to damnation). *The Counselor* also critiques the ethical failures of late capitalism more explicitly than most of McCarthy's earlier works. Written and produced in 2013, *The Counselor* is not specified by the date of its narrative action, but, as I discuss in Chapter 3, the narrative is rooted in the early decades of the twenty-first century. So important is the specificity of the vehicles each character drives that the film makes visual reference to the make of the car named in the script. Visual reference is fused by metonymy to the protagonist: when the Counselor gestures to his car, he says 'That's me over there' (63). The screenplay notes that the car is a Bentley. In the film, when the audience first sees the Counselor driving a car, the camera focuses on his face in close shots framed by the headrest, and specifically by the very visible British-made Bentley insignia. In the film, the Counselor wears linen pants and crosses his legs in European style, at the waist. He is not an 'all-American cowboy' as is John Grady Cole. Analogs for the Counselor in McCarthy's corpus may be closer to Chigurh, a man who is faintly European, faintly 'exotic,' as one character points out (*NCOM* 112). Whatever he is, the Counselor is a 'Bentley': a man characterized by his desire for wealth symbolized through his possession of a British-made luxury vehicle.

The scene in *The Counselor* most likely to raise reflections on the significance of vehicles in McCarthy's fiction is Malkina's provocative sex scene on the windshield of a Ferrari, at first glance a startling and inexplicable scene. Reiner's disturbed recollection of this event offers an explanation for it, as he underscores the distinction made between sexual prowess and romantic love, material acquisitiveness and self-sacrificial devotion, which is the film's central theme. An early scene between the Counselor and a diamond merchant foreshadows the Counselor's troubling penchant for recognizing his love interest Laura's non-materialistic virtue while attempting to 'buy' her anyway. Later when the Counselor's capacity for self-sacrifice is questioned, viewers understand the depth of his failure. The Counselor is asked, 'do you love your wife enough to go on the rack for her?' The Counselor believes that he does yet fails to do the one thing that would prevent her death: he does not give up his quest for material acquisition (149). It is no surprise, then, that he is failed not just by the wealth he pursues but also by the cars in which he pursues that wealth. He ends up carless and, recognizing that he is hemmed in, asks Westray what he is supposed to drive to escape (138). For him, there is no longer any escape.

In summary, in McCarthy's fiction, male characters who perceive vehicles as a source of power, escape, virility, success, or status find themselves failed by those very vehicles; the more power possessed by the vehicle, the higher the likelihood of its breaking down, being shot at, abandoned, or crushed by the natural world (as in an owl flying into the windshield), or even being a figment of the imagination of the vehicle's 'owner.' It is no surprise, then, that McCarthy's post-apocalyptic novel *The Road* imagines a world divested of machinery. There is only one working truck in the novel, and it appears as a noise that 'sounded like a diesel truck' and heralds the arrival of people in 'canister masks,' one in a 'biohazard suit' (51). The men in the truck hold rifles, and the novel's protagonists, a man and his boy, flee them. Then, the diesel motor 'quit[s]' (52). In place of a vehicle—and because there are no animals left—the father and son are ambulatory: they push a supermarket cart with a 'chrome motorcycle mirror' (4).

However, *The Road* is just as male-dominated as McCarthy's earlier fiction. So what does the absence of vehicles illustrate? If there is anything *The Road* teaches about the crisis of hegemonic masculinity in the twenty-first-century US, it is that it is a terrible and fragile construction, predicated on sovereignty over others, and it destroys what it needs to survive. For Naomi Morgenstern,

The Road is a male romance not just un-writing the conflation of the domestic with the feminine and the nation, but un-writing the role of the patriarchy altogether.[48] Linda Woodson agrees, claiming that indeed 'the father assumes all roles of protector, nurturer, and caregiver.'[49] McCarthy emphasizes props that illuminate the constructedness of masculine identity and the ephemerality of its construction. The fragility of vehicles gestures toward the fragility of what they prop up: a masculinity defined by privilege and power. More specifically, it gestures toward a masculinity defined by industrial proficiency, a 'working' class in which the products of labor, vehicles, are the closest to creation the hypermasculine man will ever get. When industrialization and globalization have collapsed, *The Road* suggests, the survival of humanity may come down to the need for male persons to 'woman up'—to perform generative and nurturing relationships with others in place of aggressive, acquisitive relationships with the natural world. In McCarthy's fiction, the most manly, 'self-made' men and the emblems of American capitalist success—cars and trucks—end in rust, rot, and decay, much like the men and the myths that made them.

Notes

1. Robert J. S. Ross and Kent C. Trachte, *Global Capitalism: The New Leviathan* (SUNY Press, 1990), 116; and Irvin G. Wyllie, *The Self-Made Man in America: The Myth of Rags to Riches* (New York: Free Press, 1966), 174.
2. Orville Prescott, 'The Orchard Keeper,' *New York Times*, May 12, 1965.
3. Dianne C. Luce, *Reading the World: Cormac McCarthy's Tennessee Period* (University of South Carolina Press, 2009), 29.
4. Leo Marx, *The Machine in the Garden: Technology and the Pastoral Ideal in America*, 2nd edn (Oxford University Press, 2000), 16, 26.
5. Marx, *The Machine in the Garden*, 29.
6. Henry Nash Smith's *Virgin Land: The American West as Symbol and Myth* (Harvard University Press, 1978) offers a thorough history of literary treatments of the symbolic heart of America, the West, as 'virgin' land. His treatment does not take into account some of the more pernicious implications of that gendered depiction, but Annette Kolodny does in *The Lay of the Land: Metaphor as Experience and History*

in American Life and Letters (University of North Carolina Press, 1975). For a more thorough treatment of the gendering of landscape in American westerns, see my book *Masculinities in Literature of the American West* (Palgrave Macmillan, 2016).
7 Wyllie, *The Self-Made Man in America*, 4.
8 Ernest Mandel, *Late Capitalism*, trans. Joris De Bres, 2nd edn (New Left Books, 1975), 110–111.
9 A brief note should be made here about why certain works are not discussed in this chapter. *Suttree* and *The Sunset Limited* do offer similar treatments of the machine, but, as the most urban of McCarthy's works, add little to the contrasting 'garden.' The final chapter of this book will delve into an extended analysis of *Suttree*. The Border Trilogy, *No Country* and *The Counselor*, and *The Road* will also receive extended analysis in chapters devoted, respectively, to each. *The Sunset Limited* and *Outer Dark* are the two of McCarthy's works that receive the least treatment in this book, largely because some judicious restraint is required, and their content does not contribute quite as much to my focus as his other works. *Outer Dark*, for instance, is an allegorical tale which does not fit this chapter's thematic focus. The world of the novel exists atemporally, although likely in the early twentieth century; its location is equally unspecified, although it is likely the coastal region of South Carolina, given references to Gullah culture and to alligators. The central action of the text is a tinker's rescue/theft of a child, abandoned but not killed, and so the book becomes an extended metaphor for the use of a human life by others for their own purposes—the child's father, who will neither claim nor kill him and is complicit in the boy's death; the 'grim triune' of violent men who consume the child; the tinker who uses the child but in use saves his life, for a time; and the mother, who searches fruitlessly for the child she would love. Thus, the novel offers a vivid meditation on human use value, but because it is so allegorical, it does not receive attention in this chapter that locates economic critique in the historical contexts McCarthy represents.
10 The language of 'souls' may seem fanciful here, but in McCarthy's lexicon, the imagistic language of a sort of universal soul acts as a code for a non-individualistic and non-anthropomorphized way of thinking and behaving in the world—a way of thinking and behaving that are treated as meritorious. The notion of souls will be dealt with extensively in Chapters 5–6.
11 Wolfram Elsner, 'Complexity Economics as Heterodoxy: Theory and Policy,' *Journal of Economic Issues*, vol. 51, iss. 4 (December 2017), 939–978: 941.

12 Rongqing Dai, 'Chaotic Order: A Consequence of Economic Relativity,' *Complexity in Economics: Cutting Edge Research*, eds. Marisa Faggini and Anna Parziale (Springer International Publishing, 2014), 117–135: 122.
13 Dai, 'Chaotic Order,' 124.
14 Elsner, 'Complexity Economics as Heterodoxy,' 940.
15 See Luce, *Reading the World*, 33; Kenneth Lincoln, *Cormac McCarthy: American Canticles* (Palgrave Macmillan, 2008), 142; and my own article 'Barracuda: Cars and Trucks in Cormac McCarthy's Fiction,' *Southwestern American Literature*, vol. 41, iss. 2 (Spring 2016), 7–18, from which material for this chapter was taken.
16 Edwin T. Arnold and Dianne C. Luce, 'Introduction,' in *Perspectives on Cormac McCarthy*, rev. edn, eds. Edwin T. Arnold and Dianne C. Luce (University Press of Mississippi, 1999), 1–16: 2.
17 Fred Brown, 'Cormac McCarthy: On the Trail of a Legend,' *Knoxville News Sentinel*, December 16, 2007.
18 This quotation is from an interview in a news article by Don Williams, 'Annie DeLisle: Cormac McCarthy's Ex-Wife Prefers to Recall the Romance,' published in the *Knoxville News Sentinel* on June 10, 1990, running on pages E1–E2, found in The Cormac McCarthy Papers, collection 92, box 5, file 1.
19 The Guy Davenport Papers, box 133, file 2. This letter is dated 12 May 1978. 'Frank' may refer to Frank Zappa.
20 The Cormac McCarthy Papers, collection 91, box 84, file 3, p. 239H, and box 84, file 4, unpaginated, respectively.
21 Lincoln, *Cormac McCarthy*, 142.
22 Michael S. Kimmel, *Manhood in America: A Cultural History*, 2nd edn (Oxford University Press, 2006), 58.
23 Kimmel, *Manhood in America*, 81.
24 Stephen Meyer, 'Work, Play, and Power: Masculine Culture on the Automotive Shop Floor, 1930–1960,' *Boys and Their Toys? Masculinity, Class, and Technology in America*, ed. Roger Horowitz (Routledge, 2001), 13–32: 18.
25 Michael S. Kimmel, 'Globalization and Its Mal(e)contents: The Gendered Moral and Political Economy of Terrorism,' *Handbook of Studies on Men and Masculinity*, eds. Michael S. Kimmel, Jeff Hearn, and R. W. Connell (Sage Publications, 2005), 414–431: 414.
26 Kimmel, 'Globalization and Its Mal(e)contents,' 417.
27 R. W. Connell and James W. Messerschmidt, 'Hegemonic Masculinity: Rethinking the Concept,' *Gender & Society*, vol. 19, iss. 6 (December 2005), 829–859: 846.

28 Ellen Hartigan-O'Connor, 'Gender's Value in the History of Capitalism,' *Journal of the Early Republic*, vol. 36 (Winter 2016), 613–635: 621, 624.
29 Peter Nolan, *Capitalism and Freedom: The Contradictory Character of Globalisation* (Anthem Press, 2007), 10, 17.
30 Wyllie, *The Self-Made Man in America*, 174.
31 Jack Halberstam, *Female Masculinity* (Duke University Press, 1998), 4.
32 The Cormac McCarthy Papers, collection 91, box 18, file 1.
33 The quotation is taken from pp. 400–401 of a Xeroxed article from *The Journal of Southern History*, found in The Cormac McCarthy Papers, collection 91, box 18, file 2.
34 A page of notes on McEvoy's actions includes a line 'Young socilist. [sic]—saying goodby. His heart is torn.' Below that, McCarthy has jotted notes on immigrants, on working poor white southerners united against unions, immigrants, black laborers, and so forth. While the notes are not clear enough to elicit conclusions about potential plot points, they suggest that the issue of labor, class, and race in the US during these critical decades was directly at the forefront of McCarthy's mind as he drafted the initial screenplay. The Cormac McCarthy Papers, collection 91, box 18, file 3.
35 Peebles, Page, Stage, Screen, 15.
36 Matthew 6:28, KJV.
37 In a scene near the end of *Suttree*, Cornelius Suttree visits his Aunt Alice in an institution for the mentally infirm, where she recalls a memory of a horse named Captain; the memory is borrowed nearly word-perfect from Martha's recollections in *The Gardener's Son* (S 434). Why McCarthy chose to reiterate this one scene in another text is unclear, but at the very least it gestures toward that scene's importance in his mind. Not only does this scene resonate thematically throughout McCarthy's works, but it also (literally) reiterates.
38 Luce, *Reading the World*, 3.
39 Luce, *Reading the World*, 29.
40 Luce, *Reading the World*, 6, 7.
41 Luce, *Reading the World*, 138.
42 Forbidden because Tennessee's anti-miscegenation laws were not overturned until the 1967 *Loving v. State of Virginia* Supreme Court decision.
43 Patty Jo Watson, Mary C. Kennedy, P. Willey, Louise M. Robbins, and Ronald C. Wilson, 'Prehistoric Footprints in Jaguar Cave, Tennessee,' *Journal of Field Archeology*, vol. 30, iss. 1 (2005), 25–43: 25.
44 Luce, *Reading the World*, 33.

45 Luce, *Reading the World*, 31.
46 James Campbell is the first scholar to note that Billy is in southern New Mexico in 'July of that year' (i.e., 1945) and that the 'false dawn' is the nuclear explosion at the Trinity Site, which occurred on July 16, 1945. See James R. Campbell, '"Seeking Evidence of the Hand of God in the World": Transforming Destruction in The Crossing,' *Proceedings of the 2nd Annual International Conference on the Emerging Literature of the Southwest Culture*, privately distributed (University of Texas at El Paso, 1996), 13–17: 16.
47 Edwin T. Arnold, 'Cormac McCarthy's *The Stonemason*: The Unmaking of a Play,' *Southern Quarterly*, vol. 33, iss. 2–3 (Winter–Spring 1995), 117–129: 121.
48 Naomi Morgenstern, 'Postapocalyptic Responsibility: Patriarchy at the End of the World in Cormac McCarthy's *The Road*,' *Differences*, vol. 25, iss. 2 (2014), 33–61: 54.
49 Linda Woodson, 'Mapping "The Road" in Post-Postmodernism,' *The Cormac McCarthy Journal*, vol. 6, special issue on *The Road* (2008), 87–97: 88.

2

War and the wanderer: the rise of empire in *Blood Meridian*

> The years between the Civil War and the Spanish–American War [in the US] can then be reformulated to emphasize the conjoint processes of nation-building, industrialization, the achievement of substantive independence, and the foundation of an overseas empire.
> (A. G. Hopkins, *American Empire: A Global History*)

> So little are the Homeric heroes presented as developing or having developed, that most of them—Nestor, Agamemnon, Achilles—appear to be of an age fixed from the very first. ... But what a road, what a fate, lie between the Jacob who cheated his father out of his blessing and the old man whose favorite son has been torn to pieces by a wild beast!
> (Erich Auerbach, *Mimesis: The Representation of Reality in Western Literature*)[1]

'His origins are become remote as is his destiny,' says the narrator of the feckless protagonist of Cormac McCarthy's first western. '[A]nd not again in all the world's turning will there be terrains so wild and barbarous to try whether the stuff of creation may be shaped to man's will or whether his own heart is not another kind of clay' (*BM* 4–5). Before penning these words, McCarthy had, more or less, divested himself of his Appalachian roots and journeyed south to a new terrain, a new geography, and a new literary project. His research and extended travels in the US–Mexico border region were largely funded by a MacArthur Fellowship, and in 1985, he published the fruit of his journeys, *Blood Meridian: Or, the Evening Redness in the West*, a novel frequently identified as McCarthy's masterpiece and one of the great novels of American literature. In *Blood Meridian*, McCarthy depicts a panoramic landscape imbued with vitality, rage, and horror, and the men who traverse that land are equally barbarous. It is a novel about war and it is a novel about wandering.

Blood Meridian is a quest narrative whose grail is ambiguous, an odyssey whose sailors have no home to which to return, and a biblical morality tale with no clear moral or conclusion. It is notoriously difficult to interpret, even though it is regarded by most scholars and by McCarthy's legion of fans as among his best work. Because it is an (the?) American western, whatever its conclusions, critics tend to concur that *Blood Meridian* speaks directly to American national character and to the lasting implications of the American frontier era: the great push to claim what is now the American southwest and west in the mid- to late nineteenth century. This chapter will explore *Blood Meridian*'s aesthetic and thematic claims about war, human agency, and the dawn of the American age of empire. More broadly, this chapter serves as the lynchpin for the first section of this book, which examines the rise of US economic imperialism as it is depicted in McCarthy's historical novels and his post-historical novel, *The Road*. Reading economic systems as complex adaptive systems requires an integrated understanding of the relationships between resources, productivity, profit, power, and the complex effects of those relationships on human and nonhuman communities and spaces. The argument of this book is that literature can code those complex systems in graspable symbols and evocative narrative structures. Building on the examination of symbolic referents for capitalism and manhood in America in the previous chapter, this chapter turns attention to the more nebulous territory of literary aesthetics and the structural representation of economics.

Blood Meridian is widely recognized as a literary masterpiece, which makes it an obvious candidate for a methodological approach that reads the rise of economic imperialism in the US at a stylistic level. However, this approach wades directly into muddy interpretive waters. Many critics find that *Blood Meridian*'s gorgeously written scenes of epic brutality render efforts to find constructive meaning frustratingly elusive. Vereen Bell, one of the first scholars to write on McCarthy, claims that its linguistic feats 'transubstantiate' the 'material world,' refiguring the cruelty of its content into something utterly other to human experience.[2] Steven Frye calls *Blood Meridian* an 'extended nightmare in human language.'[3] It is certainly true that the violence in the novel is rendered with shocking beauty; what shocks even more is the meticulous historical accuracy of that violence. J. Howard Woolmer, an early, enthusiastic fan of McCarthy's, hunted down an excerpt published in the literary journal *Triquarterly* before the novel manuscript even went to press. On reading 'The Scalphunters,' Woolmer questioned McCarthy about the accuracy of the genital mutilation in the piece. With distasteful anti-Semitism, he queries whether genital mutilation isn't 'a Middle Eastern thing, like eating halvah?' McCarthy cites research that shows the Comanche also practiced genital mutilation, suggesting that genital mutilation is not the purview of any singular people group, but—'Like eating halvah? Jesus, Howard.'[4]

So what should we make of a horror too beautiful to look away from? Most scholars believe that the darkness in *Blood Meridian* holds a mirror up to the darkness at the heart of the American national project. James Bowers, for instance, asserts that the novel attempts to 'lay bare national myths through the ethnic, racial, and social tensions of 1850s America.'[5] Mark Eaton claims that McCarthy's westerns as a whole 'make visible those violent episodes' of US history that are too often sanitized or presented with a patina of nationalist glory.[6] *Blood Meridian* poses an undeniably bleak vision of the American southwest in the mid- through late nineteenth century. In McCarthy's apocalyptically violent version of the American west, there is no glory. So fantastically rendered is this world, however, that the novel seems to be a critique of more than just US history and cultural memory: it offers a study of human evil itself. In John Jurgensen's *Wall Street Journal* interview with McCarthy and John Hillcoat, who directed the film version of *The Road*, Hillcoat comments to McCarthy, 'I remember you said to me that "Blood Meridian" is about human evil, whereas "The Road" is about human goodness'; McCarthy concurs.[7]

Judge Holden is the novel's gargantuan, hairless, dancing personification of human evil. He may be the 'evil archon' of American literature that Rick Wallach identifies in his seminal article with that title; he may be a personification of the gnostic demonic, entities 'who have turned away from the divine so completely that they no longer feel the pain of separation and rejoice in their own depravity,' as Petra Mundik's meticulous examination of gnostic influence in the novel suggests. He may represent 'conscious evil,' an intentional commitment to immoral acts in human form, as opposed to natural havoc, as Russell Hillier contends.[8] Judge Holden may be any or all of these readings. At the end of the novel, the judge confronts the kid, now a grown man, and talks to him about human agency and violence. 'Only that man who has offered up himself entire to the blood of war,' the judge says, '... only that man can dance' (331). In the following scene, in a shithouse, the judge gathers the man whom he once named as his oppositional force 'against his immense and terrible flesh' (333). That allusive language is the only cue to the man's fate. The judge then returns to the saloon, alone. In a telling shift into the present tense, the novel proper closes: 'He is dancing, dancing. He says that he will never die' (335).

Who is Judge Holden? By his own assertion, and coded into the modal language of the novel, he is the one who has offered himself entire to the blood of war. In notes for an early draft, McCarthy typed a quotation from the pre-Socratic philosopher Heraclitus: 'War is the father of us all and out [sic] king,' and a few more lines, before ending: 'War is god.' McCarthy noted to himself: 'Let the judge quote this in part and without crediting source.'[9] In the published novel, the line becomes: 'War is the ultimate game because war is at last a forcing of the unity of existence. War is god' (249). The judge, then, is war's truest acolyte, the mouthpiece of Heraclitus's ontological claim about human violence, and the (metaphorical?) god of war's closest approximation in human form—the personification of what John Emil Sepich calls the 'universal energies, superrational and mad folly, that are war itself.'[10]

But it is not war alone that renders the judge the sole dancer on the world's stage. It is that which drives war: human societies' avaricious consumption of resources. In McCarthy's economic philosophy, the mechanics of capitalism are the engines of modern warfare, and the value systems that underlie capitalist endeavors are the same value systems that the judge embraces and embodies. War is not *mere* violence but rather is a state of violent conflict between articulated social groups—nations, states, or tribes. The judge claims that war predates *Homo sapiens*, but the logic of his assertion is true only if violence in the animal kingdom can be considered *war* (248). With the arguable exception of ant colonies, there is little evidence that any other species practices the scale and strategy of human warfare. War is a function of organized, populous societies with a purpose and a strategic endgame, whether that purpose is acquisitive (a desire for material or geographic gain), retributive (revenge for perceived loss or injury to the social group), or ideological (an assertion of religious, ethnic, or national superiority). The industrial revolution drove the empires of Europe through the early nineteenth century, but by the mid-nineteenth century, when this novel commences, the US had turned its attention too to such ambitions. *Blood Meridian* is a novel about war, but interpreting its claims is difficult because its most articulate character, Judge Holden, purports to love warfare, and his claims are in the service of war; his views are not necessarily the novel's.

Michael Lynn Crews's bibliographic study of McCarthy's sources offers a suggestive inflection to the specific quality of the evil that drives the violence permeating *Blood Meridian*. McCarthy's notes include a reference to Geoffrey Chaucer's 'The Pardoner's Tale.'[11] Crews suggests that the moral of Chaucer's tale, where violence visits three greedy young men who search for Death and find gold, is that '*Greed is the root of evil.*'[12] Hillier describes the novel's articulation of this point by connecting the judge's espoused worldview with the narrative's perspective. He cites the judge's claim that 'Everything's for sale' (*BM* 295), and then shows that 'the novel's world seems to endorse this grim principle, especially regarding the value of life.' Living creatures are fully commodified; '[u]nder the judge's gaze,' Hillier points out, 'a human or creaturely life loses any intrinsic worth and becomes just one more item in his inventory of the extant.'[13] The judge offers his philosophy about war and commerce: the nature of humanity is greed and violence, and war is the strategic function of societies to acquire more at the expense of others. There can be no other interpretation of human predilection; all societies, given time and numbers, will engage in war in order to profit.

In his Appalachian novels, McCarthy pays subtle yet insistent attention to the military uses of industrialization in early twentieth-century Appalachia. *Blood Meridian* offers an extended and rich analysis of the explicit connections between war and empire, the military industrial complex fused with and inseparable from the economic interests of the US from the nineteenth century on. However, what has confounded scholars and challenged readers' ability to make sense of what the novel *does* with this claim about human greed, the rise of empire, and American violence is that judge's voice dominates the narrative so completely, even though the judge himself claims that the novel has an oppositional force, the kid. If the kid opposes the judge, what philosophy does the kid espouse to counter the judge's? It is clear that the judge 'marks' the kid from their first meeting: the judge turns and watches the kid as he passes, and smiles (14). At their final confrontation in the saloon, the judge greets the kid, saying, 'The last of the true. I'd say they're all gone until now saving me and thee' (327). It is less clear, however, that the kid shares the view that their relationship is oppositional. When the kid refuses to shoot and kill the judge, even at the ex-priest's urging, the judge tells him that he knows the kid will not kill him because there is a 'flawed place' in him. 'You reserved in your soul some corner of clemency for the heathen,' the judge says, and that minimal amount of compassion makes the kid too weak to effectively counter the self-professed acolyte of war (299). However, there is little textual evidence that the kid expresses mercy or clemency toward any non-white actors, even if there is equally little evidence that he actively joins in the slaughter or scalp-taking. In their final confrontation, the judge tells the kid, 'I recognized you when I first saw you and yet you were a disappointment to me' (328). A disappointment he may be to the judge; he is surely more of a disappointment to readers. The novel is no *High Noon* (1952), and the kid is not a noble embodiment of white-hat altruistic good as one might expect in a western. In short, the problem with reading the kid as the sole force counter to the judge is that, if he is, then all that the judge stands for—greed and war—are 'suzerain' (*BM* 198).

There are oppositional forces in the novel; it is just that the kid is an imprecise representation of them. The kid serves as a gestural placeholder, objecting to the judge's claims of precedence and sovereignty. When the judge finds him in a cell in California, the rest of their gang gone, he refutes the judge's verbal manipulations and refuses to subscribe to the judge's philosophy of war (307). The kid does not, however, articulate a position counter to the judge, and the kid certainly does not outlive him. Instead, the kid passes through the narrative as a human referent for a larger conflict, because the judge's arguments are not ultimately aimed at humans. The judge does intend to conquer the people he meets, but more importantly, he aims to conquer the natural world. 'Only nature can enslave man,' the judge says. And that is why he intends to be 'suzerain' over it (198). The judge externalizes the most extreme ideological argument underlying an industrialized capitalist economy and conflict in the service of global imperialism: to rule over everything and to use everything (from people to vegetal and mineral resources) for one's own gain. The kid sees this argument as dangerous, but it is not the kid who stands against the judge. It is nature itself.

In contention in *Blood Meridian* are two different and competing types of violence. Human-made violence, particularly elevated to the level of tribal or group conflict (war), is a mechanistic and wholly destructive violence. Natural violence, by contrast, is cyclical, balanced, and regenerative. Violence is part of the natural life cycle of biological organisms, but human-created violence—specifically its apogee, warfare—operates on a different plane entirely. Near the beginning of the novel, the kid runs into an ex-slaver who tells him that humanity is the 'meanest' of animals and the most dangerous because of its technological capacity. Humanity is 'a creature that can do anything. Make a machine. And a machine to make the machine. And evil that can run itself a thousand years, no need to tend it' (19). By the end of the novel, the kid, now a forty-five-year-old man in 1878, talks with a hunter who recalls his participation in the extermination of American bison. The hunter concludes, 'They're gone. Ever one of them that God ever made is gone as if they'd never been at all' (317). After his assertion, the omniscient narrator remarks that, once again, 'stars were falling' (317). The reference to meteoric activity represents a narrative punctuation mark, linking this last year of the kid's life with his first, born during the Leonid meteor shower of 1833. Meteor showers do not herald doom in a purely scientific sense, but the human tendency to ascribe prophetic warning to such meteorological events suggests that the violence of the novel may be a self-fulfilling prophesy: the destructive capacity of human beings is at odds with the violence of the natural world, orchestrated within a fragile ecosystem that balances destructive and creative forces. It is humanity that preys to the point of extinction.

Even more importantly, however, the meteorites at the end and the symbolic significance of natural phenomena throughout the novel represent McCarthy's emphasis on natural-world portents that evokes an older form of narrative: the epic. Paying attention to the heavy-handed symbolic resonances in the novel matters because the novel's projection of reality is fully externalized. That is to say that its treatment of realism is what Erich Auerbach would define as 'epic.' In *Mimesis*, Auerbach explains how the Homeric epic externalizes interpretation, so that 'all events [are] in the foreground, displaying unmistakable meanings.' This narrative mode operates in contradistinction to biblical narrative, which distills disruptive social forces into a teleological ethos. Biblical narrative shifts between events brought into focus and those merged into 'background' in order to generate a 'multiplicity of meanings and the need for interpretation,' and, among other attributes, this narrative mode demonstrates 'a preoccupation with the problematic.'[14] Mimetic art in the Western tradition, following the biblical model, is representational as it reflects external 'reality,' but it is also interpretive: it seeks to present its subject matter *as* reality, and so it aims to interpret that which is or ought to be seen as 'real.' In *Blood Meridian*, the use of natural phenomena to present interpretations of events that might otherwise remain un-interpreted or interpreted solely by the judge forces readers to reorient themselves from assumptions that privilege human sentience. Readers may begin to resist readings that attribute nature's agency to pathetic fallacies rather than understanding them as 'acts of gods,' as would be expected in Homeric epic. The novel is structured to produce *biblical* interpretative modes using *epic* stylistic devices. Only by paying attention to these subtle stylistic devices can readers identify the true oppositional forces at play: humanity and the nonhuman world.

Setting the stage: warriors and wanderers in the material world

It is not an accident that scholars find *Blood Meridian* equally Homeric and biblical in its 'feel.' In a review of the novel, Gareth Cornwall calls *Blood Meridian* America's 'ambiguous national epic' and claims it 'owes direct debt' to the *Iliad* and *Aeneid*. Richard B. Woodward calls it the 'bloodiest book since *The Iliad*.' Steven Shaviro calls it 'epic in scope' and comparable only to *Moby Dick* in American literature. Leo Daugherty says the novel bears the 'affect of Hellenistic tragedy.' David Williams insists that the novel shares not just an epic 'feel' but the same force, scope, and project as *The Iliad*. Nearly every description of the book's prose also calls it 'biblical': James Wood's oft-cited review of McCarthy's works, 'Red Planet,' claims that *Blood Meridian* effectively 'ventriloquizes the King James Bible.' A Kirkus review disparagingly notes that the novel 'strains for prophetic, Bible-like tones.'[15]

The novel in fact operates through these two representational modes simultaneously. Specifically, through its aesthetic style, which evokes both Homeric and biblical cadences, *Blood Meridian* illuminates two possibilities for engagement with the natural world and the material history of nations. As I asserted in the previous chapter, McCarthy's craft lies in his meticulous fusion of theme and form. This chapter exemplifies that claim, first, through analysis of *Blood Meridian*'s aesthetic indebtedness to the Homeric epic with a correlative emphasis on war and nation building, alongside a refusal of the claims of the subtler complexities of human morality. The resonance of epic modes in the novel illuminates the nature, causes, and consequences of war. Second, this chapter turns to the novel's claims about nations and moralities—the biblical as opposed to epic claims on human nature—in order to argue that the novel's aesthetic style critiques the judge's claims through its evocation of these two foundational modes of representational reality and their divergent propositions for meaning-creation. This reading, then, focuses on witnessing the ravages of war and, perhaps, imagining a way out from under the nihilistic philosophy of the god of war.

Before commencing an in-depth examination of the novel's epic and biblical modes, it is important to take a moment to clarify the significance of the kid's role in the narrative respective to the judge's. While the judge is the embodiment of war, whatever its ultimate interpretation, the kid does not seem to embody any particular ideology or national character. Instead, he primarily serves as an observer of the violent engagements between warring groups. In McCarthy's fictional universes, there are two basic character types: witnesses and agents. In the first category are those who exist on the surface of the world, often described as wanderers, pilgrims, mendicants, or itinerants; they bear witness to the ravages of humanity, usually without taking interventionist action. They do not seek to leave a mark on the world. Some members of this category *do* intervene in what they witness, usually with salvific intent if not accomplishment (like Billy Parham's wolf- and brother-saving quests, for instance), but these characters are not, for the most part, present in *Blood Meridian*. In the second category, characters seek to shape the world to their own agency. In *Blood Meridian*, the wanderers are typically without strong ideological commitments to particular groups or philosophical claims. By contrast, agents tend to have either a nationalist or philosophical rationale for warring, or both: Captain White's ideology of Manifest Destiny is in service of the racial and national claims of superiority of white America, while Judge Holden does not ascribe to any particular nation's claims of sovereignty but adheres to a cosmic claim about the need to embrace violence in order to be the 'one beast and one alone' (331).

War: *Blood Meridian* as epic

In a characteristically incisive comment, Peter Josyph frames *Blood Meridian*'s aesthetic power as Homerically epic—and suggests the implications of that mode's rejection of Judeo-Christian narrative morality. Josyph wonders whether readers must 'check our *ethos* at the door to fully enjoy McCarthy's *epos*.'[16] He is not wrong to pose that question. Auerbach, after all, claims that the Bible's implicit treatment of human nature—jealousy, grief, and so on—is more complex than the externalized worlds of Homeric epics. 'The

Homeric poems,' Auerbach says, 'though their intellectual, linguistic, and above all syntactic culture appears to be so much more highly developed, are yet comparatively simple in their picture of human beings ... Delight in the physical existence is everything to them, and their highest aim is to make that delight perceptible to us.'[17] The judge embodies this mimetic mode and its philosophical implications when he calls on the kid to recognize the joy of the dancer who surrenders himself to the god of war. Pleasure in violence outweighs any attempt to divine deeper meaning from human suffering or striving. 'The gods of vengeance and of compassion alike lie sleeping in their crypt,' he says (331, 330).

Like all epics, *Blood Meridian* is a novel about war, and its characters are, without exception, wanderers. Some are agents as well as wanderers, and some bear witness as they wander, while others simply ... wander. Yet, while many scholars name the *Iliad*, *Odyssey*, and *Aeneid* in descriptions of the novel's literary indebtedness, remarkably few name the pseudo-historical myth of Jason and the Argonauts, that foundational national-historical narrative about Greek exploration of the Black Sea coast that laid the roots for the rise of Greek international trade and set the stage for three thousand years of Greek colonization and empire.[18] Yet *Blood Meridian* specifically connects the epic project at the heart of its narrative with Jason's quest for the Golden Fleece, where the fleece symbolizes national wealth and prosperity. In the novel, there are four specific references to explorer or settlers as 'argonauts,' with an additional two references in the sub-headings of chapters 12 and 17 (151, 241). All references to 'argonauts' are to predominantly Anglo-American groups moving west, underscoring the classical, mythic rhythms of this book whose oceans may be desert but whose themes are war and conquering. The first reference comes as Captain White's crew arrives in Chihuahua City, Mexico. There, the Americans see 'patched argonauts from the states,' these travelers 'bleeding westward like a heliotropic plague' (78). When they hunt the Gileños and come upon a wagon train that has been decimated, they find '[f]ive wagons smoldered on the desert floor,' and they dismount and walk 'among the bodies of the dead argonauts in silence, those right pilgrims nameless among the stones' (152). Dead American settlers are twice more described as 'argonauts' while White's group follows their trail to find their killers (153). Lastly, when the ex-priest Tobin and the kid leave the judge and get lost in the desert, they are found and rescued by Indigenous Digueños, who 'led the refugees into their camp at San Felipe.' There, the kid and ex-priest find an Indigenous population 'dressed largely in the cotton shirts of the argonauts who'd passed there' (300–301). 'Argonaut' is not a common referent for a settler, particularly in the context of American settlement of the southwest and California. Instead, McCarthy's use of 'argonaut' makes it a neologism, a shorthand term drawing a line between the project of these American settlers and the Greek myth about a hero and his crew in search of glory along the rich coastal regions of Greece in order to fund their imperial desires.

'Argonauts' are not the only kinds of wanderers in this epic. There are thirteen direct references to 'pilgrims' in the novel, as well. When the kid is introduced, he is identified as one of many 'pilgrims' heading to the newly created American southwest (5); dead Americans are, variously, argonauts and pilgrims (152). Sometimes, characters use 'pilgrim' to indicate the vulnerability or poverty of a settler, such as when the ex-priest Tobin tells the kid about how he and Glanton first met the judge. 'We cut a parcel of crazy pilgrims down off the Llano,' he says; these 'pilgrims' spoke Dutch, and the judge responded to them in kind (123). Similarly, the 'remnants of a wagon train' beset by cholera, syphilis, and the colorful brigand Caballo en Pelo are twice referred to as 'pilgrims' (253, 260). The only time the term is used in its fullest sense, referring to individuals on religious pilgrimage, is when the kid is twenty-eight. He sells his skills to accompany a party of people across the Mojave east from San Francisco. As he rides ahead of the civilian train, the kid comes across a group of men 'naked to the waist in black capes and hoods who flailed themselves with whips.' A man wearing white and carrying a cross follows, 'all of them barefoot.' The 'troubled sect' is referred to as pilgrims and as penitents, and seems indeed to be a band of penitential mendicants based loosely on 'los hermanos penitentes' (313–315).[19]

Mostly, 'pilgrim' is a term used by the narrator to describe the nature of those who wage war: they are acolytes of destruction. The first allusion of this type appears in perhaps the most famous passage of the book, when the narrator muses that the Glanton gang 'slept with their alien hearts beating in the sand like pilgrims exhausted upon the face of the planet Anareta' (46). In their respective studies on gnostic references in the novel, Daugherty and Mundik concur that the 'planet Anareta' refers to the Renaissance idea of a place (planet) that destroys human life.[20] Later in the novel, when the scalp-hunters cross a 'lake of gypsum,' they see dust spouts and wind cyclones, and 'some said they'd heard of pilgrims borne aloft like dervishes in those mindless coils to be dropped broken and bleeding upon the desert again.' The narrator muses that in such a place, the 'pilgrim lying in his broken bones may cry out and in his anguish he may rage, but rage at what?' (111) When they enter the town of Carrizal in Mexico, the narrator interjects again with a similar anecdote in the conditional mode ('In the days to come ... would'), and wonders whether 'all trace of the destruction of these people would be erased' so that there 'would be nothing, nor ghost nor scribe, to tell to any pilgrim in his passing how it was that people had lived in this place' (174). In other words, the narrative explicitly codes the purpose of the wandering in which the wanderer is engaged, at least in terms of emphasizing its endgame or ambitions.

In addition to the type of language used to describe wanderers, McCarthy externalizes their characterization through physical marks on their persons, similarly to how Auerbach describes the purpose behind *The Odyssey*'s extended foray into a description of Odysseus's scar: 'the basic impulse of the Homeric style,' Auerbach explains, is 'to represent phenomena in a fully externalized form.'[21] Like Odysseus's scar, the 'HT' and 'F' branded on Toadvine's forehead and his cropped ears alert readers to his essential character before he has opened his mouth (11). The lettered brands stand for 'horse thief' and 'felon,' and the mutilation suggests his punishment for the crime of thievery. While Odysseus' scar represents courage, Toadvine is a thorough scoundrel, and moreover has engaged in theft of the most important piece of property a man seeking to travel in a pre-automobile world possesses, a horse. Because he is indelibly marked, Toadvine sells his body as a mercenary. Bodily maiming, then, suggests the uncivilizing effects of these men's embodiment of the purpose of Manifest Destiny: they travel outside the law not to enact it or to civilize, but to engage in yet greater theft.

Reading the novel's adaptation of a Homeric mimetic process for its descriptive mode draws attention to McCarthy's focus on the project of empire. While epics aim to transcend the limits of the specific nation-claims of the empires whose hero tales they sing, *Blood Meridian*'s critique of the US's imperialism is significant because it extends that critique to the nature of empire itself through an economic argument about sovereignty and money. It offers an extended, panoramic critique of Manifest Destiny, but similarly to earlier American narratives about cities on hills and divine mandates, 'Manifest Destiny' in history as in literature has never been solely about America. Deborah Madsen identifies the double-sided coin of the early Puritan notion of exceptionalism, namely, that these early colonies were ones upon which the 'world's eyes' were turned, and they were poised for either greater glory or failure than any people, depending on their faithfulness to their covenant to create a reformed church and a holy society organized around that purpose. Manifest Destiny was the notion that the new nation would be tasked with 'saving the world from itself' by existing as an ideal moral and political society.[22] Thus the creation of the new US republic was not a repudiation of the crisis of colonial power but was a product of crises that afflict imperial states generally. In *American Empire* (2018), A. G. Hopkins argues that the myth of American exceptionalism too often obscures the commonalities between the geopolitical developments in the US in the latter part of the nineteenth century and European colonial powers generally. 'The years between the Civil War and the Spanish-American War,' he says, demonstrate the US's geopolitical behavior directly modeled on the processes of 'nation-building, industrialization, the achievement of substantive independence, and the foundation of an overseas empire' that the British Empire piloted earlier. However, Hopkins points out a key difference: the US empire waxed in an era substantially different from the heyday of the British Empire because technological capacity was outstripping the countercolonial forces of democratization.[23] American economic and military influence around the world has far more dire consequences for emerging economies, natural resources, and global stability than the British Empire had.

Since the earliest scholarship on *Blood Meridian*, scholars have interpreted its dark *epos* as an indictment of US imperialism, focusing on an historical context in which that urge to conquer and colonize Mexican and Indigenous lands was couched in terms of divine mandate. In 2016 Dan Sinykin built on Eaton's 2003 article, situating McCarthy's southwestern fiction within an historical reading of the rise of US imperialism in the mid-nineteenth and into the mid-twentieth centuries. Sinykin reads *Blood Meridian*'s apocalyptic metaphor for the American southwest as a sun that is at both its height (its meridian) and its 'sunset' as speaking to the economic and political crises of 1985: he claims that the novel 'denounce[s] Ronald Reagan's "Morning in America"' through its dying sun imagery.[24] Kate Montague concurs, underscoring the significance of the novel's production during the Reagan era while depicting US expansionism across the continent, both historical moments that vilified the 'other' in order to 'simultaneously open ... up new flows for capital into and out of the nation-state.'[25]

One thing scholars agree on is that *Blood Meridian*'s indictment of the rise of US economic imperialism also critiques its contemporaneous, Reagan-era context. What shape that critique takes, and what specifically the novel critiques, is more variously debated. For the most part, scholarly approaches to the novel understand that the critique is, somehow, fundamentally about economics. Nicholas Monk suggests that the judge personifies insatiable consumption, and the kid stands in opposition to him because 'neither he nor his possessions can be reduced to commodities and traded.'[26] James William Christie argues that *Blood Meridian* can best be understood as a novel about labor; he sees the oppositional relationship between the kid and the judge as representing the forces of constructive acts (work) against destructive acts (violence). In Christie's reading, the novel fails to find a way to organize work with craftsmanship. Like Daugherty, he reads the novel's epilogue as a return to the 'order of work' out of the darkness of violence, yet, Christie says, the novel ultimately 'sees McCarthy's own authorial position implicated with that of the lost poets or the kid's father, whose words serve to separate the kid from the order of craft to which he is heir.'[27] Christie illuminates an important point: the divergent possibilities of making and destroying as coding how McCarthy values work and war, respectively. However, Christie's focus on labor perhaps oversells the point. The kid is not a laborer; he is a scalp-hunter. And while his instincts toward creative engagement with the material world and his disinclination toward shooting unarmed people and children mark him as distinct from the judge's philosophy of total war, he is ultimately merely the judge's victim, not an apologist for another, contrary philosophy of constructive labor.

John Mark Robison picks up on the notion of labor as redemptive in the novel, but contextualizes it historically. He focuses on currency, arguing that coins represent 'not … the exorcising of violence from the marketplace but rather a subtler encoding of it.' Like Christie, Robison reads the kid's oppositional position to the judge through his diverging economic philosophy, although Robison focuses on currency rather than work. In Robison's reading, the kid's final exchange of his last two dollars for the necklace made of severed human ears that Brown used to wear is a symbol representing 'that he has valued human relationship over currency,' and it is a value system that the judge 'cannot understand and cannot allow to continue.'[28] Once again, a desire to read the kid generously results in an interpretation of the novel that both undersells the narrative's reverence for *techne*, in the classical Greek sense of the word—the art of making that incorporates 'making' from engineering to fine arts—and oversells the kid's active engagement with 'making' rather than destroying. After all, a necklace made of human ears is not an obvious or easily interpretable referent for meaningful human relationships.

Raymond Malewitz offers perhaps the best reading of the narrative's deeply embedded reverence for ingenuity and craft. He discusses the material symbols representing creative acts of craftsmanship as evidence that these men who can manipulate the natural or artificial landscapes around them—Comanches splicing telegraph wire, or Judge Holden making gunpowder from urine and saltpeter, as two examples—'resonate with older, mythic notions of American identity.'[29] The language of things provides the novel's semiotic register for US economic, racial, and imperial aims. As Wallach notes, *Blood Meridian*'s 'semiotic systems are indeed imbedded concentrically within each other.'[30] If we focus specifically, as Robison does, on currency, it becomes clear that *Blood Meridian* uses coins as a shorthand visual referent for the rise of nations, the formalization and codification of international relations between the US, Spain, and Mexico: when Glanton's group attempt to navigate the marketplace in Mexico, they have coins of many mints from three countries (France, Spain, US) and Mexico (264). Robison points out that the kid's final year, 1878, was when the US centralized its printing of currency.[31] The history of currency and its significance was not lost on McCarthy; his archived papers include an entire page of notes on different specie used as currency in the contested borderlands in the mid-nineteenth century, from Spanish doubloons to US dollars.[32]

Currency, then, represents the desire for wealth that drives conquest and, through currency's heterogeneity in that historical moment, the 'flickering' nature of value itself. In a fevered state while he is in prison awaiting hanging, the kid dreams about the judge, and in his dream he sees another man, 'an artisan or a worker in metal.' The judge stands over this 'coldforger who worked with hammer and die' and who is a 'false moneyer with his gravers and burins' imprints a face onto the coin.[33] That face will 'render this residual specie current in the markets where men barter.' It is here, finally, that the judge's symbolic role is indicated: 'Of this is the judge judge' (310). The kid has conjured the image of a coiner looking for the face of the god, king, or ruler—the one who defines value and who is the arbiter of wealth in the given system, and in his fevered state, he realizes that the judge is this arbiter. The judge's sole power, in other words, is to determine the currency of the marketplace. What is the judge's currency? War is the 'ultimate trade,' as the judge says (248). The frightening tautology of the judge's philosophy is that violence is the currency of war and the most violent in war are the most powerful, the market 'winners.'

Throughout the novel, characters point to the dangerous and destructive philosophy of empire, where wealth is achieved through dispossession and violence and only in the emptying out of the conquered (lands, bodies) is war satiated. Toward the beginning of the novel, the kid shelters with a hermit who tells him, 'This is a hungry country' (17). The old hermit reveals that he was once a slaver who '[m]ade good money' and stopped only because he '[j]ust got sick of it. Sick of niggers' (18). He then hands the kid a blackened, dried heart, and says it 'costed me two hundred dollars'—meaning this was the price put on the 'black son of bitch it hung inside of' (18). The capacity to reduce a human to a dollar amount is a nihilistic power; the man tires of the exercise of it once the ultimate commodification of the body has been achieved. He can carry his $200 in the form of a human heart with him, and in so doing he renders humanity cheap to the point of meaninglessness. A human life reduced to labor value alone is a commodity with an expiration date. Later, when the kid is recruited to join Captain White's endeavor, the recruiter tells the kid that the recruits 'wont need no wages' because they get to keep the '[s]poils of war' (30). The kid, despite the hermit's warning about the 'spoils' of the slave trade, goes up 'Commerce Street' to the main plaza to sign up for war (30). Captain White explains the purpose of the project as killing Mexicans and Native Americans not solely for racial reasons tied to Manifest Destiny, but also for monetary reasons: they are meant to create a pass to California that will free 'American' settlers from 'tolls' (34). And so it goes through the rest of the novel: currency is rendered valueless with changing nationalities; material wealth disappears in the next act of violence, such as when scalps are traded for money, a mine plundered only to have the donkeys carrying the wealth fall to their deaths in a ravine, 'silently as martyrs' (195). Humans, like the slaver's commodity, are reduced to a body part (a scalp, an ear) for money, such as when the kid, near death, comes on the 'remains of the scalps' in a bonfire 'burned unredeemed' (that is, unpaid for), or when the kid buys back a scapular made of human ears with the last of his money (216). The epic records the glories of war, but dead bodies make for poor bards; in the end, they are the most accurate accounting of a war's cost.

This interpretation is undercut by the forcefulness of the text itself, not by the kid. The more important question posed by the novel can be found when we explore the limitations of the Homeric mode as an explanation for the interpretive complexity of this American western. The characteristic elements of the novel that derive from the Homeric tradition emphasize the judge's argument that war is the progenitor of all human deeds, that warriors are the ones whose tales are told, and that the aims of empire are the only story that exists. The judge's arguments, however, are not the only arguments at play. The biblical elements create a crosscurrent that provides a texture and depth impossible to ignore. *Blood Meridian* is an epic about men but it is a biblical morality tale about nature.

Because nature is not a character, the novel poses its arguments stylistically. These 'biblical' passages differ from descriptions of violence, shifting the novel into a mode focused on the moral implications of the commerce of war.

Witnessing: *Blood Meridian*'s landscape and nonhuman agency

In a stylistic analysis of *Blood Meridian*, Arthur Bingham notes that the novel 'does much to debunk the romantic image of the American west.' This 'odyssey,' he says, strips any romanticizing from the narrative beyond its structural premise—a boy's journey to adulthood through adventure and the dawn of a nation. Bingham's linguistic study focuses on analyzing how the novel 'foregrounds' acts of violence by using shorter clauses linked by the conjunction 'and' while, by contrast, nonviolent passages are characterized by lengthier clauses, which 'iconically help[s] to create a feeling of temporal length.' Surprisingly, Bingham notes, nonviolent passages possess an equal or greater number of preterit narrative verbs and syntactic methods of foregrounding. Descriptions of landscape, one would think, would be *background* information but they are stylistically foregrounded. Bingham explains this anomaly by suggesting that violent passages are still foregrounded, as we would expect, because of semantic content alone.[34] He compares two sentences in which key information is backgrounded, one violent and one nonviolent, to make his point that readers interpret as 'foreground' that which is syntactically background on the basis of semantic content. The first example is 'When Glanton and his chiefs swung back through the village people were running out under the horses' hooves' and the second, 'they rode out with the flames lighting all the grounds about and shadow shapes of the desert brush reeling on the sands' (162, 169). Both sentences follow the 'when → -ing' construction, where the main subject-verb clauses ('Glanton and his chiefs swung back' and 'they rode out') are syntactically foregrounded as primary actions and other actions happen in the background: while Glanton rides, 'village people were running,' and while they ride, 'flames [were] lighting.' Despite the similar syntactic form, Bingham argues, ordinarily readers mentally 'foreground' the backgrounded action of the first sentence because it *matters* that villagers are attempting to flee as they are being mown down, whereas the nonviolent sentence's backgrounded material simply suggests the visual violence of a natural landscape and readers impugn no agency to the flames casting terrifying shadows.

Bingham's explanation for how McCarthy's violent and nonviolent scenes both foreground violence seems to make sense, insofar as a book about warfare and American expansionism would theoretically foreground violent acts committed by and against its American protagonists. Syntactically, though, this does not appear to be the case. If a reader were to approach the text without anthropocentric assumptions about significant versus insignificant action, they would find that the text codes violent scenes as 'exciting' through comparatively short sentences. Sentence style throughout the novel mimics the temporal frame of the action—elongated for journey scenes, and truncated for action scenes. However, in terms of foregrounded action, nonviolent scenes are just as likely to present agents acting as violent scenes are. In *Blood Meridian*, the difference is that the agents in nonviolent scenes are natural elements rather than human. Furthermore, many scenes centering on violent human actions syntactically background the human agents of violence and foreground the recipients of that violence.

A comparison of the first extended scene of the kid's journey with Captain White's group and the scene of that group's first violent encounter with Indigenous people reveals this syntactic inversion of readers' expectations:

> They rode on and the sun in the east flushed pale streaks of light and then a deeper run of color like blood seeping up in sudden reaches flaring planewise and where the earth drained up into the sky at the edge of creation the top of the sun rose out of nothing like the head of a great red phallus until it cleared the unseen rim and sat squat and pulsing and malevolent behind them. (44–45)

> A rattling drove of arrows passed through the company and men tottered and dropped from their mounts. Horses were rearing and plunging and the mongol hordes swung up along their flanks and turned and rode full upon them with lances. (53)

In the first, nonviolent scene, the main action ('they rode') is linked by coordinated conjunction ('and') to the action of the sun: the sun 'flushed' and then 'rose out of nothing' and 'sat squat and pulsing and malevolent.' In this single complex sentence, the sun is syntactically given three active verbs ('flushed,' 'rose,' 'sat') to the men's single action verb ('rode'). The sun, moreover, is explicitly assigned agency: it is 'malevolent.' By contrast, the first action scene foregrounds the action of non-agents (the subject of the sentence is 'arrows'). In the next sentence, the putative protagonists, Captain White's group, are invisible; their frenzy is implicit in the actions of their horses, which are 'rearing and plunging' as the enemy ride up alongside their ranks.

The narrative as a whole suggests that readers would be well served by paying attention to the 'wrath' of the natural world. For example, in Bexar, Texas, the kid listens to Captain White's impassioned defense of Manifest Destiny and he decides to join White's company, terrorizing Mexicans and Native Americans along the contested new national border (32–36). Later, the kid and his companions enter a cantina, where they meet 'an old disordered Mennonite,' a man sworn to a pacifist religion in one of the most violent geographic regions and eras (39). Like many of McCarthy's wandering prophets, the old man offers an ominous warning that none of the novel's characters take heed of. 'The wrath of God lies sleeping,' the Mennonite tells them. 'It was hid a million years before men were and only men have power to wake it' (40). God's wrath, which lay sleeping before humans evolved, is the natural world's violent resistance to their destructive progress.

Thus, in a scene that seems to serve as a symbolic answer to the Mennonite's prophesy, the kid finally arrives in California and journeys north to San Francisco, where he witnesses the great fire of 1851 that started in a warehouse and burned $10–12 million of goods—products whose value was lost entirely because the fire occurred before insurance markets were established in the city. The convergence of these two factors, a boom economy at the height of the gold rush and a new, fragile infrastructure, contributed to the economic disaster of the fire.[35] The kid sees the fire from a distance, where 'the shape of the city burned against the sky and burned again in the black waters of the sea where dolphins rolled through the flames, fire in the lake, through the fall of burning timbers and the cries of the lost' (313). This apocalyptic scene, in which dolphins frolic as men scream and burn and the city collapses, depicts a natural world that is granted an agency and a violence at least equal to the agency and violence attributed to men in this novel.

What happens, then, if readers let the narrative cues guide their interpretation of the text and read the active verbs of landscape scenes *as* action? In this reading, landscape and atmospheric phenomena are ascribed an agency that suggests that men operate in a world inimical to them. There is a fundamental and violent opposition at the heart of this novel, but the specific categories of men who war against each other is nearly incidental; the larger conflict is between humanity and nature. Of course, such agency can be read as merely metaphoric (i.e., 'the sun's heat makes it seem malevolent'). The nature scenes certainly seem to be described with no clear moral to be drawn ('dolphins frolic, a city burns, a kid watches'). As Auerbach reminds us, though, biblical narrative is syntactically primitive in comparison to Homeric epics. Biblical narrative is characterized by sentences with little causal relationship or connection, and scant or no attention to 'background' information such as landscape or scars, yet within the thinness of the narrative lies a profound moral complexity. Even without attention to background, biblical characters are treated as though they possess depth. By contrast to Homeric heroes who show no growth or change, Auerbach points to the riven, complex worlds of biblical heroes such as David and Saul. 'How fraught with background, in comparison,' Auerbach exclaims. 'How entangled and stratified' they are, compared with the flat and glorious Achilles, Nestor, or Agamemnon.[36]

In *Blood Meridian*, no humans are granted emotional complexity. But the active, foregrounded nonviolent passages of the novel, if they are read non-anthropocentrically, suggest a living, vivid cast of characters who are granted rage, foreknowledge, and pathos—an emotional register significantly superior to that of the human characters. Another comparison of a nonviolent with a violent passage demonstrates this distinction in emotional register:

War and the wanderer 91

> That night they rode through a region electric and wild where strange shapes of soft blue fire ran over the metal of the horses' trappings and the wagonwheels rolled in hoops of fire and little shapes of pale blue light came to perch in the ears of the horses and in the beards of the men. All night sheetlightning quaked sourceless to the west beyond the midnight thunderheads, making a bluish day of the distant desert, the mountains on the sudden skyline stark and black and livid like a land of some other order out there whose true geology was not stone but fear. (47)

> And now the horses of the dead came pounding out of the smoke and dust and circled with flapping leather and wild manes and eyes whited with fear like the eyes of the blind and some were feathered with arrows and some lanced through and stumbling and vomiting blood as they wheeled across the killing ground and clattered from sight again. Dust stanched the wet and naked heads of the scalped who with the fringe of hair below their wounds and tonsured to the bone now lay like maimed and naked monks in the bloodslaked dust and everywhere the dying groaned and gibbered and horses lay screaming. (54)

From the standpoint of an epic, the second, violent section 'foregrounds' the action clearly, beginning with a temporal deictic ('now') that fastens the action to the present, rendering the wild brutality always happening, always immediate to the reader. The pathos of the dying animals follows with descriptions both heightened and syntactically backgrounded through strings of participle phrases, 'eyes whited' and 'some were feathered' and 'some lanced through' and 'stumbling and vomiting' and, finally, 'dying groaned and gibbered' and 'screaming' (54). This information suggests that the background effect—animals dying (secondary, one would think, to the men)—is omnipresent, pervading all action. But consider what is missing: the actual foregrounded action. Animals die onscreen, while the men who kill are syntactically implicit.

By contrast, the landscape in the previous section is animate and seems to be attempting to communicate its prophetic terror to the animals: the static electricity built up in the lightning storm 'came to perch,' Pentecost-like, on the horses and men; the lightning 'quake[s] sourceless'—sui generis in its frenetic message (47). The landscape quakes, trembles, and sets fire to the night, like a voiceless

Cassandra, while in scenes of battle, animals, and not humans, are granted the dignity of their own terror and suffering.

Conflict may be instigated by men, the novel's stylistics suggest, but it is the land and nonhuman animals that witness, that shriek warning to the human inhabitants. It is the nonhuman world that suffers the ravages of human violence onscreen. We again find concretization of this notion in the following nonviolent and violent passages:

> They rode on. The horses trudged sullenly the alien ground and the round earth rolled beneath them silently milling the greater void wherein they were contained. In the neuter austerity of that terrain all phenomena were bequeathed a strange equality and no one thing nor spider nor stone nor blade of grass could put forth claim to precedence. The very clarity of these articles belied their familiarity, for the eye predicates the whole on some feature or part and here was nothing more luminous than another and nothing more enshadowed and in the optical democracy of such landscapes all preference is made whimsical and a man and a rock become endowed with unguessed kinships. (247)

> The savages built a bonfire on the hill and fueled it with the furnishings from the white men's quarters and they raised up Glanton's body and bore it aloft in the manner of a slain champion and hurled it into the flames. They'd tied his dog to his corpse and it was snatched after in howling suttee to disappear crackling in the rolling greenwood smoke. (275)

The first scene is one of the most frequently cited scenes in the entirety of the novel. In it, the omniscient narrator explicitly points out that the landscape is inimical to human survival, but defies human comprehension, interpretation, or explanation. If the judge serves the god of war with the method of mammon, intent on suzerainty, then the landscape here stands in stark defiance: 'the [human] eye predicates the whole on some feature or part,' the narrator says. But the landscape's 'optical democracy' defies hierarchizing efforts of men (247). By contrast, in this second climactic scene, the Glanton Gang is finally decimated. Here, syntactic coordination belies a semantic hierarchy present in every line. The Indigenous warriors are 'savages,' an epithet used by their white enemies to describe them as primitive, as 'lower' forms of humanity. In this instance, they triumph: they build the fire on which they will burn their chief enemy, who is borne 'aloft in the manner of a slain champion' and, it should be noted, in a Homeric (specifically, Hector-like) image. The dog is compared to the wife of a powerful maharaja in India, thrown on the pyre with her husband, as she is his property. Once again, warring factions of humans glory in violent acts of suzerainty over the other while the suffering of animals takes center stage.

Who is witness to the democratic, nonhuman suffering and brutality of the natural world? Earlier I claimed that many of the 'wanderer' characters in McCarthy's fiction act as witnesses; the kid, who is clearly a wanderer, is not one of those witnesses. At the end of the main narrative arc, the kid wanders for some years, during which time he is often taken for 'a sort of preacher but he was no witness to them, neither of things at hand nor things to come' (312). Those who wander carry a currency of information, but through these years, the kid 'seemed to travel with no news at all, as if the doings of the world were too slanderous for him to truck with, or perhaps too trivial' (312). Indeed, for all that the kid is a 'pilgrim among others,' he a wanderer who sees but does not witness the panoramic history-making of this endeavor. The 'mindless violence' that broods in him at age fourteen suggests that he is, in some imperfect way, 'like a son' to the judge (5, 3, 306). At fifteen years old, in New Orleans, the kid rents a room behind a tavern and beats the drunks there every night to feel his own power, a power that is expressed in terms of empire: in this cosmopolitan port city bar, he finds and conquers '[m]en from lands so far and queer that standing over them where they lie bleeding in the mud he feels mankind itself vindicated' (4). His commitment to violence ends in the judge's violent embrace. If *Blood Meridian*, in true epic form, is only about the deeds of men, then there is no witness remaining at the end. Maybe there never was one.

But the kid's failure to bear witness is *not* a failure of the novel as a whole. Near the beginning, the kid passes a 'shadowed agony in the garden' that he sees but does not comprehend before he sails down the Mississippi (5). Readers, unlike the kid, will note that Christological reference applied to Black men working in a cotton field and will hear that intertextual echo of souls singing from that great, muddy, soul-deep river, singing from the cotton. Biblical cadences form as these two isolated moments merge to form an interpretive morality tale: those who refuse to witness the world may nevertheless be held to account for what they have seen. Finally, at the novel's end, the now-grown man pushes open the saloon door. He 'looked back a last time at the street ... and at the last pale light in the west'—a sunset that he has failed to note as a key moment of foreshadowing (324). Astute readers, by contrast, will note the ominous last light of the sun, as the narrator who has consistently foregrounded the phenomenological activity of the natural world insists that they should. The kid's sun sets before he is aware, and before he has time to reckon with his life's deeds. Readers have seen it setting for some time.

The significance of landscape transcends its use merely as metaphor. The agency expressed by natural phenomena and their capacity to 'speak into' and interpret the actions of the text emphasize how landscape is foregrounded in the narrative. Luce points out that McCarthy specifically alludes to several landscape paintings of famous vistas referenced in *Blood Meridian*, and that the meticulously rendered images are not 'background' to the meaning of the text at all. Rather, Luce says, 'the unusual prominence of [the novel's] descriptions of the land, asks us to join the narrator in his undertaking to see the west, human nature, and the violent claiming of an American empire with an intensity of vision and sobriety of gaze that counters the impression we may initially have of the narrator's ethical objectivity.' Luce suggests that the agency ascribed to the natural world is meant to be understood as conveying the narrator's 'sense of alternatives to blood and conflict'—a sense that, ultimately, no humans in the novel seem to grasp. She cites as a powerful example the kid's arrival in San Diego and his first glimpse of the Pacific Ocean, 'out there past men's knowing, where the stars are drowning and whales ferry their vast souls through the black and nameless sea' (304). Luce points out that these whales exist beyond the 'western limits of the land,' and so beyond the 'suzerainty' of Glanton's gang.[37] In other words, in the foregrounded passages describing the natural world's witness to the deeds of the violent men of this narrative, readers find the novel's true oppositional force: a life force possessed of 'souls,' of 'fear,' and of a capacity to regenerate as well as destroy.

It should be emphasized here that the biblical mode of the text lies in the syntactic foregrounding of nature passages, not in the linguistic rhythms of the King James Bible, which are largely due to the judge's moralizing, and the judge is a false purveyor of morals. He tells the men at one point, 'Your heart's desire is to be told some mystery. The mystery is that there is no mystery.' The ex-priest mutters that the man is 'a bloody hoodwinker,' suggesting that the judge's disingenuous claim is thin even for men who cannot quite see through his showmanship (252). The judge's most explicitly religious tone emerges when he provides a biblical-style parable for the group and interprets it with his own creed of absolute commitment to violence. The parable is set in the Alleghenies 'when it was yet a wilderness' and involves a harness maker (not incidentally, a man whose job entails domestication and control of animals) (142). The harness maker takes up robbing passersby while disguised as an 'Indian' to supplement his income; the narrative seizes again on a brief yet provocative 'flickering sign' in which a white man puts on the aspect of a group he considers 'barbarous' in order to inhabit barbarity. As the story goes, however, one young traveler sees through the harness maker's disguise and tells him he 'was a loss to God and man alike and would remain so until he took his brother into his heart' (143). The traveler encourages the harness maker to confront his racist views of an internal hierarchy of human value as well, instructing him to see a Black man who is passing by as 'not less than a man among men' (143). The harness maker seems to grow in his nascent ethical inclinations, and, in the manner of all biblical narratives, without explanation syntactically or semantically, the harness maker kills the traveler, Esau-like, with a rock (144). The judge suggests that this violent man who rejected the wisdom of a wandering stranger might be any one of their progenitors: the man's son, the judge says, grew up and 'went away to the west and he himself became a killer of men.' The traveler's son, who grew up with a dead 'saint' for a father, became equally violent (145). The equivalency of these wicked men, the judge explains, reveals the moral of the tale. Violence is not only part of human nature, but part of *nature*. 'Wolves cull themselves,' he says, and 'is the race of man not more predacious yet?' (146) But the 'bloody hoodwinker' fails to point out that fallacy, that wolves are not as predacious as men. They do not decimate entire species, at least, not like men rendering wild American bison extinct in under a decade. Nor does the judge's description capture the self-sacrifice or altruistic care for other animals that whale pods exhibit, as observed by a recent study that found whales intervening to save other species from shark attacks, suggesting that whales use their size altruistically in their ecosystems.[38] The judge's morality tale ends in an ironic violation of the tale's moral, rather than an exemplification of it. His interpretation does not correlate to the narrative's focal emphasis on animal and natural world agency, on the compassion of animals for others, even other species—like Glanton's dog's kindness to the 'idiot' and loyalty to Glanton (275). At the beginning of *Blood Meridian*, the narrator claims that the kid is journeying into the heart of the American national project to determine 'whether the stuff of creation may be shaped to man's will or whether his own heart is not another kind of clay' (4–5). In the end, the kid fails to reckon with the larger implications of the two types of men he meets on the road—the travelers who take each other 'into their heart,' and the harness makers who seek to thieve, to control, and to be suzerain.

With its push across the newly claimed southwest, the young US in *Blood Meridian* expresses a will to power that exemplifies the instincts of the harness maker writ large. The narrator suggests that the nation, with its industrial ingenuity and love of violence, is in the process of creating a destructive force that is not yet perfected. As the gang rides south, the narrator claims that 'although each man among them was discrete unto himself, conjoined they made a thing that had not been before and in that communal soul were wastes hardly reckonable' (152). This man-machine will crank toward the west coast, laying waste to animals, humans, and whole civilizations. The irony is that the desert on which the gang crosses, as the judge points out, 'calls for largeness of heart' (330). Thus, it is not the animate, vivid, and active landscape that is 'ultimately empty,' but the men who decimate it. Everywhere to which these men do not bear witness is teeming with life; that life bears witness to their smallness of heart and self-destructiveness, and it will live on after even the judge has stopped dancing.

Notes

1. Quotations from A. G. Hopkins, *American Empire: A Global History* (Princeton University Press, 2018), 7; and Erich Auerbach, *Mimesis: The Representation of Reality in Western Literature*, trans. Willard R. Trask (Princeton University Press, 2003), 17.
2. Vereen M. Bell, *The Achievement of Cormac McCarthy* (Louisiana State University Press, 1988), 131.
3. Steven Frye, *Understanding Cormac McCarthy* (University of South Carolina Press, 2009), 93.
4. The Woolmer Collection of Cormac McCarthy, collection 92, box 1, file 4.
5. James Bowers, *Reading Cormac McCarthy's* Blood Meridian (Boise State University Press, 1999), 8.
6. Mark A. Eaton, 'Dis(re)membered Bodies: Cormac McCarthy's Border Fiction,' *Modern Fiction Studies*, vol. 49, iss. 1 (Spring 2003), 155–179: 157.
7. John Jurgensen, 'Hollywood's Favorite Cowboy,' *Wall Street Journal*, Arts & Entertainment, November 20, 2009.
8. Citations for this paragraph, in order, as follows: Rick Wallach, 'Judge Holden, *Blood Meridian*'s Evil Archon,' *Sacred Violence*, vol. 2, 2nd edn, eds. Wade Hall and Rick Wallach (Texas Western Press, 2002), 1–14: 1; Mundik, *A Bloody and Barbarous God*, 32; and Russell M. Hillier, *Morality in Cormac McCarthy's Fiction: Souls at Hazard* (Palgrave Macmillan, 2016), 16.
9. The Cormac McCarthy Papers, collection 91, box 35, file 1, p. 249.
10. John Emil Sepich, 'The Dance of History in Cormac McCarthy's *Blood Meridian*,' *The Southern Literary Journal*, vol. 24, iss. 1 (1991), 16–31: 24.
11. The Cormac McCarthy Papers, collection 91, box 35, file 7.
12. Crews. *Books are Made out of Books*, 164, italics his.
13. Hillier, *Morality in Cormac McCarthy's Fiction*, 30, 29.
14. Auerbach, *Mimesis*, 23.
15. The quotations, in order, come from the following: Gareth Cornwall, 'Ambivalent National Epic: Cormac McCarthy's *Blood Meridian*,' *Critique: Studies in Contemporary Fiction*, vol. 56, iss. 5 (2015), 531–554; Woodward, 'Cormac McCarthy's Venomous Fiction'; Shaviro, '"The Very Life of the Darkness,"' 146; Leo Daugherty, 'Gravers False and True: *Blood Meridian* as Gnostic Tragedy,' *Perspectives on Cormac McCarthy*, rev. edn, eds. Edwin T. Arnold and Dianne C.

Luce (University Press of Mississippi, 1999), 159–174: 168; David Williams, 'Blood Meridian and Classical Greek Thought,' *Intertextual and Interdisciplinary Approaches to Cormac McCarthy: Borders and Crossings*, ed. Nicholas Monk (Routledge, 2012), 6–23: 7; James Wood, 'Red Planet: The Sanguinary Sublime of Cormac McCarthy,' *New Yorker*, July 25, 2005; and 'Blood Meridian by Cormac McCarthy,' *Kirkus Reviews*, February 15, 1985.

16 Peter Josyph, *Adventures in Reading Cormac McCarthy* (Scarecrow Press, 2010), 72.
17 Auerbach, *Mimesis*, 13.
18 For more information on this, see C. Doumas, 'What did the Argonauts Seek in Colchis?,' *Hermathena* no. 150 (Summer 1991), 31–41.
19 For more information, see 'Los Hermanos Penitentes: History of the Penitent Brothers,' *World History Online*, American History, August 11, 2017, accessed September 1, 2018, https://worldhistory.us/american-history/los-hermanos-penitentes-history-of-the-penitent-brothers.php. McCarthy dashed off a note on this historical monastic sect, although rather than being interested in the history of the sect, he seems keen to record the carnivalesque attributes of the group: 'penitents—uproar o tinieblas ['oh darkness,' referencing Job 22:11]—rattles, bullroarers, chains, men naked to waist in black caps [sic] whip of braided yucca,' he writes on a page of notes during the drafting of *Blood Meridian*. The Cormac McCarthy Papers collection 91, box 35, file 5.
20 See Daugherty, 'Gravers False and True,' 163; and Mundik, *A Bloody and Barbarous God*, 8.
21 Auerbach, *Mimesis*, 6.
22 Deborah L. Madsen, *American Exceptionalism* (University Press of Mississippi, 1998), 20, 2.
23 Hopkins, *American Empire*, 7, 736.
24 Dan Sinykin, 'Evening in America: *Blood Meridian* and the Origins and Ends of Imperial Capitalism,' *American Literary History*, vol. 28, iss. 2 (Summer 2016), 362–380: 364.
25 Kate Montague, 'Baroque Meridians: Between Myth and Actuality on the American Frontier,' *Cormac McCarthy's Borders and Landscapes*, ed. Louise Jillett (Bloomsbury Academic, 2016), 95–106: 95.
26 Nicholas Monk, '"An Impulse to Action, an Undefined Want": Modernity, Flight, and Crisis in the Border Trilogy and *Blood Meridian*,' *Sacred Violence*, vol. 2, 2nd edn, eds. Wade Hall and Rick Wallach (Texas Western Press, 2002), 83–104: 88.
27 Christie, 'Days of Begging, Days of Theft,' 58, 61.
28 Robison, 'The Authority of Currency,' 31, 43.

29 Raymond Malewitz, '"Anything can be an Instrument": Misuse Value and Rugged Consumerism in Cormac McCarthy's *No Country for Old Men*,' *Contemporary Literature*, vol. 50, iss. 4 (Winter 2009), 721–41: 721.
30 Wallach, 'Judge Holden, *Blood Meridian*'s Evil Archon,' 7.
31 Robison, 'The Authority of Currency,' 33.
32 The Cormac McCarthy Papers, collection 91, box 35, file 7.
33 The archaic word 'burin' was used as a synonym for the word 'graver' and refers to an engraving tool with a metal shaft that ends in a diamond-shaped wedge to carve metal. See 'Burin, n.', *Oxford English Dictionary*.
34 Arthur Bingham, 'Syntactic Complexity and Iconicity in Cormac McCarthy's *Blood Meridian*,' *Language and Literature*, vol. 20 (1995), 19–133: 19, 25, 29.
35 'Early History of the San Francisco Fire Department,' *The Virtual Museum of the City of San Francisco*, Municipal Record, City and Council of San Francisco, 2017, accessed January 22, 2018, www.sfmuseum.net/hist1/fire.html.
36 Auerbach, *Mimesis*, 12, 17.
37 Dianne C. Luce, 'Landscapes as Narrative Commentary in Cormac McCarthy's *Blood Meridian: Or, the Evening Redness in the West*,' *European Journal of American Studies*, vol. 12, iss. 3 (2017), 1–24: 2, 20.
38 See Bryan Nelson, 'Humpback Whales Around the Globe are Mysteriously Rescuing Animals from Orcas,' *Mother Nature Network*, July 30, 2016. McCarthy references this idea explicitly in *Whales and Men*.

3

Professionals: late capitalism and the illegal drug trade in *No Country for Old Men* and *The Counselor*

> The hope of achieving a humane, truly democratic, and ecologically sustainable capitalism is becoming transparently unrealistic.
> (Ellen Meiksins Wood, *The Origin of Capitalism*)

> [I]n a social field where murder has become a way of life 'that's life' also refers to perhaps the only way in which the fully human—understood as radical freedom and creative performance—comes alive ... when the *sicario* kills his capitalist.
> (Rebecca Biron, 'It's a Living: Hit Men in the Mexican Narco War')[1]

The previous chapter examined Cormac McCarthy's historically earliest novel, studying its representation of the US's rise to virtuosic economic power and imperial behavior, with violent land grabs justifying the philosophy of Manifest Destiny. This chapter turns to McCarthy's two most contemporary texts, *No Country for Old Men* and *The Counselor*. Thematically, these two texts continue the critique of economic imperialism laid out in *Blood Meridian*; their narrative action is located along the US–Mexico border from the 1980s through the early 2010s, a time period during which the US was globally economically dominant, and during what was likely the meridian of its arc as an economic empire. Both storylines also focus on a drug deal gone wrong, an ordinary man's greed precipitating his path to damnation, overt and implicit discussions of greed, commodification of the natural world and of humans, and border crime policy. As indicated in Chapter 1, *No Country* and *The Counselor* are not only similar in terms of plot; they are also McCarthy's most explicit treatments of US economic policy in the late twentieth and early twenty-first centuries. Furthermore, both narratives are similarly 'cinematic,' relying on visual cues to code their arguments about agents and systems. Symbols of wealth—coins in *No Country* and diamonds in *The Counselor*—represent the complex web of licit and illicit markets that exploit laborers, perceive humans as capital, and reduce value and meaningfulness to utilities on a global exchange. Equally important is what is not shown: in both of these narratives, the moment of choice where a character elects to operate within a corrupt economic system is missing, and this crucial missing scene is the hinge on which the tragedy of both tales turns. The absence of that moment points to the most pernicious attribute of late capitalism: its claims of inevitability. After all, what use is critique if an alternative cannot be imagined?

Raymond Malewitz explains that throughout McCarthy's corpus, but perhaps most clearly in *No Country*, McCarthy's aesthetic 'testifies to the departure of artisanal forms of production and the subsequent arrival of industrial capitalism's anarchic world of commodities.'[2] This notion of commodity is one to which I now turn. As Thomas Piketty points out, 'since the 1980s, global wealth has increased on average a little faster than income,' but incremental increases in wealth and income parity have a profound effect, compounding interest on capital at rates significantly higher than income wages are capable of earning, thereby coalescing global capital under the control of fewer individuals. Such a trajectory, Piketty warns, 'can potentially give rise to a global dynamic of accumulation and distribution of wealth characterized by explosive trajectories and uncontrolled inegalitarian spirals.'[3] Writing in an era of increasing global wealth inequality, McCarthy zeroes in on drug wars and illegal drug trade as potent examples of the predatory practices of a deregulated market system that commodifies human bodies in terms of market use value.

The reason why McCarthy chooses fictionalized depictions of illicit market agents and commodities in order to comment on licit global capitalism in the twenty-first century may seem murky at first glance. Ernest Mandel offers insight into this narrative conflation of licit and illicit markets when he argues that the history of capitalism shows a perpetual correlation between the two, since '[c]apital innately tends to combine international expansion with the formation of national markets.'[4] Mandel cites the Opium Wars in India and the US expansion into Mexico in the mid-nineteenth century as examples of the 'contradictory attitudes' of bourgeois capitalists, to consolidate the nation-state on one hand and to expand the exchange of goods on a free and open market through the dissolution of national boundaries on the other. Despite the illicit market expansions in the nineteenth century that he names, in general multinational corporations did not dominate global economics prior to the Second World War the same way as they did after. In late capitalism, 'the multinational company becomes the determinant organizational form of big capital.'[5] While licit and illicit economies have distinct and different functions, the key players of late capitalist licit economies—multinational corporations—share certain features with illicit economies, notably in the centralization of surplus capital, where labor forces may remain rooted within distinct nation-states while capital flows upward to the multinational corporation's shareholders and 'bosses.'

The black market drug trade on the US–Mexican border makes an unusually apt analogy for the form of multinational corporation-driven markets emerging in the late twentieth century that Mandel describes. According to Rebecca Biron, the American southwestern drug thriller genre, including both true crime and fictional accounts of cartel violence, exposes the internal logic of late capitalism through its depiction of shadow, illicit economies that parallel the darker aspects of licit economies. The drug thriller reduces the international licit capitalist marketplace to a simplified, and horrifying, illicit version of itself: a consumer class whose entire function in the economic ecosystem is to consume until death, and a production class that eliminates competition and 'excess' human labor waste to coalesce capital.[6] Furthermore, illegal drug markets, rather than being an effect of transitional or emerging economies, have a long and complicit history with licit capitalist markets; they form an irreducible aspect of legitimate market economies, both shaping and 'creat[ing] opportunity,' as John Fitzgerald argues. Illicit drug trade has been implicated in global capitalism since the rise of the opium trade in the eighteenth and nineteenth centuries.

'Control of the illicit drug market is really about regulation of rational decision-making through a combination of punishment, deterrence and liberal market forces,' Fitzgerald explains, and so illegal markets function precisely in the same way as legal markets in terms of economic strategies and principles. He pushes his argument further, claiming that they are in fact a necessary component of the regulation of licit markets. In the shift toward late capitalism following the economic collapse created by the global oil boom in the 1970s, the global economy moved toward a greater fluidity of labor and capital across national boundaries. Then, with new digital technologies emerging around the turn of the century, capital became increasingly displaced and globalized, located within neither spatial nor material boundaries. As capitalism increasingly thrives on the dissolution and reincorporation of 'sovereign borders, sovereign bodies, sovereign ethnic groups,' the illegal drug markets replicate and anticipate this movement in emerging economies. Illegal drug markets turn the consumer into one aspect of the product itself, creating and controlling supply and demand, dissolving the bourgeoisie into the ever-narrower ranks of those who control capital surplus. Illegal drug trade 'dissolve[s] the social into pure market relations,' thereby 'capturing a social order and subsuming the function of the social into productive capital for the drug market.'[7] *No Country* and *The Counselor* tell stories in which that shadow economy built on addiction, the exploitation of suffering, and economic fragility is explicitly linked to its legal twin, visually depicting the irreducible interrelation of an illicit economy of transnational drug trade with the deregulation of licit market capitalism in the US during this time period. Beyond merely offering a critique of a pernicious neoliberal reduction of the human laborer to a labor commodity on a global marketplace, however, McCarthy's drug thrillers draw attention to a crucial and frequently missing element in such critiques: a failure to imagine viable, bioregionally sustainable alternatives.

Overwhelmingly, capitalism continues to be represented as a function of innate human nature—that 'homo economicus' imagined by Adam Smith, John Stuart Mill, and other eighteenth- and nineteenth-century political economists. Mark Fisher, coopting an oft-cited aphorism from Fredric Jameson and Slavoj Zizek that it is easier to imagine the end of the world than the end of capitalism, names this myth of inevitability 'capitalist realism.'[8] He analyzes works of apocalyptic literature, such as P. D. James's *Children of Men*, which attempt and, to an extent, fail at this very project; their failure, Fisher contends, demonstrates our need to challenge the fatalism driving neoliberal justifications for market capitalism. *No Country* and *The Counselor* expose this failure to imagine alternatives to capitalism, or more precisely to neoliberal justifications for value systems imposed by a free market. While McCarthy's imagined alternatives to late capitalism's excesses are explored in Chapter 5, this chapter examines two narratives that expose the absurdity of a collective failure to question 'capitalist realism.'

In many respects, *No Country* and *The Counselor* are both classic tragedies tracing the failed arcs of successful men. In the case of *No Country*, Llewellen Moss, Sheriff Ed Tom Bell, and Anton Chigurh each exhibit a tragic failure in their respective narratives. Peebles points out that McCarthy's early draft screenplay of *No Country* 'originally conceived of Llewelyn Moss and Ed Tom Bell as a can-do pair of tough guys, overcoming the odds and Bell's personal losses in their victorious quest to bring the villain to justice.' The published novel, however, is a tale that violates genre expectations, 'taking on the structure and tone of tragedy' rather than offering the consolations of a crime thriller where the good guys solve the crime and the bad guy is punished.[9] *The Counselor* is even more explicitly modeled along the lines of Aristotelean tragedy, with one significant exception, as Steven Edward Knepper argues. The Counselor ends his tale searching fruitlessly for his murdered fiancée 'among the mourners,' just as Lear cradles Cordelia's body and Oedipus winds up 'a blind beggar,' but unlike Lear or Oedipus, the Counselor is neither descended from the gods nor royalty; he is a professional.[10] So too are the main characters in *No Country*: Llewellen Moss is a welder, and Bell takes rather unwarranted pride in his capacity as a rural Texas lawman (232). Russell Hillier characterizes Bell as a morally flawed man, 'inflexible, fastidious, and punctilious,' who at one point mocks a 'big city' Austin cop's standard American vernacular, suggesting that he does not do 'real work' like rural officers such as Bell.[11] Anton Chigurh, the antagonist and yet, in many respects, the most compelling character in *No Country*, is also the most successful, and he takes commensurate pride in his professionalism as a hitman. When he offers his services to a drug boss, Chigurh claims that, unlike those who 'exaggerate their own capabilities,' he is not exaggerating his skills (253).

No Country's flamboyant antagonist Chigurh in many ways is the closet correlative to The Counselor's flawed eponymous protagonist. While Chigurh is irredeemably 'bad' and the Counselor initially comes across as a morally gray romantic hero, it is important to note that the Counselor has exploited his legal position as a defense attorney to capitalize on his connections with ambitious and upwardly mobile criminals by the time the narrative commences. Both Chigurh and the Counselor work for a late capitalist marketplace defined by its closed system of good production and consumption, Chigurh as a hired hitman for drug cartels and the Counselor as a defense attorney in a criminal justice system that promulgates itself through the creation and maintenance of a criminal class. In this regard, they are emblematic of a new, ideal capitalist: both men play the role of the laborer *par excellence*. However, in a key aspect of their ambitions, they also work *against* the system: Chigurh takes out his own cartel boss's other hitmen in order to climb the ladder in his shadow market, and the Counselor helps create a new drug-running franchise that competes with an established, more violent cartel. By refusing to be mere 'cogs' in a machine, they showcase their identity as professionals more than mere laborers: they seek to succeed in the flourishing market of drug running, a system that exemplifies the self-perpetuating practices and reveals the excesses of global capitalism. Despite their professional success—or indeed, because of it—both men come to lose something ineffable and vital, and, their narratives suggest, what they have lost may not be regained. Through depictions of professional men who are skilled laborers and whose productivity in their respective fields is laudable, yet whose work is murderous, McCarthy suggests the pernicious implications of a market system in which labor and the human body are fungible.[12]

In addition to the arguments implicit in characters' narrative arcs, both texts rely on visual cues to extend their arguments, primarily through concrete metaphors for commerce—coins and diamonds, respectively—which represent the failures of licit and illicit markets and the human cost of late capitalism. While *No*

Country is a novel and *The Counselor* a screenplay, *No Country* got its start in life as a screenplay.[13] From an aesthetic standpoint, McCarthy's writing in general is so cinematic that it seems intuitive to think of his novels as transformable into screenplays. That the reverse occurs—the author writes screenplays that he then turns into novels—should not be surprising. Stacey Peebles notes that when the editor Lawrence Bensky submitted a publication recommendation for the manuscript that would become *The Orchard Keeper* to his editorial board, someone (perhaps Albert Erskine) wrote one word: 'film.' Around 1987, McCarthy drafted a near-complete screenplay called *No Country for Old Men*.[14] This early version bears few similarities to the novel published in 2005, nor to the Coen brothers' 2007 Academy Award-winning film adaptation, but it does suggest that McCarthy's vision of the narrative was informed by the cadences of the screen.

McCarthy's screenplays tend to display an unusually static approach to the visual medium, characterized by lengthy, poetic, often idiomatic and always densely philosophical monologues or dialogues. His screenplays and dramas are also characterized by the use of strong visual metaphors and mythic, literary, or biblical allusion to convey philosophically dense arguments, an approach Dianne C. Luce notes in one of the first scholarly pieces published on McCarthy's first produced script, *The Gardener's Son*.[15] Given these factors, it is perhaps unsurprising that McCarthy's screenwriting has received a more mixed reception than his novels. *The Counselor* in particular evoked consternation: even good reviews of the film seem baffled by its departures from expected rhythms and tropes of crime thrillers. In an otherwise positive review for the *New York Times*, for instance, Manohla Dargis asserts, 'Mr. McCarthy appears to have never read a screenwriting manual in his life.' In a more critical review for the *Guardian*, Peter Bradshaw calls the film a 'sub-David Mamet Esperanto of tough-guy worldliness.' Bradshaw laments a lack of 'sexiness'— snappy dialogue and sustained action that he expects from a film of that genre.[16] Anyone familiar with McCarthy's works could have pointed out to Bradshaw that none of McCarthy's screenplays are likely to be lauded for their 'snappy dialogue' or sustained action. Instead, they require careful attention to metaphor and allusion, and audiences willing to engage in the sort of analysis one might expect of a dense literary novel. Neither *No Country* nor *The Counselor* is pure entertainment of the 'shoot 'em up' variety. Rather, both novel and screenplay use the trappings of the crime thriller genre to delve into complex and allusive critiques of the US in an age of fetishized commodification.

Failure of the professional in *No Country for Old Men*

After the lyrical prose of the Border Trilogy, McCarthy turns in *No Country for Old Men* to a new aesthetic style—a grim, stripped-down prose, periodically injected with Sheriff Bell's stream-of-consciousness musings on an ostensibly 'new' violence born in the latter part of the twentieth century, as the post-Vietnam US struggled with its role as a global economic empire, incompatible with the 'city on a hill' imagery of its founding. The sparer syntactic style demonstrates the novel's cinematic approach to its themes; *No Country* relies on visual metaphor and narrative juxtaposition to offer what Stephen Tatum calls a novelistic *'corrida'* that 'indexes both directly and indirectly the political, financial, moral or ethical, and even linguistic crisis emerging along the US–Mexico border in the wake of the Vietnam War.' *No Country* works as a morality tale about neoliberal policies driving illegal drug trade between Central and North America and the War on Drugs that was meant to end it. The drug economy of the US–Mexico border region in the 1980s 'appears as the illegal image of a globalizing world system,' Tatum concludes.[17] Malewitz puts it this way: 'In McCarthy's late-capitalist denouement to the dream of the mythic West, animal prey becomes human prey, animal tracks become automobile tracks become signals, cattle-smuggling becomes drug-smuggling, and horses become off-road vehicles.'[18]

No Country is more than a morality tale about the corrupting influence of drugs. It draws attention to the larger global systems represented by the drug wars of the 1980s. Sheriff Ed Tom Bell offers a disingenuous, Fox News–like opinion on why so many American citizens have turned to drug use in a series of fragmentary monologues interspersing the main narrative action. It is because the country has begun to '*overlook bad manners*,' Bell surmises. '*Any time you quit hearin Sir and Maam the end is pretty much in sight*' (304, italics in text). This improbable slippery-slope argument is undercut by other characters in the novel, and most explicitly by Bell's Uncle Ellis, who points out that for all Bell's declarations of the 'newness' of this drug-wrought violence, no evil is new in human history. Instead, Ellis suggests, the violence along the US–Mexican border is part of an historic failure to reckon with the unfathomable corruption and violence of US history. 'How come people dont feel like this country has got a lot to answer for?' he asks (271). Perhaps prompted by Ellis's views on the historical culpability of the US, Bell admits that the commendation he received for his service in the Second World War was given to him as part of a military strategy to make a mundane loss of a strategic position into a heroic and tragic loss. In reality, Bell says, he survived because he ran away from his comrades, abandoning them to certain death. He describes his failure to act in solidarity—to stay with his men, even if he had died doing so—as breaking an 'oath': 'it's a blood oath to look after the men with you and I dont know why I didnt.' This failure is described in mercantile terms, as a theft of something valuable. 'I didnt know you could steal your own life,' Bell says, suggesting that his failure to die with his men 'steals' the ineffable value of his life (278). These assertions connect Bell's internal morality with an idealized expression of kinship or love for others, a mathematics of solidarity that runs throughout McCarthy's corpus—namely, the idea that 'we cannot save ourselves unless we save all ourselves,' as Ben Telfair puts it (*TS* 113).

Ben's assertion that salvation must be system-wide or it does not exist at all suggests the pervasive influence of Buddhist and gnostic thought in McCarthy's corpus, as it nearly word for word reiterates the pivotal assertion of the nineteenth-century abbot Soyen Shaku, the first Zen Buddhist master to teach in the US. 'We cannot save ourselves unless others are saved,' writes Shaku. 'We must help one another, we must expand our vulgar ego-centric ideas, we must expand ourselves so that the entire universe is identified with us, and so that our interests are those of humanity.'[19] Bell's failure to adhere to a principle of solidarity in which no life is valued above another's, even one's own, cannot be taken lightly or dismissed easily in the larger fabric of McCarthy's moral universe. His assertion that a man can 'steal his own life' by failing to live with and for others sheds light on an alternative value system glimpsed in a novel otherwise committed to revelation of its opposite in the form of a barren landscape where survival of the fittest plays out in gunfights and car chases.

Critics of the novel have tended to focus on its protagonists, the working-class welder and Vietnam veteran Moss and the grief-stricken, aging Second World War veteran, Bell.[20] By contrast, examinations of Chigurh typically treat him as little more than a trope—a larger-than-life antagonist in the vein of Judge Holden but without the same panache. John Vanderheide, for example, reads the novel as a postmodern examination of the soulless practices of late capitalism, with Bell and Chigurh as oppositional agents. Chigurh is an 'utterly joyless' character who represents a 'complete identification as a bourgeois subject, flatly fulfilling the bourgeois ideal of 'rational labor in a calling.' Brad Bannon examines the role of currency as a metaphor for a type of capitalist predeterminism, spending most of his article analyzing Bell and Moss. He mentions Chigurh only to claim that Chigurh's escaping capture by paying a boy $100 for a shirt represents the idea that the 'circulation of specie thus becomes the prevailing measure of contemporary life ... determining both the shape and the outcome of all human interactions and events.'[21] Most critics concur on these two points: first, that Bell merits the bulk of critical attention in the novel; and second, that Chigurh represents the critical argument at the heart of the novel. Michael Tavel Clarke claims that this strategy of offering a simplistic 'brute' (antagonist) has begun to characterize McCarthy's works in a particularly postmodern way. 'Brutes,' he says, 'no longer serve to ease readers' anxieties about the plot of decline because brutes are no longer central characters who undergo proletarianization. Instead, brutes (e.g., Eduardo in *Cities of the Plain*, Pérez in *All the Pretty Horses*, and especially Chigurh in *No Country*) are now the villains who ensure or contribute to protagonists' decline while themselves frequently enjoying upward mobility.'[22]

However, I argue that Chigurh is a consummate professional rather than a mindless 'brute' and merits a far richer examination than many critics have given him. In contrast to Chigurh's meticulous kills, the protagonists are lackluster practitioners of their chosen vocations; Moss never welds anything and Bell enforces no laws and fails to catch the bad guy. Chigurh is given fewer chances to articulate his philosophy of labor and his ethics than is Bell, but he is nevertheless offered a substantial number of near-monologues, and his theories of labor are at least as articulated as Bell's. Chigurh claims to serve the amoral agency of capitalism, the 'invisible hand' of a market represented through games of chance, specifically coin tosses. Morality, by implication, lies not in choice, since the system self-regulates without intentionality but with mathematical 'purity.' Morality, if such a concept exists, derives from the individual's submission to the laws that govern the system, and in evidence of this rationale, Chigurh lets games of chance determine whether he will murder another person. He stakes human life on the system, a faithful acolyte if ever there was one. Undercutting Chigurh's avowals, the visual semiotics of the novel link currency with the ineffable 'soul' through narrative 'jump shots' in which the omniscient perspective cuts from an image of a coin to an image of the eyes of the victim at the moment of their death.

Examining Chigurh in light of visual descriptive cues reveals a much more interesting figure than many scholars have reckoned with. The narrative introduces Chigurh with attention to his capacity to move with a skill born of infinite practice: he escapes from handcuffed imprisonment by squatting, rocking back, passing his bound arms underneath, and leaping to his feet before the surprised deputy can protect himself, and, the narrator notes, pointedly, '[i]f it looked like a thing he'd practiced many a time it was' (5). The exhaustive descriptions of his actions force readers into the role of observer. In the next scene, the narrative reinforces this dynamic: Chigurh steals a deputy's police car and uses the sirens to pull over a 'late model Ford sedan'; he asks that car's driver to step out, murders him with a cattle bolt, and then says out loud to the corpse, 'I just didnt want you to get blood on the car' (7). At first glance, this scene reinforces Chigurh's fulfillment of a 'mindless killer' or 'brute' type that Clarke describes. To a certain extent, he is—but it is important to note that he is not merely a 'mindless' automaton, a killing machine without humanity. If he were, the act of killing the driver would have completed his transaction.

His attempt to explain himself demonstrates his philosophy that the car's driver is a thing, to be used to further Chigurh's aims, but it also indicates that he feels a need to explain himself. 'Cold-bloodedness' suggests a refusal of empathy or compassion, but Chigurh engages nearly all of his victims in dialogues, often offering them a statistically possible way out in the form of a coin toss. In so doing, Chigurh suggests that his choice—to kill or not to kill—lies in some agency external to him, against which he has no power. Empathy has nothing to do with Chigurh's persona, not because he is cold-blooded, but because he has no choice to be otherwise. He operates rationally within a system whose demands include reduction of risk and reduction of profit owners in order to maximize and condense capital surplus. In this regard, Chigurh demonstrates himself to be a consummate example of the laborer in an unregulated market.

Coin tosses for a victim's life recur throughout the novel; in each of these scenes, Chigurh explicates his lack of agency within a capitalist system. For example, when Chigurh stops at a gas station in Sheffield, Texas, he reacts with insult to the proprietor's query about where he comes from. 'I guess that passes for manners in your cracker view of things,' Chigurh says—a startling statement not just in terms of its rudeness, when Chigurh is usually unfailingly polite, but also in its use of a derogatory epithet against white Americans (52). The epithet does not necessarily indicate that Chigurh is non-white, as he is described as having eyes '[b]lue as lapis,' but it certainly suggests that he perceives the encounter to be marked by racial animus on the proprietor's part (56). He takes the opportunity to engage with the gas station proprietor in a lengthy dialogue about coins, a dialogue that is quickly revealed to be Chigurh's admission of a desire to kill the proprietor, and also his determination to allow the mathematics of probability to determine the man's fate, rather than Chigurh's personal preference. Chigurh takes one of the coins that he has stacked like 'poker chips'—underscoring his use of probability and chance—and calls on the proprietor to call heads or tails (53). According to Chigurh, reducing the proprietor's survival to a game of chance reveals that human lives function the same way as coins: transactional and instrumental. 'Anything can be an instrument,' he says. The coin in this case is meant to render 'an accounting' (57). This is no revenge killing; the man intruded on his trajectory, and now he will be held to 'account' for the impact of his intersection. In this instance, the gas station attendant calls the coin correctly and lives.

Even though he uses coins to exemplify his economic philosophy, Chigurh claims that the pursuit of money does not drive his death-dealing. The distinction is significant, because while Chigurh literally reduces human lives to coin tosses, fully equating a human life's value to a single coin, he does not sacrifice humans *to* the acquisition of wealth. The novel underscores this point in a scene in a Houston high-rise office building. In that office, an American drug lord hires another hitman, Carson Wells, to hunt Chigurh, who has become 'a loose cannon' with a kill count that includes two men who 'werent ours' along with two others who 'did happen to be ours' (140, 141). The 'colossal goatfuck' of violence rippling outward from the drug deal gone wrong has Chigurh at its epicenter, the cartel boss tells Wells, but why Chigurh is on this killing spree remains unclear (141). Wells, sent to hunt the hunter, successfully tracks Chigurh, and in their confrontation, readers are offered an explanation for Chigurh's spree. In this scene, Chigurh has gotten the better of Wells and is about to murder him. Wells offers Chigurh $14,000 to let him live, but Chigurh explains that he is not interested: money is 'the wrong currency,' he says; what he is after instead is some form of agency (173). He let himself be captured by the deputy (a reference to his first scene in the novel), Chigurh tells Wells, 'because I wanted to see if I could extricate myself by an act of will' (174–175). Wells is confused by this admission, and Chigurh tells him, 'You think that I'm like you,' that his reason for killing civilians and drug dealers is 'just greed. But I'm not like you,' Chigurh says. 'I live a simple life' (177). Why, then, does Chigurh kill on behalf of the cartel? As Biron argues, hitmen play a pivotal role in the illicit economies of drug cartels; they permit the production class to 'communicat[e] through messaging based on fear,' thereby turning 'human lives into ... symbols with no intrinsic meaning.' Hitmen patrol the borders of the classes, reducing competition, eliminating consumer-class members who fail in their function. Biron notes that 'in a social field where murder has become a way of life "that's life" also refers to perhaps the only way in which the fully human—understood as radical freedom and creative performance—comes alive ... when the *sicario* kills his capitalist.'[23] In Biron's words, then, Chigurh kills because he is in search of freedom.

After killing Wells, Chigurh tracks the cartel boss who ordered Wells to kill him and kills that boss, but once again, he explains that his motivation was not the obvious one (revenge). It was to establish 'bona fides' with the boss's boss, an unnamed man in another office to whom Chigurh finally gives the money, the McGuffin that has driven the action of the novel (251). Chigurh tells that final boss that he will now work for him as his hitman. 'Not everyone is suited to this line of work,' Chigurh explains. 'The prospect of outsized profits leads people to exaggerate their own capabilities,' but Chigurh, not driven by a need to accumulate surplus profits, desires only to excel at his role in the hierarchy (253). Chigurh is not only a consummate professional hitman; he is also the consummate laborer. He kills because that is his function in a market that is driven by a need to maximize profits by minimizing the number of competitors who might share in those profits.

To return to his conversation with Wells, it becomes clear that his desire to 'free' himself by 'an act of will' reflects his larger quandary, namely that he *does* experience a longing for agency that would break the bonds of his role as laborer. In Chigurh's final scene, he confronts Carla Jean, the last person tied to the cash and therefore his last victim. She pleads for her life, telling him that he can choose to show mercy to her. Chigurh disagrees: he cannot 'make [himself] vulnerable,' he says (259). Despite his portrayal as an automaton, a laborer-cog in the illicit drug market wheel, Chigurh's more complex desire for autonomy, for a choice that seemingly has been denied to him, haunts him.

This desire is coded visually into scenes in which Chigurh commits murder, when the narrative perspective shifts from paying attention to the minutiae of the murder to focusing instead on the drain of humanity from the eyes of the victim. With his first victim, the deputy, Chigurh watches blood roll down from the bolt hole between the dead man's eyes 'carrying with it his slowly uncoupling world visible to see' (7). When he murders Wells, the narrator notes that, as he dies, '[e]verything that Wells had ever known or thought or loved drained slowly down the wall behind him' (178). When the narrative perspective shifts to focus on the 'essence' draining from a person in the moment they are reduced to a coin flip, a coherent visual metaphor for the novel's critique of the great 'evil' that has overtaken the US in these later decades of the twentieth century emerges. This argument crystallizes in Chigurh's final confrontation with Carla Jean, an innocent bystander—an unusual choice for a final showdown in a novel starring a hitman and a sheriff that underscores the novel's interest in the ordinary human cost of the economic system, rather than merely on questions of justice or the law. Here, as in previous scenes, the narrator pays close attention to the physical details of the coin toss:

> He straightened out his leg and reached into his pocket and drew out a few coins and took one and held it up. He turned it. For her to see the justice of it. He held it between his thumb and forefinger and weighed it and then flipped it spinning in the air and caught it and slapped it down on his wrist. Call it, he said. (258)

Carla Jean refutes his claim that he has no agency. 'You make it like it was the coin. But you're the one,' she tells him. 'Perhaps,' Chigurh admits. But, he says, 'I got here the same way the coin did' (258). Chigurh acknowledges that the object that represents material history is never *just* an artifact, because the record of history is never amoral: history is a record by which we mourn the dead, or justify killing the living. If we reduce beings to their use value, then that which is 'drained' in the moment of their death—their ineffable being (a soul?)—is no more and no less valuable than any other artifact; the use of a thing is its value. Although Carla Jean initially poses an alternate theory, namely that Chigurh has agency and can refuse the demands of his job, Chigurh badgers her into acknowledging his position. 'Do you understand?' he asks her, and, again, 'Do you see?' until at last Carla Jean sobs, 'I do. I truly do.' Once she admits that she sees his argument's validity, he says 'good,' and then 'he shot her' (260).[24] Chigurh's philosophy of economics is significant because he is the only character who lives authentically in line with his economic vision, regardless of any latent desires for agency or human connection or the capacity to be vulnerable. The fact that Chigurh survives and 'rides off' into his own future is ominous: his commitment to the reductive violence of the illegal drug trade presages that shadow economy's reach into the twenty-first century—the theme of *The Counselor.*

The drug trade and global capitalism in *The Counselor*

While *No Country*, set in the 1980s, is a story about the drug cartels and one hapless lawmen, in *The Counselor*'s twenty-first-century world there are no lawmen at all, just cartels, hitmen, prostitutes, and other black market operators. The screenplay extends Chigurh's worldview into an abbreviated material history of the West as a system poisoned by its reduction of human beings to their use value in a deregulated market. In one of the screenplay's first scenes, the unnamed Counselor visits a diamond merchant in Amsterdam to purchase an engagement ring stone for his fiancée, Laura. As the Counselor peruses diamonds, the merchant muses aloud about moral virtue, economic value, and determinism, concluding with an assertion about the frailty of the transitory world. 'En este mundo nada es perfecto,' he says (17). In response, the Counselor offers a guess about his interlocuter's ethnic and religious identity: 'You are Sephardic' (17). The Counselor deduces the diamond merchant is a Sephardic Jew on the basis of a single Spanish phrase and an association of Jews with diamond dealing. Such a caricatured portrayal of a Jew—and moreover the Counselor's assumption of an innate relationship between Jews and material wealth—is troubling, particularly in the context of the rise in anti-Semitism in Europe and the US that has emerged alongside global shifts toward isolationism, nationalism, and neo-fascism in the early twenty-first century. David Harvey summarizes this trend in *The New Imperialism* (2003), explaining the rise of a 'world-wide anti-globalization movement' which allied itself in the early twenty-first century with populist movements and, together, 'threaten to transform grassroots resistance into a series of ... intensely nationalist' movements.[25] What may seem a bit of casual racial stereotyping in the screenplay provides the first visual reference to the narrative's exposition of the rapacious appetites of global capitalism, its history of violent dispossession, and capitalism's mythic narrative of inevitability.

While the film did not perform well in the box office, its commercial failures are not necessarily failures of theme or content.[26] Populated by characters consumed by competition, aggression, and greed, the film poses a series of brutal, vivid visual metaphors, each one representing distinct movements in the history of market capitalism, the system which famously finds competition, aggression, and greed 'good.'[27] First, the Jewish diamond merchant in Amsterdam conjures ancient histories of oppression in a system created and driven by Western European elites whose hands, as the merchant says, 'are always dripping blood' (19). Subsequent references to black market drug dealing, sex trafficking, and computer hacking represent global capitalism's shifts in the late twentieth and early twenty-first centuries. Somewhat tongue-in-cheek, Jacob Agner calls *The Counselor* a 'trashy spectacle' of a film. Agner specifically analyzes the film's visual emphasis on trash in the context of late capitalism, arguing that 'what triggered the critical gag-reflex' was ultimately its point: a vivid articulation of the 'limits of genre pleasure.'[28] McCarthy's screenplay is even more ambitious than that, although certainly it does critique the American entertainment industry. The seemingly isolated scene in Amsterdam at the beginning of *The Counselor* is a critical interpretive key to the narrative's larger project: an impressionistic history of the monstrosities of global capitalism that gestures toward the looming crisis of late capitalism. Its most telling critique, however, lies in a narrative strategy in which a crucial absent plot point reveals the fundamental justifying myth of global capitalism: that it is inevitable, and that no alternative exists which can be imagined. In the screenplay, the preconditions for the staged drama are already set; the damaging consequences of rapacious exploitation roll on, and any alternative is already too late. While many authors offer literary critiques of neoliberalism, warn of its excesses, or mourn the reduction of the working class to global human capital, *The Counselor* forces viewers to confront the preconditions of their own participation in the assumed inviolability of capitalism.[29]

David Deacon claims that *The Counselor* extends *No Country*'s argument, depicting 'a more complete neoliberal modernity, and the increasingly routine fixture of neoliberal logic through the spirit of entrepreneurship, which erodes the integrity of law ... by marketizing its output.'[30] Aesthetically, the screenplay realizes its project through a fragmentary and imagistic contemplation of the human cost of capitalism, concluding with an apocalyptically dire vision. This compressed history pivots around a single erasure, the narrative moment in which the Counselor must have chosen to engage in drug dealing. Like Chigurh's inexplicable 'loss' of agency, *The Counselor* erases the one moment that must have generated the action of the film.

This compressed history begins with visual reference to a transnational economic system born out of the systematic alienation and oppression of Jewish communities in Western Europe. The German economist and sociologist Werner Sombart's *The Jews and Modern Capitalism* (1913) makes a case for the significant and unique role that Jewish banking communities had in laying the fiscal groundwork for capitalism in the fifteenth and sixteenth centuries. Sombart tracks Jewish economic practices—an interest in unlimited competition, speculation and market share bargaining, and international banking—to two unique aspects of Sephardic Jewish life in Western Europe in the late Middle Ages: first, that Jews were excluded from the commercial centers of European communities and thereby forced to build their own capital; and second, that they were expelled from nearly every European state throughout the fourteenth and fifteenth centuries. '[T]he rise to economic importance,' Somberg writes, 'of the [European] countries and towns whither the refugees fled, must be dated from the first appearance of the Spanish Jews.'[31] That Sombart went on to write works praising the rising National Socialist Party in the 1930s in Germany indicates the problematic nature of economists' enthusiastic reception of his earlier work, but does not negate the kernel of truth in his economic history of capitalism in the West. Jewish communities lent money at interest while anti-usury laws for Christians were more or less consistent across Christendom, and because Jewish communities tended to deal with liquid wealth rather than property (which they were often forbidden from owning), even when they were geographically dispersed, Jewish lenders were able to offer competitive rates and to be less affected by local shocks to the market.[32] Jewish communities found an early foothold in the diamond and precious-gem industry in the sixteenth century, as its newness meant fewer of the guild restrictions that excluded Jews from owning and operating businesses in most other sectors of the European economy. Amsterdam quickly became a major hub of the diamond trade, and Jews monopolized the cutting and processing of raw diamonds.[33] Later, Antwerp would supersede Amsterdam in preeminence. Today, centers of diamond dealing have been globally dispersed, and online trade is more common than in-person shopping.

So why does McCarthy's Counselor show up in Amsterdam in 2013 to discourse with a Sephardic Jew about the death of cultures and heroes while also buying a diamond for his fiancée? If all the script needed to do was suggest a connection between Jewish communities and the diamond industry, it need have traveled no further than New York City, whose Orthodox Jewish community's control of that city's diamond industry is well documented.[34] However, the Counselor appears in Amsterdam, discoursing with a Sephardic Jewish diamond merchant who 'knows Spain,' even though Spain exiled its Jewish community in 1492, a temporal distance that would logically suggest that the Jewish diamond merchant's knowledge of Spain is coincidence rather than diaspora (*Co* 18). However, the diamond merchant describes his 'knowledge' of Spain in terms of historic exile: 'At one time,' he explains, 'I thought that she [Spain] would return from the grave. But that is not to be. Every country that has driven out the jews [sic] has suffered the same fate' (18). This cryptic pronouncement of economic and cultural karma suggests that Spain's current failure to recover from the global economic crisis in 2008 somehow resulted from the expulsion of Jews in 1492. If this scene is read as an atemporal metaphor, the Sephardic Jewish diamond merchant posits a fascinating, metonymic critique of capitalism. The rise of capitalism in Western Europe was influenced by the growth of Jewish lending, and Jewish lending was successful largely because Jews were denied rights to own valuable physical property. The 'grave' in which Spain lies now is likely a reference to the economic slump Spain suffered after the ravages of the global financial collapse in 2007–2008, a financial crisis largely due to two incompatible fiscal endeavors colliding: first, the bundling and sale of mortgages for middle- and low-income Americans by international banks enjoying an era of historic deregulation and, second, consumer over-confidence.[35] To put it even more abstractly, capitalism was born as a system that required an 'other'—a class of people disenfranchised from property ownership and from centers of political and economic power. It is a system that renews itself through crisis, perpetually disenfranchising working-class laborers while concentrating surplus capital in an ever-smaller class of global economic elites. Harvey says, 'Put in the language of contemporary postmodern political theory, we might say that capitalism necessarily and always creates its own "other."' Capitalism's increasing reliance on what he calls 'overaccumulation through dispossession' is the ethical crisis of the twenty-first century.[36]

The Jewish diamond merchant warns the Counselor that the diamond—valuable because it is rare—represents the nature of value itself. In a capitalist market system, financial value is based on accumulation and dispossession; capital must be coalesced so as to be rare—the dispossession of the many in favor of the few who possess ever more. However, there are other value systems. In the merchant's non-materialistic religious and ethical worldview, abstractions like love and life are valuable because they are fleeting and rare, albeit rare in a metaphysical rather than material sense. 'At our noblest,' the diamond merchant says, 'we announce to the darkness that we will not be diminished by the brevity of our lives' (20).[37] The merchant explicitly announces this scene's role as thematic foreshadowing, saying, 'I suppose every diamond is cautionary' (20). Explaining that the first facet cut on a diamond creates an ineradicable change in the stone, he suggests that the first cut represents the first step in all human endeavors. '[W]e see a troubling truth' in the metaphorical first cut, 'in that the forms of our undertakings are complete at their beginning' (17). The metaphor of diamond cutting seems obvious, yet it is less so upon examination. What, after all, is the first 'cut' that the Counselor makes? What choice took the Counselor down this road? The thing that matters—the choice about which the merchant cautions—is absent entirely from the dialogue. It is absent as well from the screenplay as a whole.

The Counselor buys his diamond, and the scene cuts abruptly to the American southwest, where the Counselor's complicity in a drug-dealing scheme is revealed. The shift from diamond merchants in Amsterdam to Mexican cartels and drug dealing in the US in the twenty-first century visually suggests that the history of global capitalism explicates the market forces driving the illegal drug industry. In Dominic Corva's analysis of the 'hyperpunitive criminal justice practices' in the US from the 1970s on, neoliberal economic policies created a perpetual 'criminal' underclass. Corva describes the convergence of Republican and Democratic penal policies from Ronald Reagan's War on Drugs to Bill Clinton's 'tough on crime' policies as fueled by 'late 20th century capitalist media practices oriented toward producing social spectacles for profit, and the depoliticization of social relations that produce "crime" and "criminals" by their transformation into bipartisan electoral capital.'[38] *The Counselor* offers a scene that, much like the diamond merchant's shop, provides a compressed visual allusion to this system: the Counselor performs a deed that seems initially like an act of mercy—he pays off the $400 ticket of a young man whose mother, Ruth, is already in prison and whom the Counselor represents. That young man will become the courier known as 'the Green Hornet,' who links the drug shipment to its delivery center because of the debt he owes to the Counselor. The young man's role in the narrative is primarily as a victim of criminal circumstance, but it is important to unpack what his story represents.

Ruth explains to the Counselor that her son was bringing her $12,000 but because he was speeding, police pulled him over and confiscated his money. The Counselor points out the legality of this theft: the US government can legally seize any cash in excess of $10,000 found in the process of an arrest or investigation. Cynically, he quips, 'Welcome to America' (70). Because his money was confiscated by law enforcement, the young man cannot now post bail, thereby becoming a willing victim to the Counselor's offer to post bail … for a favor. The young man's story presents a concise description of the fiscal processes by which the criminal justice system in the US creates a persistent criminal underclass, without which the entire system's financial infrastructure would collapse. Forfeiture provisions authorizing law enforcement agencies to seize drug-related assets, including any money over $10,000, have encouraged the many budget-restricted agencies around the country to 'use the proceeds for their budgetary needs.'[39] This provision ensures that the War on Drugs must continue in order for many law enforcement agencies to be able to afford to operate. The Counselor at one point explains the closed circuit of criminality and profit in the American criminal justice system, in case audiences have missed the critique embedded in the narrative. Westray tells the Counselor about his planned drug transportation scheme, where they will smuggle 'six hundred and twenty-five kilos. Pure uncut' of cocaine in a sewage truck across the border. Westray then describes the financial breakdown: the cocaine 'goes for about fifty dollars an ounce in Colombia and the street price in Dallas can be as high as two grand' (*Co* 53).[40] The Counselor remarks, 'If the drug wars stop this will dry up, right?' (56) As long as policing and penal systems profit from the illegality of the product, the illegality of the product drives up the profitability of trafficking the product.

The Counselor also underscores the humanitarian crisis at the heart of neoliberal policies: laborers reduced to human capital. A failure to recognize and respect the dignity of others lies at the heart of Westray's admission of his own guilt and his indication of what he perceives as the Counselor's complicity as well. Westray tells the Counselor that Mexican cartels are depraved; hundreds, '[t]housands, more likely' of young girls are killed '[f]or fun. Snuff films' (58, 59). Westray explains that he hates his own corruption; he 'could live in a monastery,' except for his fatal weakness: 'women' (61). He then recites a fragment from a famous nineteenth-century poem, 'Tom Gray's Dream' by Retta Brown: 'the only thing ultimately worth your concern is the anguish of your fellow passengers on this hellbound train' (62).[41] The poem is about an alcoholic man (Tom Gray), who wakes up on a hellbound train; the devil tells the train's passengers that they condemned themselves by scorning justice and taking advantage of the weak. This is the quandary at the heart of *The Counselor*: Westray recognizes his moral turpitude in finding sexual gratification through trafficked women, but recognition is not enough to curtail desire. He can recognize an alternative to this cycle of supply and demand—a value system based on compassion for others—but he fails to embrace it.

The most explicit image of dehumanization is the murder weapon that Reiner tells the Counselor about early in the drama and which Malkina later employs: a 'bolito,' a 'mechanical device' that forms a noose which, once dropped over a victim's head, tightens 'until it goes to zero' (35–36). McCarthy crafts for this narrative a murder device that, first, operates mechanically after being initially started by a human, and second, reduces its human victims from being (1) to nothingness (0). That metaphor, the binary system as a description of a human being reduced to an object (a corpse), is no accident. *The Counselor* turns its attention in its final act from the War on Drugs to an even more recent symbol of global capitalism: digital capital. In the script's closing narrative arc, Malkina meets with Lee, a 'twenty-five year old Chinese American' computer hacker who specializes in bank decryption through the creation of viruses (167, 171, 173). The role of informatics and computational technologies in the form and function of global capitalism in the twenty-first century cannot be over-emphasized. It is not just labor itself that has become de-located; in the contemporary world, information 'replaces material goods as the principle [sic] commodity.' For Seb Franklin, modes of computational activity such as hacking or the creation of computer viruses are potentially disruptive because 'they retain a connection with the Romanticist notion of the individual or group that is undercut by the predominance of the dividual [the de-humanized laborer in the digital marketplace] and the data bank characteristic of control societies.'[42] Computation is a single human command replicated automatically—much like the function of the 'bolito.' Hackers and creators of computer viruses, Franklin says, are agents who intervene in automation, interrupting and subverting the intended command of the programmer—and thus hacking represents a Romantic ideal of the individual against a global market. However, after discussing the potential of global communication, networking, and computer programming, Franklin warns that the dominant use of informatics in global capitalism is still controlled by multinational corporations.

Malkina represents both the possibilities and the failures of disruptive digital technologies. She answers the hacker Lee's question about her nation of origin by claiming 'Soy pura Portena,' identifying herself as from Buenos Aires but also suggesting in the colloquial use of that expression that she is a person always on the move (169, 83). Later, she predicts the collapse of the European

Union and the rise of China in a new era of globalization and asserts her intention to profit from this shift in economic dominance (177). Malkina physically represents the disruptive global south; she is an immigrant from South America who operates through disruptive technologies that liberate capital from the banking centers of the northern hemisphere. The disruption that she represents, however, is not an overturning of the system but a replication of it, merely with different agents. Like the Counselor, Malkina fails to imagine a value system apart from accumulation of wealth at the expense of others, the men she betrays, the lives she destroys.

At the end of the screenplay, Malkina offers a poetic monologue on the beauty of predators hunting their prey. 'The hunter has a purity of heart that exists nowhere else,' she says, gesturing to her pet cheetahs (183). Yet humanity is different from other predator species. 'I suspect that we are ill-formed for the path we have chosen,' she says, indicating that humans have chosen a path of relentless predation, but are hindered perhaps by compassion, or perhaps by a moral system that values something other than the 'hunt.' She concludes that, despite momentary weakness, humans persist in predation anyway. '[T]he slaughter to come,' she says, 'is probably beyond our wildest imagining.' In *The Counselor*'s concluding line, Malkina tells a paid sex worker that she is 'famished' (184). Malkina's voracious appetites—sexual, physical, and material—represent her role as a willing participant in the rampant consumerism of late capitalism. In this closing dialogue with her 'escort,' Malkina completes the metaphoric circle by indicating that she will translate her non-material digital wealth into diamonds, 'the easiest way to compress wealth' since diamonds 'weigh nothing at all' (178). On the one hand, her claim is technically untrue, since the original form of that wealth was digital, a medium that literally weighs nothing. But diamonds, as the novel's earlier scene has indicated, represent material history. As pure carbon, super-compressed, they represent the temporal compression of the history of capitalism, humankind's most comprehensive expression of insatiable consumption. In the full extension of this metaphor, the only form of wealth purer than digital wealth is compressed carbon, a single human life. Like Chigurh, Malkina briefly indicates her complicity in the system. She tells the escort that the one thing she wants more than anything is to possess her own life: 'I imagine that I would like my innocence back,' she says, 'But I would never pay the price which it now commands on the market.' The escort, a man whose body has been ceded to her as a commodity, nods understandingly and says, 'Your own life' (182).

The ominous warning of the Jewish diamond merchant echoes: 'Once the first facet is cut there can be no going back' (17). Reiner repeats this warning to the Counselor later on: 'You pursue this road that you've embarked upon,' he says, 'and you will eventually come to moral decisions that will take you completely by surprise' (34). Both times, the temporal mode of the warning misses its mark: the Counselor has already made his decision to engage in drug trafficking, since he is, first, in Amsterdam to purchase a diamond with money from drug trafficking, and second, he is meeting with Reiner to discuss their caper. Malkina's closing dialogue reveals the screenplay's argument: if the 'good' is a sort of spiritual possession of one's own life—a state of autonomy that is achieved through moral or ethical 'innocence,' in which the individual is incorporated into a healthy communal life—then that good has been stripped away from individuals and societies through the pernicious exploitation of global capitalism. Greed and consumption are its virtues, and once an individual has become complicit in the global exchange, it no longer matters whether they are a part of the system or a disrupter of the system.

Alyssa Palish points to the film's visual emphasis on that critical missing moment of choice: there is no precipitating event in the film. 'Even before the opening credits have rolled,' she says, 'we see a motorcyclist burning down a road … The motorcyclist, we will realize later, is already heading toward what the Counselor has set in motion.'[43] Not only is the moment of choice and the precipitating action erased from the film, but the rationale for that choice is likewise obscured. Reiner at one point asks the Counselor why he chose to embark on their fated venture. The Counselor says, 'Same as you. Greed,' but Reiner disagrees: 'I don't think so. … I tried to appeal to your greed two years ago. No deal. Now it's too late' (119, 120). Reiner explicitly calls out the significance of what is erased from the storyline: the protagonist's motivation and the story's precipitating action. The film's McGuffin are the kilos of cocaine, which audiences see only once toward the end of the action (153); by implication, the cocaine could be any substance: diamonds, oil, drugs, even bitcoin. The gem trade, oil markets, drug trafficking, and e-currencies are all examples of markets that have operated licitly and illicitly, both concurrently and causally; in each case, the human cost has been untenable.

Arjun Appadurai, extending Benedict Anderson's notion of the 'imagined community' to the context of a world in global flux, where stable local communities and kinships are increasingly rare and are 'everywhere shot through' with streams of 'human motion,' claims that 'imagination is now central to all forms of agency, is itself a social fact, and is the key component of the new global order.'[44] Appadurai focuses on the importance of the 'social imaginary,' discussing the increasing complexity of a world characterized by the labor and migratory flows of late capitalism in terms of challenges and opportunities. By contrast, McCarthy's views of global capitalism in *No Country* and *The Counselor* are bleak, focusing on the dark aspect of a world in flux, and a form of capitalism characterized by vast multinational organizations that prey on small laboring communities, extending to all corners of the globe. Imagination falters in the face of its vast reach.

As is typical of McCarthy's work, however, the texts' bleakness is shot through with subtle hints of alternatives to this failure of imagination. In a scene near the end of *The Counselor*, the Counselor attempts to bargain for Laura's life with a cartel 'jefe,' who reminds audiences once again of that crucial missing scene in which a choice was made. The Counselor made his choice, the jefe claims, and now must endure the consequences: 'There is only the accepting,' he says. 'The choosing was done long ago' (147). The jefe then references Antonio Machado's *Campos de Castilla*, a poem collection grieving the death of the poet's wife, to substantiate his claim that '[t]here is no rule of exchange' in the practice of love or the experience of loss. 'Grief transcends every value,' the jefe says. 'A man would give whole nations to lift it from his heart. And yet with it you can buy nothing' (148). The jefe points to the underlying flaw in the Counselor's narrative: it is not a single moment or choice that has condemned the Counselor, but rather his failure lies in his worldview, a philosophy in which all things, including human beings, are material goods in a cosmic exchange. Just as he attempts to put a diamond on Laura—metaphorically as well as literally—so also the Counselor fails to realize that he is trying to give his material possessions, even his body, in exchange for a person when, instead, all that had been required of him was to love that person.

Ambitious and skilled in their respective systems, Chigurh and the Counselor represent the destructiveness and inhumanity of the philosophy of 'good greed.' Their attempts at success are marked by failure: in Chigurh's case, a failure to control his own destiny; in the Counselor's case, the loss of the woman he loves. These narratives suggest the limits of agency within a system that replicates itself through the commodification of the laborers who perpetuate it. The tragic failure of the professional is his belief that his professionalism will enable him to navigate the market economy's excesses without losing more than he can afford to lose; he will not be able to do so. How and why the professional fails becomes a history of market capitalism spelled out through image and metaphor, gesturing toward failures of interpretation, of critical thought, and of ethical judgment in the US as it enters the twenty-first century.

Notes

1 Ellen Meiksins Wood, *The Origin of Capitalism* (Monthly Review Press, 1999), 121; and Rebecca Biron, 'It's a Living: Hit Men in the Mexican Narco War,' *PMLA*, vol. 127, iss. 4 (2012), 820–834: 832.
2 Malewitz, 'Anything can be an Instrument,' 722.
3 Thomas Piketty, *Capital in the Twenty-First Century*, trans. Arthur Goldhammer (Belknap Press of Harvard University Press, 2017), 549, 556.
4 Mandel, *Late Capitalism*, 311–312.
5 For the purposes of this argument, 'late capitalism' refers to the shift from traditional market capitalism, which was driven by international trade but primarily located in national centers, to transnational or 'global' capitalism in the digital age. Global capitalism, with its diffusion of manufacturing around the world and the concentration of capital surplus funneled through a worldwide financial marketplace to an increasingly small number of power brokers and economic elites, provides an easy target for critique. For further definitions of late

capitalism, see Mandel, *Late Capitalism*, 316; David Harvey, *The New Imperialism* (Oxford University Press, 2003), 73; and Ross and Trachte, *Global Capitalism*, 6.
6 Biron, 'It's a Living,' 832.
7 John Fitzgerald, 'Illegal Drug Markets in Transitional Economies,' *Addiction Research and Theory*, vol. 13, iss. 6 (2005), 563–577: 565, 566, 567, 571.
8 Fisher, *Capitalist Realism*, 4.
9 Peebles, *Page, Stage, Screen*, 67, 66.
10 Steven Edward Knepper, '*The Counselor* and Tragic Recognition,' *The Cormac McCarthy Journal*, vol. 14, iss. 1 (2016), 37–54: 44, 45, italics in screenplay.
11 Hillier, *Morality in Cormac McCarthy's Fiction*, 224, 225. Hillier is one of few scholars to read Bell as a satirical depiction of a particular and pernicious form of Texas policing and carceral policy, rather than as a simplistically rendered, politically conservative, straightforward protagonist. I have similarly argued in *Masculinities in Literature of the American West*, 127–146, that *No Country* inverts the 'white hat' sheriff archetype in westerns through Bell's satirical depiction. My reading of Bell suggests that what McCarthy is doing in *No Country* is consistent with a particular movement in southern and Texas crime novels' treatments of the sheriff as a figure representing white supremacy in the post-Reconstruction South, which Nahem Yousaf explores in 'A Southern Sheriff's Revenge: Bertrand Tavernier's *Coup de torchon*.' Yousaf examines the transatlantic movement of two Jim Thompson novels to a French film director's narrative set in Senegal in the 1930s in order to illustrate a through-line which depict sheriffs—in Thompson's case, Texan sheriffs—as deeply implicated in lynch mobs and white violence aimed at 'keep[ing] black southerners in their place.' See 'A Southern Sheriff's Revenge: Bertrand Tavernier's *Coup de torchon*,' *Translatlantic Exchanges: The American South in Europe, Europe in the American South*, eds. Richard Gray and Waldemar Zacharasiewicz (Austrian Academy of Sciences, 2007), 221–238: 222.
12 Again, here I use the term 'labor' as Hannah Arendt used it, where labor is the production of commercial goods necessary to sustaining life, and differentiated from work, the making of durable things that might outlive the span of a human life. As Arendt claims, 'the mark of all laboring is that it leaves nothing behind, that the result of its effort is almost as quickly consumed as the effort is spent.' She points out that in antiquity (and, one would add, in the antebellum South) '[t]he burden of biological life … can be eliminated only by the use of servants.' Only

by the use of cheap or 'free' labor—with people reduced to the function of their labor—could slave-owning families 'rise above' the cycle of labor and consumption. Arendt, *The Human Condition*, 87, 119, 126.
13 Peebles, *Page, Stage, Screen*, 59.
14 Peebles, *Page, Stage, Screen*, 18, 59.
15 Dianne C. Luce, 'Cormac McCarthy's First Screenplay: *The Gardener's Son*,' *Perspectives on Cormac McCarthy*, rev. edn, eds. Edwin T. Arnold and Dianne C. Luce (University Press of Mississippi, 1999), 71–96: 75.
16 Manohla Dargis, 'Wildlife is Tame; Not the Humans: "The Counselor," a Cormac McCarthy Tale of Mostly Evil,' *New York Times*, October 24, 2013; and Peter Bradshaw, 'The Counselor: Review,' *Guardian*, 1November 14, 2013.
17 Stephen Tatum, '"Mercantile ethics": *No Country for Old Men* and the Narcocorrido,' *Cormac McCarthy*: All the Pretty Horses, No Country for Old Men, The Road, ed. Sara L. Spurgeon (Continuum, 2011), 77–93: 79, 59.
18 Malewitz, 'Anything can be an Instrument,' 728.
19 Soyen Shaku, *Sermans of a Buddhist Abbot: Addresses on Religious Subjects*, trans. Deisetz Teitaro Suzuki (Open Court Publishing, 1906), 109. Petra Mundik points out that Ben's quote in *The Stonemason* refers to the Akashic ledger book, the mystical compendium of all human events, acts, and thoughts throughout history, accessible only in a dream state. Mundik, *A Bloody and Barbarous God*, 353, n.5.
20 I am one of these critics; in *No More Heroes: Narrative Perspective and Morality in Cormac McCarthy* (Louisiana State University Press, 2011), I focus on Moss's character and trace how it is his greed that initiates his involvement, but his act of mercy that is his doom. And in *Masculinities in Literatures of the American West* (2016), I address Bell's problematic refusal to acknowledge his responsibility in his failures and the novel's subversion of the ethos of the 'white hat/black hat' moral paradigm of the western.
21 John Vanderheide, 'Varieties of Renunciation in the Works of Cormac McCarthy,' *The Cormac McCarthy Journal*, vol. 5, iss. 1 (2005), 30–35: 34; Brad Bannon, 'Divinations of Agency in *Blood Meridian* and *No Country for Old Men*,' *The Cormac McCarthy Journal*, vol. 14, iss. 1 (2016), 78–95: 93.
22 Clarke, 'The New Naturalism,' 64.
23 Biron, 'It's a Living,' 832.
24 I have elsewhere argued that Carla Jean's reluctant agreement with Chigurh does not indicate her actual concurrence with his worldview.

Instead, because of the narrative point of view, external to Chigurh and regarding Carla Jean's increasingly frantic pleas, readers 'come to precisely the opposite conclusion' about the inevitability of fate driving Chirgurh's actions. See *No More Heroes*, 126.
25 Harvey, *The New Imperialism*, 74.
26 The film based on McCarthy's screenplay *The Counselor*, directed by Ridley Scott, was released in 2013 to high expectations. A visually flashy crime drama, the film was nevertheless panned by critics. *The Counselor* follows an unnamed cartel lawyer ('the Counselor') as he enters into an agreement with a cartel-affiliated nightclub owner, Reiner, and Reiner's dangerous former call-girl partner, Malkina. Reiner and the Counselor plan a drug deal along with Reiner's more reluctant associate, Westray. The Counselor makes little attempt to separate his deepening involvement with the cartel from his Catholic, wholesome fiancée, Laura. When the drug shipment is found and stolen by unknown parties, Westray warns the Counselor that the cartel will hunt them down. Laura is kidnapped as punishment for the Counselor's failure to return on the stolen goods; she is later executed, a snuff film of her brutal murder given to the Counselor as notice of her death. Malkina, meanwhile, has determined that Westray made off with the funds from the drugs, and she hunts him down in London, hires a hit-woman to kill the man, and decrypts his bank accounts to steal the money back.
27 The famous 'greed is good' speech of Gordon Gekko (Michael Douglas) in Oliver Stone's 1987 film *Wall Street* echoes here.
28 See Jacob Agner, 'Salvaging *The Counselor*: Watching Cormac McCarthy and Ridley Scott's Really Trashy Movie,' *The Cormac McCarthy Journal*, vol. 14, iss. 2 (2016), 204–226: 205, 206, 214. The vivid and prolific scenes of trash that Agner identifies suggest the importance of the theme of over-consumption—of which 'trash' is an inevitable consequence. Beyond actual trash, however, the more blatant scenes of hunting, killing, and eating provide visual metaphors for a global economic system based on predation and over-consumption. For example, Malkina is introduced with her pet cheetahs strolling around her, a tattoo of 'an Egyptian cat' on her neck. The tattoo is likely meant to be an image of Bast, the Egyptian goddess of warfare (*TC* 12). Malkina's cheetahs recur as suggestive metaphors throughout the screenplay, hunting prey in the background (e.g., 184). Additionally, scenes not involving actual killing usually involve people eating in restaurants: the Counselor and Laura become engaged in a restaurant, and Malkina and Laura meet in a café at a shopping mall, combining an

image evoking the excesses of capitalism with actual food consumption (23, 44–5).
29 McCarthy is certainly not rare in the world of literary giants tackling this subject. Literary texts that engage and critique the effects of capitalism are in generous supply, but some notable examples that express the breadth and diversity of such texts include Don DeLillo's *White Noise* and *Cosmopolis*; Ngũgi wa Thiong'o's *The Devil on the Cross*; China Miéville's urban fantasies; and Mohsin Hamid's *How to Get Filthy Rich in Rising Asia*. However, *The Counselor*'s focus on exposing the failures of its audience to imagine a way out of the system merits extended study, in my view.
30 David Deacon, '"Some Unholy Alloy": Neoliberalism, Digital Modernity, and the Mechanics of Globalized Capital in Cormac McCarthy's *The Counselor*,' *European Journal of American Studies*, vol. 12, iss. 3 (2017), 1–16: 2.
31 Werner Sombart, *The Jews and Modern Capitalism*, trans. M. Epstein (E. P. Dutton & Co., 1913), 14.
32 Maristella Botticini, 'A Tale of "Benevolent" Governments: Private Credit Markets, Public Finance, and the Role of Jewish Lenders in Medieval and Renaissance Italy,' *The Journal of Economic History*, vol. 60, iss. 1 (March 2000), 164–189: 171.
33 Karin Hofmeester, 'Shifting Trajectories of Diamond Processing: From India to Europe and Back, from the Fifteenth Century to the Twentieth,' *Journal of Global History*, vol. 8, iss. 1 (2013), 25–49.
34 Richman Barak D. Richman, 'Community Enforcement of Informal Contracts: Jewish Diamond Merchants in New York,' Harvard Law School, Discussion Paper no. 384 (September 2002), 1–57.
35 Carl Levin and Tom Coburn, 'Wall Street and the Financial Crisis: Anatomy of a Financial Collapse,' Majority and Minority Staff Report, Permanent Subcommittee on Investigations, US Senate, April 13, 2011.
36 Harvey, *The New Imperialism*, 141, 156.
37 This passage in its entirety reads: 'The heart of any culture is to be found in the nature of the hero. Who is that man who is revered? In the classical world it is the warrior. But in the western world it is the man of God. From Moses to Christ. The prophet. The penitent' (*Co* 19).
38 Dominic Corva, 'Neoliberal Globalization and the War on Drugs: Transnationalizing Illiberal Governance in the Americas,' *Political Geography*, vol. 27 (2008), 176–193: 178.
39 Eric Blumenson and Eva Nilson, 'Policing for Profit: The Drug War's Hidden Economic Agenda,' *The University of Chicago Law Review*, vol. 65, iss. 1 (Winter 1998), 35–114: 40.

40 Specifically, they have 21,900 ounces, which by their calculations would net them somewhere around $43.8 million (*Co* 53).
41 Stacey Peebles notes that the Brown poem is often recited at Alcoholics Anonymous meetings. By implication, Westray describes the drive to exploit the vulnerable as a type of compulsion. The comparison to alcoholism perhaps illuminates a distinction between the compulsion driving excessive or exploitative consumption and the innateness myth of neoliberalism. If exploitative consumption can take the form of a disease like alcoholism, then it may seem to have certain 'innate' characteristics, but it is nevertheless innate only insofar as it is a predilection, a possible illness that may manifest, typically because of the compounding force of certain external factors, rather than being an essential characteristic of the species ('homo economicus'). Peebles, *Page, Stage, Screen*, 173.
42 Seb Franklin, 'Virality, Informatics, and Critique: Or, Can There Be Such a Thing as Radical Computation?,' *Women's Studies Quarterly*, vol. 40, iss. 1–2 (Spring–Summer 2012), 153–170: 153, 156, 164.
43 Alyssa Palish, 'The Moment of Choice: Cormac McCarthy's "The Counselor,"' *Los Angeles Review of Books*, November 2, 2013.
44 Arjun Appadurai, *Modernity at Large: Cultural Dimensions of Globalization* (University of Minnesota Press, 1996), 33, 34, 31.

4

Prophets: imagining the end of the Anthropocene in *The Road*

[W]e have turned a community of birth and death and life and love into a community of agony and horror. ... All this in an effort to appease a god who because he is cast in our own image is unappeasable. So that nothing will stop us except silence itself.

(McCarthy, *Whales and Men*)

Responsibility and vulnerability are asymmetrically distributed in the changing Earth system. ... 'Capitalocene' better reflects the sociohistorical drivers of the new epoch.

(Tobias Menely and Jesse Oak Taylor, 'Introduction,'
Anthropocene Reading: Literary History in Geologic Times)[1]

Some time shortly before 1992, Tony Miller, a director of photography whose work in the 1990s included the Emmy Award-winning *In the Company of Whales*, recalls meeting Cormac McCarthy at the wedding of the whale biologist Roger Payne. They chatted about 'the selfishness of American society and how it seemed to create such unequal divides,' a conversation that prompted McCarthy to bring up *Blood Meridian*, describing its attempt to 'mirror the current American loss of community values and self-interested individualism.' Miller says that McCarthy shifted to his 'love of the natural world and how it could so easily be permanently desecrated. Climate Change was surely a reality.'[2] In the early 1990s, McCarthy's interest in climate change and apparent belief that individualistic values had decentered responsible environmental policy and practice offered a fascinating glimpse into a project yet to be written: his Pulitzer Prize-winning novel, *The Road*.

The Road is a post-Anthropocene retrospective on the economic history of the US, from its use and consumption of people kept in slavery through its reckless consumption of fossil fuels. Through this retrospective, an unnamed man speculates on whether human existence can have meaning even in the face of annihilation. In the character of the man, *The Road* offers a prophetic call for critical evaluation of our value systems as environmental catastrophe looms. It also turns on McCarthy's notion of the role of narrative as a form of work, a view that reflects Hannah Arendt's description of story as that which 'separates human existence from all mere animal environment.' In *The Human Condition*, Arendt reminds readers of the need to fuse artifice to the ethical obligations of the real world, of life beyond our imagination, because only through imagination can humans orient themselves toward transcendence, or meaningfulness.[3]

McCarthy's ideas about the prophetic role of the storyteller who calls out injurious acts and attitudes and creates imagined possibilities for meaningful human engagement are distilled in *The Road*, but the novel offers little in the way of consolation. It may be prophetic, but it is more horror than holy tale. In a particularly telling scene, the man and boy find an abandoned plantation house containing preserved food. The man dishes up the cans of food and they eat at an elegant 'Empire table,' its aesthetic style calling out a long colonial history of slavery and genocide (175). As they eat at a table once served by enslaved people, the old house creaks like a 'thing being called out of long hibernation.' The man imagines ghosts of the now-collapsed colonial nation staring at them through the windows, and he concludes that they 'are watching for a thing that even death cannot undo and if they do not see it they will turn away from us and they will not come back' (177). In this complex image of consumption, intergenerational guilt, and a longing for redemption, the ghosts haunting the 'Empire table' conjure the critical questions at the heart of this novel. What is the essential nature of those who eat at the table now? Can and should their civilization be saved?

The Road is replete with images of consumption, from evocations of a fossil fuel-driven economy to cannibalism, the pinnacle of consumption run amok. The man's wife at one point claims that the survivors of the unnamed catastrophe are like the 'walking dead in a horror film,' associating their post-apocalyptic reality with zombies, the monstrous metaphor for consumers who consume constantly but without redemptive or meaningful purpose (47). Throughout the novel, the man is haunted by similar images of insatiable hunger, such as when he dreams of his son laid out on a table and dressed to be devoured (15–16, 109–110). The man and boy wander through a world turned into a mausoleum and a charnel house in equal parts. They stumble on a stalled-out truck full of human bodies and wander into an orchard that has become a slaughter yard. In the orchard, human victims have been 'field dressed like deer,' and the surrounding wall holds 'a frieze of human heads, all faced alike, dried and caved with their taut grins and shrunken eyes' (40, 76). Marauding survivors roam in bands of violent cannibals, 'bloodcults' wearing red scarves who march in a 'phalanx' with their 'spears or lances tasseled with ribbons,' evoking perhaps the Celtic mythology of bloodthirsty redcaps, or the ghoulish Scottish legend of Sawney Beane and his incestuous, cannibalistic horde (77). Taken together, these gothic horrors expose the connection between power brokerage and overconsumption or improper consumption of resources, exemplified by a colonial ruling class invoked by the 'Empire table' in the plantation house. And like all gothic fiction, *The Road* is a tale told with intent. The gothic exposes contemporaneous social anxiety in order to examine the 'causes, qualities, and results of terror,' and to assess and, perhaps, remedy that terror.[4]

Scholars often locate McCarthy's fiction within or adjacent to the American southern gothic. The Appalachian setting of his first novels highlights inherited regional characteristics of Scottish and Anglo-Irish literature, which Steven Frye calls an 'oblique sense of gray,' defined as a 'fatalistic, mystical apprehension that distinguished many Appalachian people since their first migration from northern Britain, southern Scotland, and Ulster Plantation.'[5] A 'sense of gray' is nowhere more explicit than in *The Road*; as Chris Danta points out, the word 'gray' appears in the novel some eighty-one times.[6] The destruction that has 'grayed' out the world of *The Road* is described as a global loss refracted through a localized lens. The man's questions about the capacity of humanity to be redeemed are questions deriving from a geographically, culturally, and nationally specific heritage. First, as descendants of a 'yeoman middle class' in the South—a class composed of agrarian landowners and middle-class industrialists, historically forged through the possession of the bodies of the underclass—the man and boy wander into houses once populated by slave owners and eat at the table, symbolizing their inheritance.[7] Second, industrialism and its disastrous environmental policies are represented by a 'tattered oil-company roadmap' that the man carries with him, which points to the over-consumption of non-renewable resources by the 'consumer class' in the early twenty-first century (36).[8]

While the novel's southern gothic elements have been frequently noted, I argue that it evokes more precisely elements of an Anglo-Irish gothic tradition, a distinction that critically highlights the novel's implication of the man in the consumerism that haunts the wasted world.[9] The Anglo-Irish gothic refers to a body of literature characterized by its focused attention on the implications of colonial and market-capitalist power systems in Ireland. W. B. Yeats, J. M. Synge, Lady Gregory, and Oscar Wilde, some of the most significant figures associated with the resurgence of the Anglo-Irish gothic tradition, shaped the tradition into a 'more critical, self-conscious gothic,' one which 'acknowledge[s] the historical culpability of the settler colonial system' that they at once denounced yet sought to redeem.[10] Terry Eagleton claims that in the historical moment of the Anglo-Irish ascendancy, its literature depicts a political state in colonial Ireland that sought to create itself while 'ominously evoking the truth that whatever goes up can always come down.'[11] Only through conjuring a ruling class already sliding into descent could the drivers of the Anglo-Irish literary tradition hermetically seal the racial and colonial sins of that class in the past, while gesturing toward a nationalism informed by the fusion of that ruling class with its colonial subjects as a new 'Ireland.' A similar anxiety about a colonial ruling class animates McCarthy's gothic fable about the spiraling consumption of the US in the early twenty-first century. I connect McCarthy's critique of US hegemony to the Anglo-Irish gothic tradition because *The Road* offers abstract critique rather than paying attention to the particulars of race-based colonialism in the US, which is a key characteristic of US southern gothic fiction. Leslie Fiedler suggests that slavery and race-based 'blood taboos' are such pervasive themes that the American southern gothic bears little resemblance to older European gothic traditions.[12] However, slavery and blood taboos are only spore in *The Road*; its fabulistic and mythic terrain, divested of particularity while retaining vague signposts of its Appalachian landscape, is interested in a more nebulous social anxiety.[13] McCarthy seems less interested in this novel in naming identities than in conjuring systems, not to adjudicate blame but rather to expose the pervasive fear that American economic ascent is only the precursor to descent.

Two key attributes of Anglo-Irish gothic literature that feature in *The Road* are explicated through images of destructive consumption. First, as part of the economic 'yeoman middle class' of the South, the man and his son reflect genetic inheritance from the class whose economic engines ran on the labor of enslaved others. Second, the countryside in the Anglo-Irish tradition represents threat to the ruling class in response to abuses of economic power. In *The Road*, the man is the product of industrialism and its disastrous environmental policies, and his journey through a gothic wasteland implicates him in the destructive uses of the ecosystems he mourns. The novel's use of elements of Anglo-Irish gothic fiction suggests its particular interest in exposing the destructive nature of economic imperialism in the US, or at least the anxiety on the part of its consumer class that its ascendency may have already reached and passed its zenith. Examining these gothic elements, in conversation with the novel's metaphoric use of fractal imagery, suggests its complex examination of the causes and consequences of its contemporaneous referent's consumer economy run amok as well its contemporaneous audience's failures to grapple with the implications of such consumption.

The Anglo-Irish 'Big House,' power, and corruption

'Anglo-Irish literature' refers broadly to a body of literature produced by English-descended landowners in Ireland after the Earl of Pembroke's invasion of the country in 1167. After the Act of Union, that term also came to embrace Irish-descended authors who rejected Catholicism and took up land and/or seats of power in Dublin and in England. Typically, the Anglo-Irish literary tradition refers specifically to a body of work produced by proto-nationalist and nationalist writers of Anglo-Irish descent through the nineteenth and into the early twentieth century. Maria Edgeworth's *Castle Rackrent*, published in 1800 and considered the first significant work classified as 'Anglo-Irish gothic,' is a drama about a landed Anglo-Irish family's decline as narrated by the illiterate household steward. *Castle Rackrent* displays several of characteristic attributes of the genre: a 'Big House' in decay; the ominous threat of a disgruntled working class; and an anxiety about marriage as a troubled and gendered representation of the threat of colonial union. The American southern gothic tradition at times adopts or adapts some of these themes—the Big House, a landed family's domain facing a largely hostile countryside and a rising tide of oppressed 'others,' for instance, carried across the Atlantic in such explicit forms as Margaret Mitchell's *Gone with the Wind*, which centers on a literally transplanted 'Tara.'[14] Even more critical than spatial and architectural aspects of the US southern plantation system, however, is the aspect of hegemonic power exercised by the ruling class, an attribute which is less common in southern gothic literature and seems to drive McCarthy's interest in making use of Anglo-Irish gothic generic elements.[15]

Many scholars have noted Anglo-Irish antecedents in McCarthy's work in other forms. An obvious example is his 2005 novel *No Country for Old Men*, which literally names the influence of Yeats; Frye systematically traces the thematic and aesthetic traduction of Yeats's 'Sailing to Byzantium' in that novel to suggest the poem lends more to the novel than just its title. Other critics have noted too McCarthy's aesthetic and philosophical indebtedness to Samuel Beckett in several works.[16] In addition to the influence of such major Anglo-Irish authors as Yeats and Beckett, James Potts finds evidence of 'Cormac Mac Airt' lore in *Suttree*; Barbara Brickman traces the spore of Celtic legends in *The Orchard Keeper*, and Barbara Bennett notes 'Celtic influences' in *No Country* and *The Road*. Bryan Giemza's study of McCarthy's Catholic and Irish identities provides the most thorough analysis to date, although he focuses primarily on Irish influences in *Suttree*, situating McCarthy within the category of Irish Catholic writers in the Appalachian American South.[17] Certainly McCarthy as an author has demonstrated a clear and persistent connection with 'Irish' identity, broadly, but his interest in Anglo-Irish political and economic concerns dates back at least to his unpublished screenplay *Whales and Men*, in which a central character is a landed Anglo-Irish nobleman who takes up a seat in the House of Lords in order to defend the rights of whales against consumer-driven devastation of their population. It may seem surprising that a Catholic-school-educated author of books replete with Catholic imagery gives certain characters 'Anglo' Irish roots in *Whales and Men*, McCarthy's only text set in part in Ireland, but as that text makes clear, it is the Anglo-Irish representation of a hegemonic, colonial settler ruling class, a milieu notably less characteristic of US southern gothic writing, that is more relevant to McCarthy's project.

Perhaps the most visible and characteristic representation of colonial power brokerage in the Anglo-Irish gothic tradition is the image of the 'Big House in decay.' McCarthy represents an autobiographical rejection of a middle-class upbringing associated with economic and legal power through evocations of the Big House, an image that crops up in *Suttree* and recurs in *The Road*. In his 1992 interview, Woodward remarks on the disparity between McCarthy's own 'comfortable upbringing' in a 'large white house' with 'acreage and woods nearby,' a home 'staffed with maids' and markedly distinct from the much poorer and smaller homesteads in the surrounding area. 'We were considered rich,' McCarthy tells him, 'because all the people around us were living in one- or two-room shacks.' As Woodward points out, it was the life of the shacks, 'Knoxville's nether world,' that seems to have seized and inspired the author's literary imagination 'more than anything that happened inside his own family.'[18] *The Road* returns to *Suttree*'s semi-autobiographical scion of landed 'gentry' with its protagonist, although in the later novel, the collapse of the man's familial home is taken to its most devastating extreme.[19] Toward the beginning of the novel, the father takes his son to his ancestral home, an old house with 'chimneys and gables and a stone wall' standing in isolation in a wild countryside (*TR* 21). Only after they leave it and venture south does the tale proper commence.

Also characteristic of the Anglo-Irish gothic tradition is the nostalgia that hangs like a pall over the novel. The man remembers his pre-apocalyptic childhood with melancholy. When he takes his son on a tour of the collapsing structure of his gabled ancestral home, he fits his thumbs against holes in the mantelpiece where he hung stockings as a child (21). At an abandoned gas station, the man picks up a telephone at the empty clerk's desk and dials 'the number of his father's house in that long ago' (6). A saccharine yearning for that 'long ago' that he attempts to conjure exists, certainly—an evocation of warmth and the comfort of ritual (fireplaces and holidays) mixed with a desire for contact with the departed, exemplified by his pointless dialing of a dead number. The novel clarifies, however, that the nostalgia associated with that familial history was present even in the man's pre-apocalyptic childhood. At one point, the man reflects that his obsession with locating himself and his son on maps of places now extinct stems from before the event that broke the world. 'He'd pored over maps as a child,' readers are told, 'keeping one finger on the town where he lived. Just as he would look up his family in the phone directory.' A need formed in childhood to geospatially locate himself is one that is rooted in a need to understand his relationship to his world through familial attachment. He identifies the names and addresses of family members in a phone book as though to verify that he exists in a world peopled by 'his kind,' his kin who keep him '[j]ustifed in the world' (153). *The Road* depicts a world wrested from the known: maps without names, humans without names, a world of signs shorn of referents. Yet that alienation seems to have plagued the man before the apocalypse. Nostalgia seems to be an affliction that has less to do with the actual loss of the culture or persons being mourned than with the condition of the privilege of the man's childhood, that ominous sense that what goes up comes down, as Eagleton puts it.[20]

While the man's ancestors were likely middle class, the Big House tradition implicates him in its darker history. As they move south from his ancestral home, they seek larger and more prestigious 'Big Houses' as logical sources of comestibles, drawing visual attention to the history of this region and the forms of consumption that have driven its economy. As they journey south, they stop at a 'grand house' with a 'port cochère' and a gravel drive, a former plantation house literally rooted in its own earth, 'kilned out of the dirt it stood on' (89, 90). The brick-based heritage is tainted with human corruption; the man reflects that '[c]hattel slaves had once trod those boards bearing food and drink on silver trays' (90). In this grand house, they find the most grotesque form of a world built on the commodification of human bodies: a cellar room packed with humans in varying states of being cannibalized, 'naked people' who are 'all trying to hide' from them, one man with 'legs gone at the hip and the stumps of them blackened' (93). The partially consumed victims plead with the man for help, but the man flees with his son, fearing a similar fate. Later, he explains to his child that they could not save them nor should they risk their lives to try (97). After they leave this shell of a plantation house, they see another group of people, a pregnant woman among them. The group 'vanish[es] one by one into the waiting darkness'; in the next scene, they come across a campfire with a 'charred human infant' (164, 167). The juxtaposition of the two scenes suggests a connection, although the logic of that connection is thin: consumption of an hours-old baby seems a less satisfying main course than an infant would be. The consumption of the young thus seems to reflect not just actual hunger in these scavenging hoards but also a desire to cut short the degenerate and degenerating remains of the race under discussion—in the case of *The Road*, humanity itself.

Throughout the narrative, the man attempts to articulate a role for himself and his son in this predatory world that is neither that of the consumer nor that of the consumed. While they abstain from eating the flesh of others and manage to avoid becoming food themselves, they are symbolically affiliated with structural systems of consumption: they push around the obvious metaphor of a 'grocery cart' full of their belongings (4). In another symbolic moment, the man forages a can of Coca-Cola from a supermarket and offers it to his son with a decorative solemnity that turns that soft drink's consumption into something akin to sacred ritual (19–20). The disorienting appearance of Coca-Cola—the only commercial brand named in the novel—suggests McCarthy's attention to the global economic implications of the brand. In an interview with John Jurgensen published by the *Wall Street Journal*, McCarthy explains that he was attracted to the genre of the western for his previous five novels because of its capacity to work metonymically, to gesture toward the US as a whole. 'Besides Coca-Cola,' he says, 'the other thing that is universally known is cowboys and Indians. You can go to a mountain village in Mongolia and they'll know about cowboys.'[21] McCarthy's nod to 'coca-colonization' in *The Road* suggests that, as symbolic consumers, the man and boy wander around and through, but never away from, their heritage of globally imperialistic economic practices.[22]

In *The Road*, 'big houses' point to a specific heritage, a corrupt southern slave-owning gentry, but also implicate the avaricious and aggressive practices of the US as a global power. The Anglo-Irish Big House draws attention to the countryside, to the poor and the itinerate workers left out in the cold by the concentration of power in the top echelons of society. By evoking the Big House in the form of plantation homes, *The Road* turns readers' attention to the ethical implications of a consumer middle class in the larger social and racial injustices of US history. The man and boy, despite trying to remain outside that vicious cycle, are nevertheless caught up as silent witnesses.

Fractals and fragments: climate change and consumerism

An idealized agrarian past evoked by the man is held up as a sort of wandering signifier—an image used to reference a past in which concepts such as 'humanity' or 'heroism' existed—and undermined by subtle references to its fictionality. Similarly, the road summons up a fantasy of the pre-apocalyptic verdant natural world with every mile. The man's detailed, fauna-specific knowledge locates him in a bioregional 'home' even as they travel over hundreds of miles. This wonderland now in ashes changes from hemlock groves to coniferous mountains as they head south. Once the man and boy pass through a five-thousand-foot-elevation mountain pass to descend on its southern side and head toward the coast, the fauna changes into a 'rich southern wood that once held' trees and flowers that the man can identify from memory even though their spore is now gone (34).[23] Approximately two hundred miles from the coast, the 'country went from pine to liveoak and pine. Magnolias. Trees as dead as any' (165). The man names and remembers a natural world that is no longer extant. In this way, McCarthy invokes a pastoral past and subtly deconstructs it simultaneously, since the man demonstrates no such correlative knowledge of streets, shopping malls, or cityscapes. The past he imagines is a fantasy of pristine wilderness, created and hermetically sealed in nostalgic reverence.

The subtle stripping of realism from nostalgia in the novel gestures toward more ominous thematic attention to what is at stake. The world of the novel may already be lost, but as in most apocalyptic fiction, the novel's primary focus is on a 'past' world, the contemporaneous concerns of the real-life world of the audience. In this novel, the cause of the disaster subverts any concrete assertions about the veracity of that past, suggesting that the man's evocations of pristine wilderness are just that—fantasy.

Derek Thiess analyses complexity theory and climate science in *The Road* and identifies some of those ominous implications in the fictional world's disaster, drawing attention to the 'fractal images favored by chaos and complexity theorists' that frame the novel's main narrative, such as the single articulated snowflake the boy catches in his hand at the beginning and the memory of fish with 'vermiculate patterns' on their scales at the novel's close. Fractal images, Thiess says, demonstrate that the novel 'is structured as a complex, nonlinear model that distinctly lacks initial conditions.' Because the cause of the apocalypse is never revealed, there is never the possibility for any solution or resolution. The cause of the disaster is relegated to the realms of 'irreducible complexity' that ultimately masks human commitments to practical realities. The complex yet mathematically beautiful natural world, even post-disaster, illuminates the 'apotheosis of the human experience,' a refusal to reduce the world to explicable causes and effects, or human beings to biological certainties.[24] For Thiess, such mystical application of theories of complex systems obfuscates the need for readers to respond with practical actions to address climate change, climate disaster, and the warming globe.

Thiess accurately identifies one of *The Road*'s most frustrating characteristics, its fabulistic and mystical tone. However, that tonal emphasis on the uncanny reflects a gothic sensibility, and the gothic is a genre where practical concerns are paramount, even if they are indicated obliquely. The precipitating disaster is intentionally ambiguous in *The Road*, as McCarthy indicates in one interview published in *Rolling Stone*. He says that he loosely designed the effects on the natural world in the novel to reflect a meteor strike, but he left the possibility open for the causal event to be read as human-made—which is his own best bet for the real world's fate. A meteoric or other natural disaster is always a possibility, McCarthy tells the interviewer David Kushner, but he bets that '[w]e're going to do ourselves in first.'[25] The novel's insistent ambiguity about the cause of the disaster evokes the conundrum in Robert Frost's epigrammatic 'Fire and Ice':[26] whether by natural disaster or specifically human-caused disaster, the end comes anyway. The only certainty is that, because of the destructive bent of humans in the twenty-first century, disaster is not a potentiality, but an inevitability.

At the same time, though, the man's knowledge of the natural world and his ability to identify his location on a well-worn map at each stage of his journey indicate the need for readers to recognize the implications at the heart of this gray and gothic tale. The world the man remembers is one filled with beauty: a pristine arcadia now victim to a pitiless and wasting disaster. As he and his son traverse roads, they see other remnants (rusting trains, trucks, and cars) of a civilization that consumed fossil fuels and destroyed ecosystems to create a transportation system to support yet more consumption. Eagleton's description of the Irish Famine as neither the calculated genocide nor the 'act of God' that myth-makers on either side of the aisle (isle?) make it out to be provides a helpful analogy for the kind of complex disaster that McCarthy envisions. As Eagleton says, apocryphally quoting Jean-Paul Sartre, if there is one thing the Irish Famine teaches, it is that '[t]here are no good or bad settlers ... only settlers.'[27] In *The Road*, the cause of the disaster remains ambiguous, but the land bears the scars of generations of settler occupation, of a ruling class driven by consumption of non-renewable fossil fuels, and consumption of natural resources to the point that they cannot be renewed.

It should be noted that the man's detailed knowledge of the flora and fauna of his wilderness home does not exculpate him from association with this consumer-driven settler class by way of his implied love for his indigenous land. David Cairns and Shaun Richards argue that the Anglo-Irish, as a ruling settler class, performed a type of indigeneity characterized by the creation of myths that hallowed the (Catholic) Irish peasant; by making the Irish peasant a national myth, the Anglo-Irish ruling class made themselves both estranged from and closer to the heart of 'Ireland' via the class distinct enough to recognize the essential nature of the place. 'Such an act of cultural and political deracination,' they argue, 'is posited as a necessity if entry into the nation of the "other" is to be achieved.'[28] In US history, settlers forged a performative indigeneity by making the Indigenous inhabitants of the Americas myths and coopting the language of indigeneity.[29] In the same way, the man's performative indigeneity—naming the flora and fauna—is contrasted by his reliance on an 'oil company' map that evokes colonial geography, the possession, delineation, and control of space. Gearóid Ó Tuathail, whose 1986 paper 'Language and Nature of the New Geopolitics' has shaped contemporary analyses of the rhetoric of geopolitics, points out that the field of geography derives from the Western 'imperializing project surveying, mapping and cataloguing the earth.'[30] The man's performative indigeneity, set against unmarked roads, forces the metaphor: the deracinated colonial can recognize a new geography but does not practice an authentic care for that place as its Indigenous citizens do. The man moves through his world bound almost exclusively to the settler-made roads that carve through the wilderness. In the US, roads and train tracks carved through the wilderness are some of the most frequently used images representing Manifest Destiny, the acquisition of 'Indian territory' for the economic progress of the European-descended American nation after the Mexican–American War of 1845–48. In *The Road*, the man's 'mapping' of the wasteland represents his efforts to reinscribe the territories of Euro-American acquisition in this new epoch. That colonial, non-indigenous land ownership is directly implicated in the collapse of the ecosystem, regardless of the singular cause of the disaster in *The Road*.

The man's implication in the collapse of an ecosystem may not seem significant; he was, at best, scion of an ordinary middle-class family. However, the beauty and terror of complexity lie in the relative significance of consequence to cause; the smallest changes to a complex interdependent system create profound ripple effects in that system. The man's comparatively insignificant contributions to a consumer-driven economy fueled by gas and oil ripple into his devastated present. In *Chaos*, James Gleick describes Benoit Mandelbrot's visualization of complex fractals, a mathematical description of complex replicability and individuality within a system. A polymathic mathematician, Mandelbrot 'mistrusted analysis, but he trusted his mental pictures.' He was able to recognize mathematically recursive shapes in complex data sets, and he created a program capable of mathematically describing systems from snowflakes to galaxies, seacoasts to river networks. One of the most beautiful and terrible realities of the physical universe is contained the notion that simple mathematical descriptions can capture the chaotic complexity of systems as different as weather systems and herd behavior, because complex systems tend toward complex organization; there is order within chaos, but chaotic order. In the 1980s the ecologist William M. Shaffer made the case that ecological systems do not balance in equilibrium but instead are dynamical, adaptive systems: *every* particle, each species, each weather pattern affects the dynamic whole of the system.[31] When large-scale intrusions into complex systems occur, the systems will change, and each change triggers its own dynamical reactions: chaos. The order that emerges from extreme change will be extreme, affecting every aspect of the system.

In *The Road*, attention to patterns, from maps of roads to maps of the world, suggests its genesis in the rich discussions of complexity theory at the Santa Fe Institute. The mathematical order of fractal patterns in complex sets illustrates how unpredictable dynamic change to a system can be. The novel represents this idea through repetitions of fractal images, and, at the stylistic level, a disintegration of syntactic patterns follows thematic dynamic change. The passages surrounding the two most symbolic uses of fractals in nature, the snowflake and the fish scales, demonstrate this pattern:

> He caught it [the snowflake] in his hand and let it expire there like the last host of Christendom. ... The wet gray flakes twisting and falling out of nothing. Gray slush by the roadside. Black water running from under the sodden drifts of ash. (13–14)

> Once there were brook trout in the streams in the mountain. ... On their backs were vermiculate patterns that were maps of the world in its becoming. Maps and mazes. Of a thing which could not be put back. Not be made right. (241)

In both passages, a series of sentence fragments follow the image of a fractal, semantically conveying a divergence from mathematical order. The first passage shows the change in weather systems—unusual cold—alongside changes in physical composition of matter: rainwater joins with the colloidal ash and forms 'gray' snow. The appearance of the most common phenomena has changed, and with it, weather patterns emerge which destroy vegetal and animal life. In the second passage, the chaos is philosophical rather than physical: if the species is wiped out, and the conditions for the species' flourishing are changed, nothing that has been characteristic of the old system will persist. Once changed, a complex system is changed utterly. In short, the terror of the gothic world in *The Road* is intensified through fractal images that allude to complexity theory applied to ecosystems. These images draw attention to the irreversible and catastrophic changes happening in the readers' contemporary lives to natural systems upended by large-scale disruptions on the North American continent.

The fire inside: the literary prophet as global conscience

If the Anglo-Irish gothic tradition points a finger at the complex and destructive effects of colonialism in Ireland, McCarthy's transplanted gothic narrative points a finger at the US's role in triggering a globally scaled system meltdown. However, the dissolution of systems is not the only force in the novel. While images of fractals suggest the dire implications of shattered ecosystems, the novel also offers images of unchanged systems, such as the sun still orbiting the earth, even though earth itself has changed. Persistence and change vie for dominance in *The Road* through a series of images of that which persists when the biosphere changes, images that suggest a recalibration of codes, adaptability and resilience that, if matched with an ethos of care, may provide a glimmer of hope even in a world that cannot be made right again.

The man's wife appears at a surface level to play the role of the father's dialectic opposite, as she presents an antagonistic argument to the father's attempts to articulate a reason to have hope or to find meaning in a post-apocalyptic world. Descriptions of the wife are grotesque: she first appears in a dream as a gothic corpse bride, her 'nipples pipeclayed and her rib bones painted white,' as she emerges 'out of a green and leafy canopy' (15). She literally embodies decay and the 'uncanny' (16). To some extent little more than a Jungian archetype of the negative mother complex, the woman, like Lot's wife, looks backward on destruction and cannot look forward toward the future. In his one extended memory of her, the man remembers her explaining that the moral choice would be to murder their child, rather than leaving him alive to be raped and murdered by others (49).

However, the mother's insistence on suicide is explicated by an earlier metaphoric description of the sun as a 'grieving mother with a lamp' (28). The 'grieving mother' mourns the loss of a symbiotic relationship with earth, suggesting that the wife's inversion of the generative, earth-mother archetype is part of a larger inversion of gender archetypes in the novel. In the Western cultural tradition from Plato's *Symposium* to the post-Enlightenment feminization of the planet as 'Mother Earth,' it is rare to see the sun personified as a woman or as a mother; more typically, the sun is male and the earth female. In *The Road*, the earth seems incapable of producing new life after the apocalyptic event. Women may become pregnant and bear children, but their children are turned into comestibles.

In the man and his wife's debate over the morality of suicide, her failure to survive is depicted as an intentional, rational choice made because she accepts the changed world *as it is*. When she criticizes her husband for behaving as though there may be hope left, he does not answer, and she says, 'You have no argument because there is none' (49). The man makes no argument because he cannot imagine the world other than in its current chaotic state. He does, however, demonstrate an ability to *persist* in this changed world. Their son demonstrates the key attributes of adaptation and creative imagination, suggesting his capacity to actually *survive* in this different system. Ultimately, then, the woman's failure to imagine an alternative to their reality finds its opposite not in her husband, but in their child. Just as the novel subverts images of the Big House and its idealization of an imagined agrarian past, it also obviates the terror created by its depictions of a violent and inhumane apocalyptic landscape. Alan Warner suggests that *The Road*'s 'nightmare vistas [could] reinforce those in the US who are determined to manipulate its people' through fear of terrorism.[32] A cursory reading of the novel may well support his claim, since the novel paints a vicious view of a ravaged world and power gone rogue; all 'others' the man and his son meet on the road are evil, and the man attempts to murder them if he cannot flee them first.

A more nuanced reading of the novel, however, suggests that it is fear that is to blame for this violence, and fear that makes of others an 'Other.' The novel warns against fear through the boy, who questions, 'If you're on the lookout all the time, does that mean that you're scared all the time?' (127) The boy postulates that an attitude of constant fear might cause them to miss out on finding other 'good guys' on the road (127). As the novel's moral center, he exemplifies the capacity of compassion to triumph over fear. In the first scene of substantial length that is narrated from the boy's point of view, he imagines another child his own age and expresses a desire to rescue him (71). His insistence on the existence of some 'other' who is his kin and his moral responsibility demonstrates how the boy creates a world characterized by an ethics of reciprocal care and hospitality. He insists they feed a wandering blind man, Ely, out of their meager supplies, an act that works against their self-interest and survival, as the father points out, but that characterizes a generosity capable of triumphing over base hunger (141). The boy insists on reciprocal kindness even toward those who do them wrong. When another steals their cart with its supplies, the man and his son hunt down the thief. In revenge, the father takes back their supplies and strips the thief of his clothes. The boy protests and cajoles his father until the man returns the thief's clothes (217–219). The boy's reasoning, that the man stole from them because he was 'so scared,' suggests that the boy insists on a world in which the Golden Rule is practiced through material goods. The boy distributes goods—food and clothes—to others as he would wish to be cared for himself, in a way commensurate with his ability to do so.

The boy's behavior is the novel's antithesis to a geopolitical system characterized by hegemonic power and rampant consumerism. When they find a bunker filled with food and clothes, the man tells his son that the family who left the supplies 'would have wanted' them to take and use those supplies, '[j]ust like we would want them to' (118). Because he describes the family as motivated by a reciprocal care for others, the boy assumes that the family who left it are 'good guys,' preparing a world for salvation (118). Before they eat, the boy prays to the people to thank them for the 'food and stuff' (123). In a wasteland characterized by violence and famine, the boy practices a sacred orientation of gratitude toward those ancestors who practiced hospitality and generosity, illustrating his adaptability and resilience; while the father may be able to persist into the new, strange world, his son is capable of *creating* new meaning, new codes of civility, and a new ethic of care.

The boy's equitable parsing of goods, his hospitality in the face of threat, and his efforts to make sacred the sacrifices of the dead are corrective gestures to an imperialistic economic system predicated upon the seizure of material goods from a citizen population considered 'other' to a ruling class. It is in this subtle yet profound critique of the devastating consequences of consumer-driven global market-capitalist systems that *The Road*'s harkening back to the Anglo-Irish gothic tradition—and not solely the transplanted version in the American South—is clearest. *The Road* depicts three types of people: those who consume each other, literally living off of the bodies of others; those who are consumed; and those who insist on an equitable parsing of what meager goods remain. The price for this last category, the antidote to the gothic 'salt moorland,' is high: with limited and non-renewable resources, the descent of the human species is inevitable, and those who do not hoard goods or devour others will likely die first, but the boy accepts this fate and goes on, an eternal exile who leaves no mark on his terrain (215).

Because they embody a way of life that is non-industrialized, non-materialistic, and removed from the acquisition of power or the pursuit of power over others, itinerate wanderers seem to possess the sole capacity to find a way out of the death spiral of consumer capitalism in much of McCarthy's fiction. The following two chapters extend discussion of nomadism as a corrective to individualism and to capitalist excess in McCarthy's works, but *The Road* offers perhaps the clearest articulation of the role of storytelling in codifying the world-creating, regenerative power of a homeless exile. Before he dies, the father considers his child's fragile future on the road and thinks that '[t]here is no prophet in the earth's long chronicle who's not honored here today' (233). For McCarthy, storytelling is not easily distinguishable from prophecy, an act that fuses truth-telling with linguistic artifice. When the man claims that his son is the 'word of God,' and, if not, then 'God never spoke,' he identifies the boy as the *logos*, a reference to the passage in the Gospel of St. John that identifies Jesus as breath, word, and light: life, meaningfulness, and inspiration or divine truth, respectively (4).[33] In *The Road*, the recurrent image of 'carrying the fire' represents the idea of storytelling as a ritual act of hope, an ethical choice, and a form of instantiated love in the darkness of human corruption, natural disaster, and the inevitable collapse of life systems. The man tells the boy that they are 'carrying the fire' in the form of hero stories that instruct the boy about human goodness, generosity, hospitality, and self-sacrificial love for strangers on the road (109). When he is dying, the man begs the boy: 'You have to carry the fire' (234). The boy says that he does not know how to, or where the fire is, and the man replies, 'It's inside you. It was always there' (234). After the man dies, the boy asks the first stranger that he meets, 'Are you carrying the fire?' (238) Scholars identify this metaphorical 'fire' as abstract notions of hope or goodness. Bennett links the recurring motif of 'carrying the fire' to an ancient Celtic tradition, in which a family's hearth fire was never permitted to go out so that when a family moved, its members 'carried their fire' with them. By analogy, carrying the fire in *The Road* reflects an act of heritage, of keeping family (human?) tradition alive.[34] While the Celtic roots of the phrase are suggestive, there is an even more specific association of carrying the fire in rites of rebirth and renewal. In ancient Christianity, from the time of Constantine through the Middle Ages, religious families would extinguish their hearth fires for the duration of the Paschal Vigil. When the flame was rekindled at the end of the Vigil, worshippers gathered for the

Vigil would relight their tapers from the Paschal flame and carry that fire home to renew their own fires once again.[35] In his Easter Vigil homily in 1997, Pope John Paul II linked the notion of Jesus as *logos*, 'word made flesh,' to light, suggesting that the imagery of the fire during the Easter Vigil represents the believer's hope in life itself. 'At the beginning [of the liturgy],' he explains, 'the "new fire" is blessed, and is used to light the Paschal candle, which is then carried in procession to the altar. The candle ... moves forward at first in darkness, until the moment when, after the intonation of the third "*Lumen Christi*," light returns to the whole Basilica.'[36] In *The Road*, McCarthy retells the Paschal Vigil through the image of fire and the language of prophetic storytelling: in a world sunk into darkness, the light and word of God made flesh is embodied in one who will rekindle light in the dark, and from whose light other travelers on the road may rekindle their own flames.

On the one hand, the dire and truly apocalyptic warning at the end, that the world cannot 'be made right again,' suggests the force of the novel's prophetic call (241). Through elements of Anglo-Irish gothic horror, the novel indicates its readers' complicity in the exploitation of natural resources that is characteristic of the 'consumer class' in the US. In its ashen wasteland, McCarthy imagines the end of such over-consumption: a world utterly changed. On the other hand, the worst of human turpitude is not the sole narrative; amid this violent depiction of corruption and consumption, all 'prophets' of human history are honored. If *No Country* and *The Counselor* dramatize the consequences of a failure to imagine alternatives, *The Road* offers a vivid alternative in a child whose commitment to ethical choice renders him an embodiment of imaginative hope. Here at the end of all things, the violent and the hungry devour themselves, but 'prophets'—the tale-tellers of human history—honor those who live not as consumers but as wanderers.

Notes

1 The first quotation is spoken by John Western in *Whales and Men*; see The Cormac McCarthy Papers, collection 91, box 91, file 6, p. 120;

Tobias Menely and Jesse Oak Taylor, 'Introduction,' *Anthropocene Reading: Literary History in Geologic Times*, eds. Tobias Menely and Jesse Oak Taylor (Pennsylvania State University Press, 2017), 1–24: 8.

2 Tony Miller, 'On the Road with Cormac McCarthy,' *Tony Miller BSC Director of Photography*, accessed March 30, 2018, www.tonymillerdp.com/on-the-road-with-cormac-mccarthy/.

3 Arendt, *The Human Condition*, 2.

4 Louis S. Gross, *Redefining the American Gothic from* Wieland *to* Day of the Dead (University of Michigan Research Press, 1989), 1.

5 Frye, *Understanding Cormac McCarthy*, 17.

6 Chris Danta, '"The Cold illucid world": The Poetics of Gray in Cormac McCarthy's *The Road*,' *Styles of Extinction: Cormac McCarthy's* The Road, eds. Julian Murphet and Mark Steven (Continuum International, 2012), 9–26: 9.

7 Of particular relevance here is Burton's contention that, while not monolithic or lacking friction, the distinctions between white yeoman middle-class and upper-class southerners were muted by the shared reliance on agriculture and its enslaved manual labor force. Burton quotes Thomas Green Clemson, son-in-law of John C. Calhoun, who claimed, 'Slaves are the most valuable property in the South, being the basis of the whole southern fabric.' A key distinction should be noted here between Anglo-Irish literature, in which the threat of a rising, majority-Catholic middle class threatens the agrarian gentry class of Anglo-Irish landowners, and literature of the US South, in which the distinctions between the yeoman middle class and upper class bear class—but not racial—distinctions. That is, the yeoman middle class in the US shared with upper-class plantation owners the dubious distinction of relying on possession of the bodies of (Black) others for its existence; only the landed gentry in the Anglo-Irish tradition share that distinction—a class defined by their actual 'rule' of the country, yet possessing the economic characteristics of both yeoman middle and upper classes in the US South, and defined over and against the (Catholic Irish) 'other.' The father in *The Road* is clearly part of an affluent middle-class family; yet his complicity in the engines of consumption that drive the history of the US South is, if anything, exacerbated by his middle-class status. He is, by that token, a member of the 'consumer class,' implicated in the US's shifts toward global economic imperialism in the latter part of the twentieth century. See Orville Vernon Burton, *In My Father's House Are Many Mansions: Family and Community in Edgefield, South Carolina*, Fred W. Morrison Series in Southern Studies (University of North Carolina Press, 1987), 47–103, 38.

8 For a succinct description of the globally disproportionate consumption of natural resources by the American middle class in the early twenty-first century, see 'Use It or Lose It: The Outside Effect of U.S. Consumption on the Environment,' *Scientific American*, EarthTalk, 2016, Accessed January 23, 2021, https://www.scientificamerican.com/article/american-consumption-habits/. McCarthy himself seems interested in global implications of US consumption. On a page of notes found in a folder for *The Road* in his collected papers, McCarthy has jotted what appear to be his own musings on contemporary geopolitics, an unusual enough venture, and one that seems to have little relationship to the ahistorical world of *The Road*. In this page of notes, McCarthy muses that the 'answer to the problems with the Muslim terrorists would seem to be to halt fossil fuel consumption.' McCarthy goes on to point out that even this cutting-off of the major export of the Middle East, however, would not work in the long run, as the 'people of Islam' (presumably he refers here to mainly tribal, rural areas in certain Middle Eastern countries) are 'fighting for their lives,' and moreover for the survival of their culture and way of life, inexorably being deteriorated by 'Hollywood movies, McDonald hamburgers,' and so on. This page of notes does little to illuminate the cause of the destruction in *The Road*, but it does much to gesture toward McCarthy's awareness of the geopolitical risks of dependence on foreign oil, as well as suggesting his perhaps empathetic notion that economies driven by fossil fuel have supported the rampant capitalism inimical to the pace of life of a tribal, nomadic culture. This latter interpretation of the note is consistent with similar themes in McCarthy's writing from his earliest novel, *The Orchard Keeper*; Dianne C. Luce points out that McCarthy's father, as an attorney representing and working for the TVA, was, in McCarthy's eyes, complicit in the 'engineering decisions' of the company that 'destroyed the farmlands of hundreds of families and permanently altered the traditional culture of the region,' and this critique of economic complicity plays out through images of industrialization and ruin in the novel. Luce, *Reading the World*, 20. See The Cormac McCarthy Papers, collection 91, box 87, file 5.

9 Scholars who have noted the novel's southern gothic characteristics include Frye, *Understanding Cormac McCarthy*; Luce, *Reading the World*; Wesley G. Morgan, 'The Route and Roots of *The Road*,' Adapted from a paper presented at 'The Road Home: Cormac McCarthy's Imaginative Return to the South,' Knoxville, TN, April 26, 2007; and Bryan Giemza, *Irish Catholic Writers and the Invention of the American South* (Louisiana State University Press, 2013). I also

offer an overview and summative discussion of American southern gothic influence in McCarthy's fiction in my article 'Cormac McCarthy, Tennessee, and the Southern Gothic,' in *The Cambridge Companion to Cormac McCarthy*, ed. Steven Frye (Cambridge University Press, 2013), 41–53. Such scholarly concurrence suggests that, particularly in his Appalachian novels, McCarthy is indebted to the American southern gothic tradition. While that influence is surely at play in *The Road*, in other regards, McCarthy's 2006 novel is distinct; it dislocates its action from a named, physical space, globalizing the cultural referents in a way that calls out American slave-holding history but forces a transnational comparison of power brokerage that is particularly resonant in the Anglo-Irish gothic tradition. Because class and consumption are so central to the Anglo-Irish gothic—with the landed gentry class being explicitly centered in depictions of 'fallen houses'—this chapter examines those resonances in *The Road* to illuminate its often subtle implications of the US consumer class in the causes of the fictional world's mysterious demise, and the real world's perhaps imminent one.

10 Julian Moynahan, *Anglo-Irish: The Literary Imagination in a Hyphenated Culture* (Princeton University Press, 1995), 147.
11 Terry Eagleton, *Heathcliff and the Great Hunger*, Studies in Irish Culture (Verso, 1995), 33.
12 Leslie Fiedler, *Love and Death in the American Novel* (Dalkey Archive Press, 1966), 397.
13 Perhaps the only element of the novel that is closer to the American gothic tradition is its location of the action in the 'wilderness' at the borders of the home (rural or 'frontier' America vs. the urban center). By contrast, nineteenth-century European gothic literature often relocates the action from a familiar home (Ireland or England, for instance) to an 'exotic' nation such as Italy or Romania. As I will discuss later, however, the important role played by 'big houses' in the text suggests a more potent association with the family home in the Anglo-Irish tradition. See Gross, *Redefining the American Gothic*, 23.
14 Helen Taylor describes how southern white nationalist groups coopted Celtic literature, such as *Rob Roy*, and claimed cultural affinity with Irish and Scottish people, culture, and literature in order to create a culturally cohesive vision of the South that was white. See Helen Taylor, 'The South and Britain,' *South to a New Place: Region, Literature, and Culture*, eds. Suzanne W. Jones and Sharon Monteith (Louisiana State University Press, 2002), 340–362: 341, 345.
15 Eagleton claims that the defining characteristic of Anglo-Irish literature is the problem of Anglo-Irish 'ascendancy,' a term which ought,

he says, 'to translate as "hegemony"' in Irish writing. See Eagleton, *Heathcliff and the Great Hunger*, 32.

16 In order, see Steven Frye, 'Yeats' "Sailing to Byzantium" and McCarthy's *No Country for Old Men*: Art and Artifice in the New Novel,' *The Cormac McCarthy Journal*, vol. 5, iss. 1 (2006), 27–41; Ellis, *No Place for Home*, 290; Ron Charles, 'Apocalypse Now,' *Washington Post*, October 1, 2006; William Quirk, '"Minimalist Tragedy": Nietzschean Thought in McCarthy's *The Sunset Limited*,' *The Cormac McCarthy Journal*, vol. 8, iss. 1 (2010), 29–46; and Lydia R. Cooper, '"A Howling void": Beckett's Influence in McCarthy's *The Sunset Limited*,' *The Cormac McCarthy Journal*, vol. 10, iss. 1 (2012), 1–15.

17 In order, see James Potts, 'McCarthy, Mac Airt, and Mythology: *Suttree* and the Irish High King,' *Mississippi Quarterly*, vol. 58, iss. 1–2 (2004), 25–40; Barbara Brickman, 'Imposition and Resistance in *The Orchard Keeper*,' *Myth, Legend, Dust: Critical Responses to Cormac McCarthy*, ed. Rick Wallach (Manchester University Press, 2000), 55–67; Giemza, *Irish Catholic Writers*, 195–240; Barbara Bennett, 'Celtic Influences on Cormac McCarthy's *No Country for Old Men* and *The Road*,' *Notes on Contemporary Literature*, vol. 38, iss. 5 (November 2008), 2–3.

18 Woodward, 'Cormac McCarthy's Venomous Fiction.'

19 In the US South, the landowning upper middle classes were the true engines of social and economic power, and thus the distinctions between plantation owners and yeoman middle-class agrarians are less significant economically and socially, and are not, for McCarthy, as significant as is the use of the yeoman middle class to metonymically represent the 'consumer' white middle class of the US. In this way, his use of the 'yeoman middle-class' protagonist reflects the common use of 'lesser gentry' in Anglo-Irish gothic literature, such as *Castle Rackrent*—a use of a character who represents not the heads of state, but the ordinary and complicit members of the class that drives the interests of the state. See Burton, *In My Father's House*, 102–103.

20 In the Anglo-Irish tradition, the Big House and its environs represent an idealized, fictionalized version of the past, an idyllic fantasy of a world prior to the 1920s and the war for Irish independence, although it is never fixed at an actual historical point. It is therefore significant to note that *The Road* both employs and subverts the nostalgia associated with the image of the Big House. See Eagleton, *Heathcliff and the Great Hunger*, 33.

21 Jurgensen, 'Hollywood's Favorite Cowboy.'

22 It should be noted that it is not clear whether McCarthy would have had J. G. Ballard's essay on 'Coca-Colonization,' in which Ballard

famously calls the beverage the 'most infamous' branded product in the world, in mind when he added this scene to his own novel. It is not a stretch, however, to imagine that McCarthy would at least be aware of a writer of Ballard's stature, particularly given Ballard's shared thematic literary interests and polymath tendencies. And as his interview with Jurgensen illustrates, McCarthy is keenly aware of the reach of Coca-Cola as part of the US's geopolitical sphere of influence. See J. G. Ballard, *A User's Guide to the Millennium: Essays and Reviews* (Picador, 1996), 213.

23 The pass in the novel is possibly the Newfound Gap at the Tennessee–North Carolina boundary, which is five thousand feet in elevation. In an 1874 travelogue, Edward King describes hiking through a five-thousand-foot-elevation gap (Newfound Gap) on his way to the North Carolina coast, a journey that is mirrored by the man and boy. Wes Morgan provides a thoroughly detailed argument in favor of finding the man and boy located around McCarthy's childhood home, passing through the Newfound Gap, and then on to the South Carolina coast. See Edward King, *The Southern State of North America: A Record of Journeys* (Blackie and Son, 1874), 483; Morgan, 'The Route and Roots of *The Road*.'

24 Derek Thiess, 'On *The Road* to Santa Fe: Complexity in Cormac McCarthy and Climate Change,' *Interdisciplinary Studies in Literature and the Environment*, vol. 20, iss. 3 (Summer 2013), 432–552: 541, 544, 550.

25 Kushner, 'Cormac McCarthy's Apocalypse.'

26 'Fire and Ice' was originally published in *Harper's Magazine*, December 1920. The astronomer Harlow Shapley claims to have inspired Frost's famous meditation on human contributions to global disaster, much as *The Road* bears the influence of many of McCarthy's scientist colleagues at the Santa Fe Institute. See Tom Hansen, 'Frost's "Fire and Ice,"' *The Explicator*, vol. 59, iss. 1 (2000), 27–30.

27 Eagleton, *Heathcliff and the Great Hunger*, 64.

28 David Cairns and Shaun Richards, *Writing Ireland: Colonialism, Nationalism, and Culture* (St. Martin's Press, 1988), 25.

29 Frederick Jackson Turner's famous thesis of the American frontier as the forge of an authentic and unique 'American' identity, presented at the Chicago World's Columbian Exposition in 1893, is the best-known articulation of this idea. Turner argues that the frontier forged 'a composite [ethnic] identity' in which 'immigrants were Americanized, liberated, and fused into a mixed race,' albeit a race 'of mixed European ancestry.' Moreover, the frontier developed a political identity—the

construction of 'democracy' through the frontier's reliance on 'individualism' and 'antipathy to control.' Thus, for Turner, the space itself not only can but must be imbued with an incorporeal yet very real identity, an identity that can occur only in the ongoing confrontation between European American immigrants and the geography of the place. The notion of essential 'American-ness' as comprising European-descended ancestry and vehement individualism that resists centralized governmental control remains tellingly pervasive to this day. See Frederick Jackson Turner, *The Frontier in American History* (Henry Holt and Co., 1962), 22, 23, 30.

30 Gearóid Ó Tuathail (Gerard Toal), 'Problematizing Geopolitics: Survey, Statesmanship and Strategy,' *Transactions of the Institute of British Geographers*, vol. 19, iss. 3 (1994), 259–272: 260.
31 Gleick, *Chaos*, 84, 315–317.
32 Alan Warner, 'The Road to Hell,' *Guardian*, November 4, 2006.
33 John 1:1, KJV.
34 Bennett, 'Celtic Influences on Cormac McCarthy's *No Country for Old Men* and *The Road*,' 2.
35 Rebecca Button Pritchard, *Sensing the Spirit: The Holy Spirit in Feminist Perspective* (Chalice Press, 1999), 88.
36 Pope John Paul II, 'Easter Vigil: Homily of Pope John Paul II,' March 29, 1997.

5

Pilgrims: nomadism and the making and unmaking of the world in the Border Trilogy

> As opposed to the images of both the migrant and the exile, I want to emphasize that of the nomad. The nomad does not stand for homelessness or compulsive displacement: it is rather a figuration for the kind of subject who has relinquished all idea, desire, or nostalgia for fixity.
>
> (Rosi Braidotti, *Nomadic Subjects: Embodiment and Sexual Difference in Contemporary Feminist Theory*)
>
> The only state that is as anomalous as pain is the imagination.
>
> (Elaine Scarry, *The Body in Pain: The Making and Unmaking of the World*)[1]

Until now, this book has moved chronologically through McCarthy's literary output, examining the implications of industrialization within the context of the US's growth as a military and economic empire; it has focused on how depictions of economic and political 'progress' are subverted by images of complex natural systems crippled by industrialization and capitalist excess, devastating both human and nonhuman communities and culminating in *The Road*'s dire image of the death of the biosphere itself. This chapter turns back chronologically to the Border Trilogy (1992–1998), three novels where storytelling is depicted as a moral imperative and where peripatetic wanderers represent sustainable and ethical life. While the previous chapter suggests the importance of our ability to imagine ecological disaster, this chapter focuses on narrative's capacity to connect readers imaginatively with the non-material value of the nonhuman other as a motivation for responsible behavior toward our ecosystems. Specifically, through depictions of human and nonhuman bodies in pain, the Border Trilogy argues that witnessing the suffering of others is a crucial first step to deciding to intercede in the unmaking of the world. McCarthy's project in the Border Trilogy in many ways reiterates Aldo Leopold's call for human recognition of the intrinsic value of the natural world, as a corrective vision to the utilitarian ethics that guides Western views of environmental policy through the lens of 'stewardship' rather than complex, adaptive symbiosis. 'For the biotic community to survive,' Leopold says, 'its internal processes must balance, else its member-species would disappear.'[2] Michael Lynn Crews notes that McCarthy made only two explicit references to other authors in his drafts of *The Crossing*; not surprisingly, one of those is to Leopold's *A Sand County Almanac* (1949). McCarthy made a marginal note 'see A. Leopold' on a draft of a scene in *The Crossing* where Don Arnulfo talks about wolves' mystical knowledge of natural order. Crews connects this scene with Leopold's story of killing a wolf in *A Sand County Almanac*, where Leopold recalls killing a wolf to preserve deer; on witnessing the dead animal, however, Leopold concludes that the wolf symbolizes a 'deep knowledge' of ecological balance that he has irrevocably upset.[3]

In the Trilogy, McCarthy weaves a narrative tapestry that illustrates this 'deep knowledge' of ecological balance and suggests the beauty of complex natural systems. The very complexity of natural systems makes them terrifyingly fragile, and sustaining them requires interdependence and multi-faceted engagement between its member species. In my reading, McCarthy suggests that complexity and contingency characterize pro-social and pro-natural system ethics; only in mutual affirmation of the interrelated life of all things does any individual find their full meaning. This alternative value system is closely tied to non-capitalist lifeways, such as nomadism, and to narrative. Of McCarthy's novels thus far, the Border Trilogy offers the richest vein of McCarthy's non-anthropocentric ethics, a value system that rejects the commodification of beings as well as the first principle of capitalism: property ownership. This non-anthropocentric ethics is represented through systematic attention to bodily suffering: to pain, grief, and loss experienced in human and nonhuman bodies.

When Karl Marx and Friedrich Engels sounded the warning that capital 'has resolved personal worth into exchange value,' they suggested a realization of the failures of utilitarian ethics. The utilitarian ethicists Jeremy Bentham, John Stuart Mill, and Henry Sidgwick all imagined possible realities in which 'communal wellbeing' would include human and nonhuman animals.[4] However, their holistic definitions of communal wellbeing failed to clarify the relationship between a largely agricultural economy reliant on animals for food, transportation, and other utilities, and humans as 'users' in the economic system. Notwithstanding Bentham's famous adjuration that utilitarian ethics must answer not to the question *'can they reason?'* but rather to *'can they suffer?,'* anthropocentric codes of ethics dominate the Western tradition, built on the belief that 'man' has been given 'dominion ... over all the earth.'[5] For Mark Fisher, the problem with late capitalist 'first world' cultures lies not solely in exploitative, inequality-intensifying economics, but also in a profound sterility of imagination, in which alternative economic systems can no longer be imagined. 'Capitalism,' he says, 'seamlessly occupies the horizons of the thinkable.' Losing the capacity to imagine alternatives affects real-world ethics in the new capitalist realism. Citing the political theorist Wendy Brown, Fisher suggests that the inherently contradictory aims of neoliberalism (amorally concerned with ends rather than means) and neoconservatism ('expressly moral and regulatory') are fused in the late capitalist marketplace, where alternatives to the system cannot be imagined and solutions are found only in the products of the market.[6] Without the capacity to imagine alternatives, bizarre unions of protectionism and economic imperialism flourish, a moral system that claims to recognize inherent value in life (such as the inviolable 'pro-life' plank in the neoconservative platform) but can imagine no alternative to a system in which all life can be quantified by its exchange value or utility in the global marketplace, to the detriment of all life on the planet. The question at the heart of any study of literary representations of economic systems, then, is whether narrative can conjure an imagined alternative, first by estranging the value systems of utilitarian ethics from its late capitalist forms, and second by imagining radically different value systems.

McCarthy takes up the tricky question of narrative's capacity to do just this, but in the Border Trilogy, the answers are not straightforward. *The Crossing* deals most directly with the subject of narrative, but it seems uncertain of the capacity of stories to distance themselves from the realities humans create—at least, to distance themselves sufficiently to recreate value systems. Dianne C. Luce finds evidence that *The Crossing* effectively argues that narrative 'carries our past, gives meaning to our present, and right intention to our future,' and 'is our primary means of accessing and perhaps communicating the thing itself: the world which is a tale.'[7] Luce suggests that McCarthy is somewhat more ambivalent about language than he is about narrative, but I believe that McCarthy thinks of language as an imperfect codification of 'deep knowledge.' Narrative, a construction made of language (a verbal work/artifact), is a tool of imperfect but necessary use (to shape the speaker's own world) and referential use (to implicate its readers into its created world). Narrative is the rickety vehicle we ride in order to arrive back at our pre-lingual knowledge of each other, the world, and how to be 'right' or to make 'right' choices in it. A central theme of the Trilogy is how, through narrative, we make our world and we unmake it. When John Grady Cole and Lacey Rawlins first head south toward Mexico at the beginning of *All the Pretty Horses*, they ride like 'thieves newly loosed in that dark electric' toward 'ten thousand worlds for the choosing' (*APH* 30). From that early scene at night looking toward the dawn, the novel draws to a conclusion as the sun is setting on a reduced and singular 'world to come' (302). By the end of *The Crossing*, Billy Parham has lost his human and nonhuman communities, and, in an 'alien dark,' he witnesses a test atomic bomb explosion. The world hovers on the brink of unmaking, until the 'right and godmade sun' rises once more on a familiar world (*Cr* 426). By the end of *Cities of the Plain*, Billy has wandered '[t]ill he was old' but without identifying what that his role in that world may be—at least, until a kindly New Mexican housewife, Betty, tells him that his love for that world is not in vain (*COP* 264, 291). His life, she says, is like his hands, scarred with 'map enough for men to read. There God's plenty of signs and wonders to make a landscape. To make a world' (291). The Trilogy journeys from worlds in their thousands to a solitary world, and then to a world on the brink of destruction, before closing on an image of hands capable of making the world anew.

This chapter examines how McCarthy codes his arguments through aesthetic focalization on pain, and specifically on bodily experience of the world and what makes and unmakes it—such as the world-making 'maps' of Billy's scars in that final scene of the Trilogy. In a scene near the end of *Cities of the Plain*, Billy runs into another itinerate Spanish speaker under a freeway overpass in central Arizona. They share a meal of crackers while the man spins a long and complicated story about a dream that he once had about a pilgrim in search of meaning. In that dream, he says, the pilgrim searched for a 'calculus' by which to measure or determine the purpose of his life. A map cannot 'locate' a person in the world, the man tells Billy, because a map is an atemporal geospatial identity. By contrast, a human life is made of time, not a 'where' but a series of 'whens': actions, choices, events. 'Yet,' the stranger tells Billy, 'in its final shape the map and the life it traces must converge for there time ends' (274). Because a human life can be measured only in the unity of map and event/time, the only way to understand it is to unify its map and its events—to map time in the form of a human life. We must learn to link space to event, place to choice, being to time. A Heideggerian hermeneutic emerges, dimly. The stranger concludes that we must 'assemble them [events] into the story which is us. Each man is the bard of his own existence. This is how he is joined to the world' (283). Narrative provides the vehicle for the joining of being (the 'what') with time (the 'when'), and the spinning of the tale provides the threads that bind human life to consciousness, and in so doing allows for a meaningful existence.

To be clear, I am not, nor do I think McCarthy is, arguing that meaningfulness is achieved through narrative, but rather that narrative is the connective tissue between the body and a sense of itself *as* meaningful. Here is where pain comes into play. In 1986, after the publication of *Blood Meridian* and while McCarthy was working on three projects that would become the novels of the Border Trilogy, he wrote to J. Howard Woolmer that he had '[j]ust finished a very interesting book.' That book was Elaine Scarry's *The Body in Pain: The Making and Unmaking of the World* (1985), about violence and suffering as linguistic and bodily acts.[8] McCarthy uses the exact phrase from her title, the 'making and unmaking of the world,' in *The Crossing*. An old man tells Billy about a priest who blamed God for his suffering and sought to face down God. The old man then had a dream of God, where God was a man bent over an invisible loom spinning a tapestry into a void. 'And somewhere in that tapestry that was the world in its making and unmaking was a thread that was he,' says the old man, 'and he woke weeping' (*Cr* 149). The making and unmaking of the world suggests the chaotic order of the natural world—the complex flux, decay, and regeneration of galaxies, ecosystems, quantum particles—and narrative as the 'one story' of which all human stories are threads (143).

Crews attempts to identify McCarthy's 'take' on Scarry, saying that he believes McCarthy finds Scarry's 'humane revulsion of violence' moving, yet that McCarthy 'parts company from Scarry's clearly pacifist leanings.'[9] Scarry's description of war as a project whose 'main purpose and outcome is injuring' repudiates any military philosophy that would justify the physical purpose of war (to out-injure the 'other') by some articulated geopolitical purpose.[10] In my read of McCarthy, however, his views of violence are hardly less obdurate in their refusal of justifying claims about virtue in violent acts. For instance, even Leopold lauds certain forms of human violence against the natural world. What is the hunter but a 'non-creative artist,' one who 'thrill[s] to beauty' just as poets do?[11] McCarthy's hunters—John Wesley Rattner, who returns his hawk-killing bounty; Billy Parham, who risks his life for a she-wolf; the fated, generous Llewellen Moss who leaves off hunting to give water to a dying man; John Grady Cole mourning a slain deer—are not poets, and despite their best intentions, they experience pain and express grief when they hunt, trap, or tame wildlife. Nor does McCarthy depict those who engage in combat as having achieved any justifying aim other than injury: *Blood Meridian* is a devastating *Iliad* of human harm.

McCarthy's depiction of injury as the sole purpose of war is consistent with Scarry's vision, as is his reluctance to ascribe any justifying purpose to injuring others, even in 'justifiable' contexts such as revenge and hunting. McCarthy's characters do frequently rely on nonhuman animals for their survival, but they demonstrate a persistent concern with the ethical and reciprocal use of others' lives, and this concern is not restricted to human lives. In an early draft of a passage where Billy Parham defends his decision to take a she-wolf back to Mexico, Billy explains his decision, saying, 'I've always had peculiar notions about animals.'[12] Billy, and to a certain extent, John Grady Cole, exemplifies this 'peculiar notion' that ethical treatment of nonhuman life is a baseline test for the validity of the ethical paradigm. If a being can suffer, then it possesses a 'soul.' In contrast to a Romantic notion of pity as the motivating factor in just behavior, this peculiarity recognizes that the incomprehensible alterity of the other does not require pity but rather a holistic valuation of beings as individuals in a complex system that needs each member species to survive. Harm to an individual living body is an unethical act and one that reflects the more ambiguous cost of unethical behavior—an unmaking of the world.

How does pain in the material body reflect immaterial or metaphysical 'value'? In *The Body in Pain*, Scarry says imagination is an anomalous human state, comparable only to the state of being in pain. Through imagination, the body is capable of realizing its own being reflexively as well as 'making' knowledge. In terms of material history, the relationship between imagination and artifact gestures toward the originator or creator, whether identified as 'God' (from religious narratives to temples and natural wonders such as rainbows), or Karl Marx's material history (identified in artifacts of market structures, civil structures, and codified, systemic ideologies). The point is that, either way, an artifact provides evidence of the imagined connection between the thing and the idea of its meaning. As an example of the way human minds work through referentiality, Scarry says that a 'particular molecular structure may be dreamed before it is seen,' a reference, one must assume, to 'Kekulé's problem,' which McCarthy addresses in his 2017 essay which begins with August Kekulé's tale about how he discovered the shared valence electron structure in aromatic isomers.[13] From the anecdote about how Kekulé dreamed of an ouroboros and discovered the benzene molecule, McCarthy posits that the 'unconscious is a machine for operating an animal,' storing humans' 'deep knowledge' for survival and for problem solving. Language evolved later, not being necessary for survival.[14] His point is not that language does not matter, but that language does not predate or produce the type of knowledge we might quantify as 'deep knowledge,' a 'reptilian' knowledge that someone is watching us, for instance. Instead, language is an imprecise and imperfect code used to translate deep knowledge into something communicable to others, an imperfect tool but necessary for us to be able to communicate with others and, perhaps more importantly, with our own unconscious.

Scarry's argument helps to elucidate McCarthy's position on language, for she describes human language and the body as distinct yet ultimately inseparable parts of a whole. Even metaphysical attributes such as imagination and empathy reside in our bodies but are created through language, which in turn translates imagination into action and into experience. Scarry summarizes her point by saying, 'the human imagination has its collective expression in civilization: it is the thing created.' There is no clear distinction between human imagination, creation, and human bodily experience of the world. As an example, Karl Marx's description of the function of human economies is couched in 'bodily language'— production, consumption, reproduction, circulation—suggesting that all human making and unmaking is expressed and experienced as both linguistic and bodily acts.[15] For Scarry, the most extreme form of unmaking is torture. A torturer exhibits the most profound unmaking of human experience and civilization, transforming tools meant to provide comfort or aid into devices for harm. She uses the example of a chair, an object created to alleviate spinal pressure but which in torture becomes a device to stretch or abuse the human body, to stress its limbs and spine to the point of agony rather than to relieve pressure. Torture is also a linguistic abnegation of meaning: the point of torture is its pointlessness, the creation of pain for an ostensible purpose (to find out the truth, to punish a wrong-doer) that is in reality unachievable through torture (torture does not result in the truthfulness of the sufferer, nor does it purify the wrong-doer or rectify wrongs done). The 'goal of the torturer,' Scarry says, 'is to make the one, the body, emphatically and crushingly *present* by destroying it, and to make the other, the voice, *absent* by destroying it.'[16] Injured and tortured bodies litter the Border Trilogy, and their brokenness represents the breaking of the world. McCarthy's metaphoric use of the broken body to convey the breaking-down of narrative and of meaningfulness is not unique to the Border Trilogy. In correspondence with Albert Erskine about a draft of *The Orchard Keeper*, McCarthy responded to a question about plot and chronology by noting that a 'cat's death should trigger general decline of everybody.'[17] Even in his first novel, then, an injured animal constitutes the event leading to the unraveling of human characters and narrative. Injured or broken bodies capture in essence what Scarry describes as 'the intense pain that destroys a person's self and world, a destruction experienced spatially as either the contraction of the universe down to the immediate vicinity of the body or as the body swelling to fit the entire universe,' she says. 'Intense pain is ... language-destroying.'[18] This point of world- and self-destruction is where the Border Trilogy focuses its aesthetic and descriptive attention.

McCarthy applies a meticulous medical and physiological precision to his descriptions of bodily injury in men, horses, and wolves.[19] The language of harm is fused to a critique of the Western tradition's tendency to read profound suffering as 'proof' of virtue. As an example, John Grady Cole is literally 'gutted' twice. In *All the Pretty Horses*, he faces down a *cuchillero* and wins, but staggers away with his belly sliced open. He walks away from the fight holding his guts: 'blood was oozing through his fingers where he held himself' (202). In his final knife fight with Eduardo, Magdalena's pimp, he again manages to kill his adversary but this time receives fatal belly wounds: 'He ... got his breath and looked down. His shirt hung in bloody tatters. A gray tube of gut pushed through his fingers. He gritted his teeth and took hold of it and pushed it back and put his hand over it' (*COP* 254). There is a reason why so many colloquial expressions in English for deep emotion and deep courage center in the gut: we are 'gutted' in great disappointment; it 'takes guts' to behave courageously; a 'visceral' experience is one felt profoundly, deeply. Language codes our unconscious knowledge of our vulnerable body, the soft, easily damaged part of us that we display to the world as we walk on two legs. It names that part of us that understands our vulnerability; it names physiological manifestations of acts of courage and experiences of suffering.

The Trilogy focuses its narrative gaze on hurt bodies as the site of torture—as in Magdalena's broken body in the morgue

(*COP* 229)—or as a spectacle in which a punished body determines the outcome of legal arbitration—as when John Grady's bullet wound is used to determine his innocence of horse theft (*APH* 289). However, while characters in the Trilogy commit acts of torture or use evidence of harm in ways that suggest their implicit belief in something meaningful occurring in the act of injury, the omniscient narrator subverts any attempt to ascribe meaningfulness to suffering by drawing thematic attention to the meaninglessness of the agony and humiliation in these scenes.[20] The Trilogy as a whole suggests the need for a radical decoding of any value system that justifies harm, focusing on the brutal politics of the US border region and the economic interests of a nation that grew from violent land acquisitions and damaging expansionist agricultural practices. The language of pain unmakes the virtues that Western ethics ascribe to the structures that underlie the economic and geopolitical realities of the border region, specifically land misuse due to growth economies based largely on meat production; the use of land in the creation and testing of atomic weapons; and borders that define nations and defy bioregional unity.

Beyond merely decoding that pain-creating and world-unmaking value system, the Trilogy offers a vision of a contrasting value system that I term 'nomadic economics,' in which the value of a being lies in both the material function of the body and the immaterial value of life (the 'soul'). 'Nomadism' describes a particular orientation toward the world, one that contrasts with the land-rootedness of Western notions of property ownership that was used to justify settler colonialism. In *Nomadic Subjects*, Rosi Braidotti defines the nomad not as a person without a home or in displacement, but rather as a 'figuration for the kind of subject who has relinquished all idea, desire, or nostalgia for fixity.' For Braidotti, nomadic life is an intellectual commitment to 'political resistance to hegemonic fixed, unitary, and exclusionary views of subjectivity.'[21] Intellectual nomadism understands the 'body or the embodiment of the subject' as 'neither a biological nor a sociological category, but rather as a point of overlapping between the physical, the symbolic, and sociological.' She suggests that, as the Western world has moved away 'from manufacturing toward a service and information-based structure,' it has created a global shift in labor. With that shift, 'first world' economies have seen a corresponding decline in welfare states and wealth equity. With this new global precarity, there is an increasing urgency in our need to imagine a non-land-rooted and non-capitalist definition of subjectivity.[22] Braidotti's definition of intellectual nomadism illuminates the connection between McCarthy's nomadic protagonists and their relationship to the natural world. That connection lies in the novels' systematic uncoding of Western land-rooted capitalist value systems and their representation of an alternative, non-anthropocentric ethics of contingency, adaptability, and complexity. Nomadic subjects are represented by wanderers, some of whom choose the 'life of the road,' and others of whom adapt to displacement. What unifies them is their rejection of fixed notions of nation, property ownership, and anthropocentric utilitarian ethics. The nomadism Billy practices at the end of *Cities of the Plain* is therefore not the only sustainable model for human communities; a Yaqui man in *The Crossing* models an orientation toward the world that emphasizes adaptability and sustainability, but the Yaqui nation is traditionally agricultural and fairly land-rooted. Like many Indigenous agricultural nations in what is now central and northern Mexico and the American southwest, Yaquis have a history of agricultural and geographical adaption to extremes of climate change in a region that has undergone periods of intense aridity.[23] Nomadism, then, describes a particular type of relationship to one's bioregion. Such an orientation may not require actual un-homing, and indeed, a 'deep knowledge' of one's bioregion privileges indigenous communal knowledge. It is instead a radical repudiation of land-rootedness that is based in notions of property ownership and that values profit over sustainability, 'suzerainty' over adaptability.

Here, again, pain comes into focus. The body in pain is the material body reduced to its most corporeal, but grief expressed by the body enduring pain—and the compassion of the witness to that grief or endurance—reflects the metaphysical value associated with life. Adaptive nomadism is the practice of a body adapting to privation, looking to preserve the material body but not at the cost of the survival of the system or its constituent species. The body in pain suggests the cost of beauty, desire, and love in a post-industrialized, anthropocentric utilitarian ethics: the aesthetic body (a flower, a beautiful girl, a horse, a hunted animal) is used for the pleasure of the capitalist witness. By contrast, nomadic witnesses engage with human and nonhuman others without exacting a price for the existence of the other's beautiful life.

Bodies in pain: on the suffering of human and nonhuman animals

As the first chapter of this book explains, McCarthy uses wild animals, and particularly those trapped by humans or in the process of being 'broken' or domesticated, as referents for the non-material value of living beings not defined by their utility to the economic hegemon. In *Animals in the Fiction of Cormac McCarthy*, Wallis R. Sanborn III summarizes the 'hierarchies ... within genera' in McCarthy's fiction, such that 'proximity to and dependence upon man results in mistreatment and death, while distance from man results in survival and fitness.' Wild animals in captivity (whether that captivity is imagined, attempted, or successful) illuminate 'man's absolute desire to control the natural world.'[24] This statement may seem broad and vague, but it finds general concurrence among McCarthy scholars. Luce is one of the first scholars to note that McCarthy drafted his unpublished screenplay *Whales and Men* while researching and drafting *The Crossing*. Although one uses whales and the other wolves, both texts highlight animal communities' 'living web,' an existential as well as material matrix in which animals' bodily experience—auditory sensitivity for whales, and sense of smell for wolves—permits a highly attuned, adaptive, and nuanced engagement with their natural environment, as well as with their own species.[25] Luce argues that whales and wolves represent the ideal of the world as it should be, while McCarthy's human protagonists experience the world as it is, alienated, post-industrialized, and in danger of its complex ecosystems failing altogether. Stacey Peebles, building on Luce's earlier work, notes that 'of all of McCarthy's works [*All the Pretty Horses* and *Whales and Men*] as well as *The Crossing* have the most to say about the potential resonance between human and animals.'[26] Nonhuman animal relationships serve as the most common image of functional communities in McCarthy's works, as well as representing the failures of human communities.

McCarthy does distinguish types of relationship between human and nonhuman communities based on the type of use or labor to which the nonhuman species is put, but Sanborn is not correct to suggest that McCarthy perceives all relations between human and nonhuman species are necessarily violent or abusive. Instead, McCarthy's view seems to correspond more closely with what Donna J. Haraway describes in *When Species Meet* (2008) as an ethics of companion species. 'To be in relation of use to each other is not the definition of unfreedom and violation,' Haraway says. Companion species labor with and for each other; that is inevitable. Moral relationships between companion species require a 'radical ability to remember and feel what is going on,' to recognize when use of another species violates their freedom, and to 'respond practically in the face of the permanent complexity not resolved by taxonomic hierarchies and with no humanist philosophical or religious guarantees.'[27] McCarthy's *Whales and Men* presents his arguments about ethics and human and nonhuman animal relations with notable lucidity. The screenplay tells the story of a philosophically minded and independently wealthy man, John Western, his girlfriend Kelly McAmon, a whale biologist named Guy Schuler, and an Irish nobleman named Peter Gregory who set sail from Sri Lanka hoping to see whales. They run into a small pod of blue whales, but when an illegal whaling ship kills the two adults, the small crew chases off the whaler and waits with the dying baby blue whale. When sharks arrive, Guy puts down the baby whale in a mercy killing and admits to Kelly that he stopped his fieldwork because he was on the brink of becoming an ecoterrorist, such is his rage against humans for decimating whale populations. John suffers an existential crisis and breaks up with Kelly; Kelly and Peter end up together in Ireland, where Peter stands for a seat in parliament and presents legislation on behalf of whales and Kelly becomes pregnant, a choice that she says represents her belief that love and human communities are worth fighting for, even if they are terribly damaged. John becomes a medical doctor working in war zones.

Throughout the script, the main characters engage in lengthy discussions about violence, community, love, and what, if anything, gives meaning to life. In an indirect reference to Scarry's work on torture, Guy says that 'our claim to need the whale's products was like the inquisitor's claim to need his victim's information.' Whaling becomes a metaphor for the inclination in humans to injure, while whale societies illustrate a purity of love that gives meaning to existence. The whale biologist Guy argues for a new ethics for dealing with nonhuman animals: 'We're prisoners to a religion of utility,' he says. What we need is a non-utilitarian view of animals: 'They are not brethren. They are not underlings. They are other nations, caught up with ourselves in the net of life and time.' Peter then critiques the limitations of human ethics as a limitation of language itself: 'Language is a way of containing the world. A thing named becomes that named thing. It is under surveillance,' he says. 'We were put into a garden and we turned it into a detention center.' To counter this dominionist approach, he claims that we need to learn to *be* with each other in the world. What humans fear most is to experience and express this radical, de-centered love, '[b]ecause,' Peter says, 'if we truly believed it existed then we would have to change.'[28]

Whales and Men spells out much of the thematic treatment of animals in McCarthy's fiction. Like the contrasting images of cars and horses, damaging human–nonhuman animal interactions represent McCarthy's critique of deeply embedded Christian dominionist thought in Western utilitarianism. In this context, Raymond Malewitz uses 'thing theory' (following philosophers including Ken Alder and Bruno Latour) to analyze McCarthy's treatment of animals as a literary 'modeling [of] nonhuman entities in ways that foreground the limitations of anthropocentric codings.' He argues that McCarthy often 'codes' the animal textually in terms of its use value in an anthropocentric utilitarian model, but the animal is then textually re- or un-coded, and finally it is rendered un-codable to human characters, and to readers. This process models for readers their mental coding of animals as 'things' rather than as subjects. While Malewitz finds the Border Trilogy and *The Crossing* specifically problematic for imposition of 'romantic conceptions of otherness onto wolf and Mexican citizen alike,' his analysis provides a helpful description of the Border Trilogy's stylistic representation of a non-anthropocentric value system.[29] For McCarthy, nomadic economics prioritizes the use of the body in relation to a complex 'matrix' of a natural system, but while its use value is contingent on its relationship to its proper function in the 'matrix,' the *being*'s value is non-material and not contingent; it is separate from its function or usefulness. I use the term 'nomadic economics' to describe this philosophy in which an individual's value is measured not through its output or profitability but rather in terms of its engagement in its 'proper' work, through proportional, adaptive, and reactive labor or behavior in relationship to its natural system.

In order to understand the Border Trilogy's patterns of uncoding the 'thingness' of animals, it is necessary to establish McCarthy's linguistic codes for value. McCarthy uses 'soul' to express an essential, intrinsic, and innate value in a being separate or separable from its 'thing' value. Given his characterization of animals as being in 'ideal' communities, it comes as no surprise that animals are frequently associated with living closer to or being more in tune with their own souls, although, as Luís the *mozo* tells John Grady, 'the souls of horses mirror the souls of men more closely than men suppose' (*APH* 111). While humans and different species illustrate different aspects of the risks of capitalist excess, the failures of Western utilitarian ethics, and the possibilities of nomadic existence, both human and nonhuman animals are fundamentally equated by virtue of this possession of a 'soul'—a value not quantifiable on the market. All living beings, in this fictional rendering of value, can be understood to possess a soul. However, beings can be alienated from their own sense of that value, and others can repudiate the value of the being by rejecting its worth, ascribing value solely to its physical body, and finally by commodifying its body. In bodily suffering, the living being loses connection to a sense of a soul, a sense of having an innate value. Conversely, bodily suffering can produce in the sufferer and, even more clearly, in the witness to suffering a recognition of the soul as that which is violated by the inducement of pain. The being who is in pain does not need conscious awareness of its own existence in order for suffering to violate its meaningfulness.

In *All the Pretty Horses*, when the dueña Alfonsa explains this concept, her explanation represents its function throughout the Trilogy. She tells John Grady about a childhood love affair with a revolutionary named Gustavo. Because Alfonsa damaged her hand as a young girl, she is 'damaged goods' on the marriage market, and as the daughter of a wealthy landowner in pre-Revolution Mexico, she is raised to know that her exchange value on the marriage market equals her value as a person. The one-eyed revolutionary Gustavo woos her anyway, explaining that suffering must lead a person 'back into the common enterprise of man' or else the sufferer's bitterness will warp their development (*APH* 235). As he speaks to her, he begins to weep, and Alfonsa says, 'I knew that it was my soul he wept for.' She explains why his sorrowing witness of her suffering changes her valuation of herself and offers John Grady a moving description of what a world might look like in which a being's value lies not in market use but rather in something non-material. 'I had never been esteemed in this way,' she explains:

> I wanted very much to be a person of value and I had to ask myself how this could be possible if there were not something like a soul or like a spirit that is in the life of a person and which could endure any misfortune or disfigurement and yet be no less for it. If one were to be a person of value that value could not be a condition subject to the hazards of fortune. It had to be a quality that could not change. (235)

Alfonsa recognizes that value must lie in something separable from the material body, so that the body might be made to suffer but 'be no less.'

Across the Border Trilogy, a living being's suffering both represents the use value assigned to the being by the one imposing suffering (that is, harm to a living being reveals the perpetrator of harm valuing the harmed being 'less') and also provides evidence that the harmed living being's value is not, in fact, 'less' for their suffering. Because horses and humans mirror each other 'more closely than men suppose,' *All the Pretty Horses* illustrates this concept in parallel passages describing John Grady's 'breaking' of wild horses and his sexual relationship with Alejandra, whose 'marriage market value' he destroys (111). The scene where John Grady proves his cowboy 'machismo' by breaking sixteen wild horses in four days is rendered in erotic language that illuminates the loss horses experience through domestication. At the beginning of his excessive display of horsemanship, Lacey Rawlins and John Grady discuss how John Grady intends to break that many horses in so short a time. Rawlins brings up his father, a 'certified peeler' who was known to 'hang and rattle a time or two' (103). Rawlins refers here to a type of bronco busting that rides horses to exhaustion. John Grady's process initially seems more humane: he rubs down the mustangs with gunnysacks that smell like him (102). However, he describes his purpose with a clear indication of his belief in his anthropocentric sovereignty over the animals: he will 'make em believe' in his ownership (103). With his purpose to dominate the horses until they no longer 'believe' in their independence, he breaks the first horse by riding it to exhaustion. The horse collapses, and

> Before the colt could struggle up John Grady had squatted on its neck and pulled its head up and to one side and was holding the horse by the muzzle with the long bony head pressed against his chest and the hot sweet breath of it flooding up from the dark wells of its nostrils over his face and neck like news from another world. They did not smell like horses. They smelled like what they were, wild animals. (103)

He 'breaks' the once-wild horse for use as a cattle horse, an act that increases the animal's use value to humans but reduces its capacity to live in 'proper' relationship to its herd. Then John Grady breaks the next horse, and the next. By the final night, he hears 'broken' horses in the paddock, and the 'wild and frantic band of mustangs that had circled the potrero that morning like marbles swirled in a jar could hardly be said to exist and the animals whinnied to one another in the dark and answered back as if some one among their number was missing, or some thing' (107). What is missing is what their suffering has alienated them from: their place in the matrix and connection through some ineffable, common 'soul.'

Luís tries to explain this notion to John Grady and Rawlins when they are in the mountains corralling wild horses: 'the horse shares a common soul and its separate life only forms it out of all horses and makes it mortal.' By contrast, he says, 'among men there was no such communion' (111). The view that animals share a common soul is not unusual in McCarthy's fiction, but McCarthy is more ambivalent about Luís's claim regarding humans. In *Whales and Men*, Kelly argues that *all* living things share a common soul; it is only that humans are deluded in thinking themselves apart from other animals. Both Peter and John reiterate this point, suggesting her claim's significance to the overall argument of the drama. Kelly also criticizes commodification of life in terms of its use value: 'Isnt existence a purpose?' she says. 'I think we confuse purpose with utility. It's as if existence itself were somehow not noble enough or sacred enough to justify its own undertaking.' In this model of existence, 'It's not that we have a soul. It's that a soul has us.'[30] In *All the Pretty Horses*, the problem with John Grady's love of horses lies in his view of them as utilities. The novel underscores the use-value problem by conflating John Grady's gaze leveled on horses with his gaze as it lands on Alejandra. After watching Alejandra dismount from her black Arabian stallion, John Grady falls asleep that night thinking of her that night and dreams 'of horses' (117–118). The textual splicing of his erotic gaze and his yearning for horses is no accident: after their first sexual encounter, Alejandra looks at John Grady and 'he saw in her face ... something he'd not seen before and the name of that thing was sorrow' (140). He does not seem to recognize—or is not willing to acknowledge—why she exhibits 'sorrow,' the loss of something vital, but the narrator describes John Grady's sexual hunger for the girl as they make out in a lake as '[s]weeter for the larceny of time and flesh, sweeter for the betrayal' (141). The narrator points out his 'theft' of her time and body, a theft John Grady admits to only in a negation at the end of the narrative when he looks at his cousin Rawlins and thinks that Rawlins, at least, has ruined '[n]o man's daughter' (255).

Alfonsa explains the connection between the breaking of horses and girls. The girl's freedom and her agency are precarious in a social system that denies her value except in her marriageability, her virginity. It is not *love* that Alfonsa wishes to deny Alejandra by coercing her into rejecting John Grady; she wishes to preserve the girl's agency through the only avenues of power that are open to her. Alfonsa makes it clear that she does not want to force Alejandra into an economically advantageous marriage, necessarily. She has 'long been willing to entertain the notion of rescue arriving in whatever garb it chose,' she says (240). By implication, it is marriage to a man who permits the girl the possession of her own soul, her own *self*, that Alfonsa desires for her grandniece. 'I only know that if she [Alejandra] does not come to value what is true above what is useful,' Alfonsa concludes, 'it will make little difference whether she lives at all' (240).

McCarthy symbolically underscores the connection between Alejandra's emotional suffering and that experienced by the inconsolable horses crying out to each other in search of what has been taken in the scene after John Grady leaves Alejandra. On his journey back to the States, penniless and alone, John Grady shoots a doe for food. As the doe bleeds out, he puts his hand 'on her neck and she looked at him and her eyes were warm and wet and there was no fear in them and then she died' (282). John Grady immediately shifts to thinking about Alejandra, and reflects that 'the world's heart beat at some terrible cost and that the world's pain and its beauty moved in a relationship of diverging equity and that in this headlong deficit the blood of multitudes might ultimately be exacted for the vision of a single flower' (282). If the symbolic association of the flower with Alejandra's lost virginity seems trite, it nevertheless speaks to the inordinate cost that John Grady's 'dominion' over horses and women exacts. In *The Crossing*, McCarthy revisits the image of a flower as representing beauty or innate value, but extends the metaphor to a she-wolf. When the she-wolf dies, Billy holds the wolf, but her dead body represents what he does not hold, her value, which 'cannot be held never be held and is no flower but is swift and a huntress and the wind itself is in terror of it and the world cannot lose it' (*Cr* 127). *The Crossing* associates the possession of a 'soul' with New Mexican wolves—the 'soul' first referenced as 'some inner fire'—similarly to how *All the Pretty Horses* describes the communal soul of horses (*Cr* 4). There is a marked difference in the wolves' proximity to their 'soul' relative to that of horses in the previous novel, as the passage suggests: wolves are *more* than a flower, and their loss more cataclysmic. Sanborn claims that 'the wolf is a warrior animal of honor, and its absence ... becomes a negative metaphor for man's ceaseless appetite for control over the natural world.' However, Sanborn identifies Billy's persistent belief that the wolf has been put 'in his care' as representing Billy's subconscious subscription to the Judeo-Christian dominionist view of nature. While he reads Billy's freeing of the she-wolf in the same way as Luce does, as a 'symbolic resistance' to American capitalism, Sanborn suggests that in Billy, the tenets of capitalism remain intact.[31] Critiquing Sanborn's claim, Malewitz suggests that the novel models the 'emergence of a thing from an object' when Billy captures the wolf, but he nevertheless concludes that Billy kills the wolf and barters his gun for its carcass because 'Billy believes that he can freely cross over into the borderless, unrestricted, and undifferentiated world of animals without altering that world.'[32] However, Billy's narrative arc is rather more dynamic than Malewitz and Sanborn suggest. Billy quickly rejects his father's dominionist use of the wolf at the beginning of *The Crossing*. Even though he has not fully grasped the significance of his lessons at the end of that novel, by the end of *Cities of the Plain*, Billy operates out of a different value system altogether, suggesting that his narrative arc spans two volumes, not one.

At the beginning of *The Crossing*, young Billy Parham rides out in search of the she-wolf because she has been preying on his family's cattle and is a threat to their livelihood. He rides with his 'heart outsized in his chest,' and the landscape around him looks 'new born out of the hand of some improvident god who'd perhaps not even puzzled out a use for [the mountains]' (31). This 'god' is 'improvident' in the sense that it does not require use, or profit, from the world; this god is not an anthropomorphic utilitarian, but instead requires only the wild joy of all its creations. As Billy rides, he imagines wolves 'and ghosts of wolves running in the whiteness of that high world as perfect to their use as if their counsel had been sought in the devising of it' (31). The wolves, and more specifically their 'ghosts,' their non-material essential being, have greater agency and a deeper knowledge of the use of this landscape than the god who created it, suggesting that in their joyous fulfillment of their proper, proportional role in the food chain in this balanced eco-system, these apex predators create as well as inhabit their world.

Scientists cannot prove that the reintroduction of wolves to Yellowstone National Park created dramatic positive effects on bioregional diversity, as some now-debunked, fatuous initial reports claimed. However, the biologist Andy Dobson offers evidence that the reintroduction of wolves did clearly have a net-positive effect. Current scientific debate about the ecological effects of the wolves being reintroduced to Yellowstone National Park sheds light on how little we know about the complex interrelationship of top-down (apex-predator-focused) versus bottom-up changes to ecosystems (like climate change). But what is clear, Dobson states, is that food webs and ecosystems function through 'a series of nested forces' that hold complex systems together; the study of biodiversity is nearly identical to the study of particle physics, the study of how divergent particles are held 'together using a mixture of centripetal and gravitational forces.'[33] The wolf alone may not 'create' the matrix of its natural system, but *absent* the wolf, the system frays or collapses. Dobson's research on the reintroduction of wolves to Yellowstone draws on current research on complex systems in studies on foods webs, biodiversity, and particle physics. This research was supported by Dobson's work at the Sante Fe Institute, suggesting the possibility of cross-pollination of ideas between his and McCarthy's own work at the Institute. More importantly, Dobson's work illustrates the irreducible complexity of natural systems. It may not be possible to determine the effects of one species on a region, because nothing operates in isolation. The precarious, ecologically balanced life of a 'wild' natural system, characterized in the Border Trilogy by 'hearts' and 'souls,' suggests a quasi-religious value system directly at odds with military-industrial forms of capitalism.

In *The Crossing*, McCarthy codes this communal, non-hierarchical value system syntactically. When the wolf is introduced, the narrative perspective shifts to her point of view, making her the only nonhuman point-of-view character in McCarthy's fiction. The wolf 'crossed the international boundary line' between Arizona and Sonora into the San Luis mountains, traveling with a wound on her hip from where her mate had bitten her because 'she would not leave him' when he was caught in a hunter's trap (24). Her loyalty is underscored when the narrator explains why she is migrating: 'She was moving out of the country not because the game was gone but because the wolves were and she needed them' (25). In addition to noting the rich interior communal life of the wolf, the narrative underscores not what she thinks, which would anthropomorphize her, but *that* she thinks—that she observes and her instincts, her 'unconscious,' responds. Billy, then, finding the she-wolf in the trap that he and his father set, comes abruptly on his first existential crisis. Caught between two competing value systems, his father's ranch and the 'soul' in the she-wolf's eyes, he chooses to free her, and in so doing, he acts against the material success of his family. The narrator notes five times that the wolf watches Billy: 'The wolf was watching him' and she 'looked at him' (53); 'She looked toward him,' 'She watched with one almond eye' (54); and finally, after he has caught her with a rope and a stick to keep her teeth at bay as he unhooks the trap, 'She looked up at him ... the knowledge of the world it held sufficient to the day if not to the day's evil' (55). Her comprehension of Billy's actions might be incommunicable, but she is capable of thought, experience, and emotional expression.

Billy's decision to free the wolf contrary to the economic interests of his family reverberates through the rest of his life. While Sanborn and Malewitz may be right that Billy's recognition of the wolf's intrinsic value is sufficient that he decides to free her but not sufficient to free him from his dominionist mindset, it is important to note that he at least comes close to recognizing the flaws of anthropocentric ethics. The scene in which the wolf dies also depicts Billy grappling with the implications of the destruction of complex natural systems. When Billy closes the dead wolf's eye, he

> close[s] his own eyes that he could see her running in the mountains, running in the starlight where the grass was wet and the sun's coming as yet had not undone the rich matrix of creatures passed in the night before her. Deer and hare and dove and groundvole all richly empaneled on the air for her delight, all nations of the possible world ordained by God of which she was one among and not separate from. (127)

As he cradles the she-wolf's head, Billy recognizes that what is lost in the wolf's death, 'the world cannot lose' (127). Two value systems collide in the wolf's death. What the world cannot afford to lose is the animal Billy's father cannot afford to let live—at least not if he is to keep his source of income, his cattle. Billy's shifting perspective, from the wolf as threat to the wolf as an integral species in the 'rich matrix' of its natural system, commences a process of decoding and re-coding of value that the Trilogy argues for.

In *The Crossing*'s opening scene, Billy holds his baby brother Boyd before him on his saddle; as they ride into the new country, he 'named to him features of the landscape' (3). Billy has learned to map the landscape and name its features from his father, who teaches him to 'learn' the land with 'astrolabe and sextant' (22). Their goal is to settle this 'new country,' which is unfenced: 'You could ride clear to Mexico and not strike a crossfence' (3). Their father fences property, grazes cattle, and cuts into the migratory route of the wolf. Yet from his early education in mapping land, trapping wolves, and ranching, Billy's story takes an abrupt turn. In this new story, the world of men preys on the wolf and does not know that it cannot afford to lose her. *The Crossing* is, in many ways, McCarthy's clearest articulation of what is at stake in the loss of the 'soul' of the wild: it is the loss of a story of another world, another reality, another system of value that is foreign to an economic system that defines value in terms of utility and ownership, and heroism in terms of violence.

If *The Crossing* is the story of Billy's awakening to the need for an ethics whose communal wellbeing includes nonhuman as well as human life, *Cities of the Plain* tells the story of a man who loses all but his instincts not to kill animals unless he is required to do so, but whose journey toward finding his own 'soul' ends with a redemptive moment in which he seems to practice a non-anthropocentric ethics. Billy's narrative arc through *The Crossing* and *Cities of the Plain* pays attention to the complexity of natural systems and proposes that an ethics of value for nonhuman others may require an intellectual, if not physical, commitment to nomadic life. In *Cities of the Plain* Billy initially seems to be a more jaded man in his late twenties, but his instinctual care for animals remains. Toward the beginning of the novel, Billy and John Grady are on the range together when they see a coyote. John Grady offers to 'get the rifle,' but Billy stops him, without explanation (11). While Billy is driving with Troy, a jackrabbit darts into the road. Billy tells the rabbit, 'Go on dumb-ass,' but Troy runs over the rabbit when it does not move (20).

The most telling symbolic regeneration of Billy's non-anthropocentric ethics is his relationship to dogs. At the end of *The Crossing*, having crossed through the Animas valley into central Arizona, Billy finds an old dog that looks like 'some awful composite of grief had broke through the preterite world' (424). Billy has lost the she-wolf, lost his brother, lost his family, and he responds with blind rage to this domesticated canine whose mutilated body is 'composite of grief.' He yells at the dog to 'git'; but while feral wolves need the company of other wolves, dogs need the company of their domesticators. At first, the grief-dog refuses to leave, but when Billy throws rocks at it, the dog runs off. Then Billy is woken in the night by the 'dim neon bow' of the first atomic explosion (425). His reaction to this terrifying image of a world radically unmade is to walk 'out on the road and call ... for the dog.' Billy 'called and called,' but the dog does not return, and Billy 'held his face in his hands and wept' until the sun rises (426). In *Cities of the Plain*, Billy and John Grady are sent to shoot a pack of feral dogs ravaging the ranch's newborn calves. This scene represents one aspect of the damage done to ecosystems when its apex predator, the gray wolf, is destroyed: packs of dogs, who do not have the instincts to limit their thinning of a food supply, now fill the power vacuum at the top of the food chain. It also serves to introduce the puppy. John Grady notices that one of the feral dogs has recently given birth, and he wakes Billy and insists Billy accompany him to find and rescue the litter. Billy, called out of his sleep metaphorically and literally, attends John Grady's rescue of a litter, including a small pup which refuses to leave its dead sibling with whom John Grady feels an immediate kinship. John Grady announces that he 'got [him] a dog' (177). When Billy finds John Grady dying in a shack at the end of the novel, John Grady is '[h]olding himself close that he not escape from himself,' an escape that he senses as 'his soul ... which stood so tentatively at the door of his corporeal self. Like some lightfooted animal that stood testing the air at the open door of a cage' (156–157). His soul departs into the uncaged freedom that is, one assumes, the collective freedom of all the 'ardenthearted' of the world. Billy mourns the dead boy, and in the following scene, leaves the ranch and his former life behind, heading out on horseback, 'he and the dog' (263). In the overarching symbolism of the Trilogy, John Grady's passion for life, despite his immature desires to possess or control it, has granted him access to an experience of his own 'soul'—a value not contingent on any metric of the marketplace, on success, or having a wife, or even winning a knife fight with his antagonist. Billy's role as witness to the ineffable value of another now permits him to travel on, carrying 'grief' with him, symbolized by John Grady's shivering, orphaned pup. Billy embodies Gustavo's proscription against bitterness, carrying his symbolic suffering with him 'back into the common enterprise of man' (*APH* 235). In language reiterating Gustavo's warning to Alfonsa, a Yaqui man at one point calls Billy an orphan, a 'huérfano still,' and warns him that in deracinating loss, he may 'become estranged from men and so ultimately from himself.' The man explains that Billy has a 'largeness of spirit ... and that the world would need him even as he needed the world for they were one' (134). He must share this 'largeness of spirit' with the world, and 'to do this one must live with men and not simply pass among them' (134). Living with the world lies at the heart of the communal and non-anthropocentric ethics the Trilogy calls forth. Living with, however, does not require rootedness—and may only be found in un-rootedness, in an adaptable, reciprocal life with and among other human and nonhuman life.

Bodies on the move: nomadism and natural systems

Beyond using nonhuman animals as a sort of litmus test for non-anthropocentric ethics, the Border Trilogy embeds animals within a bioregional analysis of the dire implications of sovereignty-based utilitarian ethics on natural systems. This notion can be seen in the Trilogy's preoccupation with fences, where fencing demarcates private property and represents a capitalist and Christian dominionist view of life and value. For example, when John Grady and his cousin Rawlins head south toward Mexico, they leave an American landscape where 'wire fence strung pole to pole like a bad suture,' the land here imagined as an injured body badly held together by the symbols of private property (*APH* 38). They find an Edenic destination in the mountainous inner region of north-central Mexico, riding through mountains until they see 'the country of which they'd been told,' a country of deep, unmarked grassland where 'vaqueros [are] driving cattle before them' (93). The problem with this open country is that it is not *theirs*, as John Grady discovers to his own, and his cousin's, detriment. Nevertheless, the trackless, unfenced land illustrates the interior bent of the boys toward a way of life where free-grazing animals suggest a land use model that does not demarcate property for private ownership. However, as Sara Spurgeon argues, the 'myth' of the cowboy on that trackless, open land is just that: a myth. It forms a gilded patina over the brutal land seizures of Spanish settlers in Mexico and European American settlers in Texas. Spurgeon rejects earlier readings that suggest that a fenced Texan landscape represents modernity while an unfenced Mexican landscape represents pastoral nostalgia, and proposes that it is 'the hollowness and non-innocence of that myth' on which John Grady 'has chosen to place his faith' that is his undoing.[34] Spurgeon's reading explicates the narrative's attention to the suffering experienced by the horses and by Alejandra as objects of John Grady's acquisitive love.

Horses represent the struggle between natural adaptation and human-caused incursions into ecosystems. Wild horses, tough and suited to their Mexican mountainous terrain, were originally brought by colonial Spanish forces to conquer the local population, and they represent the adaptability of ecosystems. The novel draws explicit attention to the colonial history of these wild horses, suggesting that the military industrial hunger of colonialism outstrips the capacity of natural systems to adjust to disruptions. Don Héctor's plan is to breed a thoroughbred, the half-brother of a Brazilian Grand Priz runner named Three Bars, to his 'wild' mares to create an indigenous Mexican quarter horse (*AHP* 114); the wild horses are, John Grady explains, 'Spanish ponies,' from 'Old Barb stock' (115). Referring to 'Uncle Billy' Anson, a British nobleman who emigrated to Texas in 1890, Don Héctor intimates that he shares Anson's vision. Anson supplied the British army with thousands of American quarter horses for use in the Boer War. Popular for their noted endurance, speed, and reliability, Anson's horses played a 'pivotal role' in shaping the American Quarter Horse Association breed (115–116).[35] Central American horses, in other words, are products of colonial invasion, and the new horse-breeding enterprise John Grady joins is inspired by the use of horses in fighting colonial wars. In *Cities of the Plain*, Eduardo taunts John Grady by explicitly naming Mexico's burgeoning economy when he claims that Mexico's imperialistic power will wax as the US's economic hegemony wanes: 'we will devour you, my friend,' he says. 'You and all your pale empire' (*COP* 253). As Spurgeon has argued, the point is not to force comparisons between the relative ethics of Spanish imperialism in Central America and settler American imperialism in what became the US southwest. Rather, the Trilogy as a whole describes various 'pale empires' in Spain and the US and the emerging capitalist voracity of Mexico as equivalent. Each represents an economic system built on violent land seizures and the use and abuse of human and nonhuman bodies, where everything—land, people, animals—has value solely based on its utility to the empire. The consequence of this invasion is ecological disaster.

In *Cities of the Plain*, John Grady discusses with 'old man' Johnson the tenuous future of Mac's ranch, and of ranching itself, in the western Texas and eastern New Mexican basin experiencing ongoing drought. Johnson explains that even the recent good rains will not be enough to rehydrate the Tularosa basin; in the end, '[f]olks ... might be glad to let the army have it' (62). The Tularosa basin in the Chihuahua mountain range east of the Rio Grande is where various streams flow in but not out, creating what was at one point lush grassland populated by the nomadic Apache nation until about 1850, when the region was claimed by US troops. After US settlement, non-indigenous cattle over-grazed the grassland until they dried it out; ranchers drilled into the aquifer for more water and dried that, too, over-salinating the region. Because of the devaluation of the property given its ecological challenges, the US army purchased part of the basin and created what is now the White Sands Missile Range.[36] This is the wider context in which Billy leaves Mac's ranch after John Grady's death. The narrator explains that Billy quits ranching altogether when drought strikes Texas, after which point he works as an extra in a film in El Paso; when money dries up there, he travels west through Arizona (*COP* 265). The significance of Billy's departure, then, is explained by his shift from working at the ranch to nomadic labor across a bioregion, which suggests that Billy's life describes the Trilogy's answer to the ecological disaster wrought by empires in the American southwest and in Mexico.

Throughout the Trilogy, McCarthy makes a case for the need for proper land use as part of an ethical commitment to communal wellbeing that takes into account nonhuman as well as human life. Mark Eaton examines the transformative role of border crossings in the Trilogy as metaphors for a critique of land use and nationalism. By showing the fragility of national identity—specifically, the identities of people increasingly alienated from national mythologies of sameness and otherness—McCarthy's border novels represent the US–Mexico borderlands as 'a *transfrontera* contact zone, an approach we should not therefore associate only with American ethnic writers.'[37] Spurgeon concurs, claiming that McCarthy's border novels are 'an indictment, bloody and accusatory, of an American national(ist) identity based on the violent conquest of both racialized Others and feminized nature.'[38] While Eaton focuses on the novels' deconstruction of national identity and Spurgeon on the binary construction of 'imperial self/colonized Other,' paying attention to the novels' treatment of nomadic communities draws these themes together. At the end of *Cities of the Plain*, Billy carries the dog symbolizing grief with him, representing his growing understanding of the need to channel grief in pro-social ways, but it is difficult to read him as engaging meaningfully with community. However, his is not the only nomadic life the Trilogy describes. In *The Crossing*, a band of people whom McCarthy identifies as 'gypsies' finds Billy when he is attempting to carry his brother's bones with him back to the States. They treat Billy's horse, who has been shot, and save its life; they then tell Billy a heavily metaphorical story about an abandoned broken airplane in the field nearby, whose tale of destruction that is the result of human greed. In contrast to get-rich-quick schemes, the group of travelers 'stood in no proprietary relationship to anything, scarcely even to the space they occupied. Out of their anterior lives they had arrived at the same understanding as their fathers before them. That movement itself is a form of property' (410). One of the travelers, Rafael, refuses payment for their aid, explaining to Billy that it is 'Para el camino,' and 'the way of the road was the rule for all upon it. He said that on the road there were no special cases' (414). Rafael indicates that there is a way to live that is characterized by reciprocity and recreative energy, and that such a life follows its own ethics and economics: to share food, goods, and services, and to receive such when in need. 'Property' is defined in Western capitalism through the concept of private land ownership, the foundational source of capital.[39] When 'property' is redefined as 'movement,' it suggests a nomadic economics whose foundational principle is fundamentally adaptive and contingent: movement can be a form of 'property' when the individual has rights to land use for their own sustenance, merely by virtue of existing on the road and having need there. Rafael's description of such an ethos and such an economics presages McCarthy's most explicit representation in the father and son in *The Road*, with the boy living out those practices with 'ardenthearted' fervor. However, that nomadic philosophy is perhaps best articulated by a Yaqui man, Quijada, in *The Crossing*. Quijada describes himself as a man who does not 'have the same loyalties' as the Mexican farmers in the region. He is not loyal to the nation-state of Mexico, since the Yaqui nation fared poorly under the Spanish, American, *and* Mexican governments (*Cr* 385). At this point, Billy is still looking for Boyd; Quijada confirms that Boyd has died, but, he says, Boyd died a hero, 'very popular with the people' (383, 384). The *corridos* sung about Boyd are perhaps not technically true, Quijada admits, but the men whom Boyd killed included a friend of the *alguacil* (sheriff) of the region. 'There is the latifundio of Babícora,' Quijado says. 'And there are the campesinos in their rags' (384). The *latifundios* were land grants that the Spanish government awarded to *conquistadores* in recognition of conquest, and with permission from the Spanish government to use Indigenous people as slave labor. Therefore, Boyd killed a powerful representation of colonial wealth, and the *corridos* sung about him are a 'poor man's history' that owes no 'allegiance to the truths of history but to the truths of men' (386). *Corridos* represent a deeper ethos, a recognition that the world does not belong to people. 'The world has no name,' Quijada says. Names for things 'exist only on maps,' and maps are drawn so that 'we do not lose our way. Yet it was because the way was lost to us already that we have made those names. The world cannot be lost' (387).

Just as maps attempt to codify the natural world for human use, narratives attempt to locate human meaningfulness. Scarry describes the ways in which imaginative language bridges loneliness between individuals and forges community out of alienation. The

Border Trilogy suggests that it is through stories that we weave ourselves into the warp and weft of our experiences and of the universe that exists outside us and will exist long after we are gone. It is only in that last observation that human language recognizes its potential for meaning: there exists a world outside our own experience. We can torture the bodies of human and nonhuman animals, destroy natural systems, and one day perhaps the biosphere. But the body in pain forces us to consider what is not present in the moment of suffering: the world beyond. Lives lived to alleviate the pain of others accept the contingency of life in a shared system. By minimizing their impact on their bioregion through adaptive and transitory patterns of life, nomadic people live in a state of change and impermanence. But impermanence, too, is just a story that we tell ourselves. As Quijado reminds Billy, the world is not going anywhere; we are the ones who are, at times, lost.

Notes

1 Rosi Braidotti, *Nomadic Subjects: Embodiment and Sexual Difference in Contemporary Feminist Theory* (Columbia University Press, 2011), 57; and Elaine Scarry, *The Body in Pain: The Making and Unmaking of the World* (Oxford University Press, 1985), 162.
2 Aldo Leopold, *Round River: From the Journals of Aldo Leopold*, ed. Luna P. Leopold, illustrated by Charles W. Schwartz (Oxford University Press, 1993, orig. 1953), 162.
3 Crews, *Books are Made out of Books*, 233, 235.
4 The Communist Manifesto quotation appears in Fisher, *Capitalist Realism*, 4.
5 Jeremy Bentham, *An Introduction to the Principles of Morals and Legislation*, Dover Philosophical Classics (Dover Publications, 2007), 311, italics his; and Genesis 1:26–28, KJV.
6 Fisher, *Capitalist Realism*, 8, 60, 61.
7 Dianne C. Luce, 'The Road and the Matrix: The World as Tale in *The Crossing*,' *Perspectives on Cormac McCarthy*, rev. edn, eds. Edwin T. Arnold and Dianne C. Luce (University Press of Mississippi, 1999), 195–220: 208.
8 The Woolmer Collection of Cormac McCarthy, collection 92, box 1, file 6.

9 Crews, *Books are Made out of Books*, 298.
10 Scarry, *The Body in Pain*, 63.
11 Leopold, *Round River*, 170.
12 The Cormac McCarthy Papers, collection 91, box 51, file 6, p. 185. In the published version of the novel, Billy does not think this about himself; a rancher tells him that he is a 'peculiar kid' and Billy responds that he always presumed he was rather ordinary (*Cr* 68).
13 Scarry, *The Body in Pain*, 323.
14 McCarthy, 'The Kekulé Problem.'
15 Scarry, *The Body in Pain*, 244, 245.
16 Scarry, *The Body in Pain*, 49, italics hers.
17 The Cormac McCarthy Papers, collection 91, box 1, file 1.
18 Scarry, *The Body in Pain*, 35.
19 For example, McCarthy corresponded with Barry King and Oren Ellis, orthopedic surgeons in El Paso and Santa Fe, respectively, in letters dated from November 1993 through January 1994, about the scene in which a Mexican doctor treats Boyd's gunshot wound. King in particular was enthusiastic about helping McCarthy get the medical and bodily details of injury, differential diagnosis, and treatment accurate to the time and to human reaction in such situations. As to his motivations to provide such lengthy help, King writes, 'I'd get a kick out of having them [medically literate readers] wonder how in the hell you know these things.' This letter from King to McCarthy is dated January 14, 1994. The Cormac McCarthy Papers, collection 91, box 55, file 2.
20 I have argued this point at greater length in 'Inside 'La Periquera': Prisons and Power in *All the Pretty Horses*,' *Beyond Borders: Cormac McCarthy's* All the Pretty Horses, ed. Rick Wallach, Casebook Studies in Cormac McCarthy, vol. 3 (The Cormac McCarthy Society, 2014), 251–263.
21 Braidotti, *Nomadic Subjects*, 57, 58.
22 Braidotti, *Nomadic Subjects*, 24, 25, 22.
23 In an overview of two thousand years of Pueblo communities' responses to climate change in the American southwest, for example, Eric Blinman describes an advanced agricultural economy that adapted drastically, including shifting from maize-based crop production to more varied crop production, in response to multi-year arid cycles. Pueblo history, Blinman suggests, offers a land-use model for contemporary communities facing exigencies of climate change for which they are unprepared. See Eric Blinman, '2000 Years of Cultural Adaptation to Climate Change in the Southwestern United States,' *Ambio*, Special

Report no. 14, Royal Colloquium 'Past Climate Change: Human Survival Strategies' (November 2008), 489–497: 489, 495–496.
24 Wallis R. Sanborn, *Animals in the Fiction of Cormac McCarthy* (McFarland & Co., 2006), 1, 2.
25 Luce, 'The Road and the Matrix,' 94.
26 Peebles, *Page, Stage, Screen*, 54–55.
27 Donna J. Haraway, *When Species Meet* (University of Minnesota Press, 2008), 74, 75.
28 In order, quoations come from The Cormac McCarthy Papers, collection 91, box 91, file 6, pp. 119, 94, 58, 59.
29 Raymond Malewitz, 'Narrative Disruption as Animal Agency in Cormac McCarthy's *The Crossing*,' *Modern Fiction Studies*, vol. 60, iss. 3 (Fall 2014), 544–561: 546, 547–548, 557.
30 The Cormac McCarthy Papers, collection 91, box 91, file 6, p. 45.
31 Sanborn, *Animals in the Fiction of Cormac McCarthy*, 131, 549, 458.
32 Malewitz, 'Narrative Disruption as Animal Agency,' 552, 557.
33 Andy P. Dobson, 'Yellowstone Wolves and the Forces that Structure Natural Systems,' *Plos Biology*, vol. 12, iss. 12 (December 2014), 1–4: 3.
34 Sara Spurgeon, *Exploding the Empire: Myths of Empire on the Postmodern Frontier* (Texas A&M University Press, 2005), 45–46.
35 'William Anson,' *American Quarter Horse Association*, AQHA Hall of Fame.
36 'White Sands National Monument, New Mexico: History and Culture,' *National Park Service*, December 14, 2015.
37 Eaton, 'Dis(re)membered Bodies,' 171, 174.
38 Spurgeon, *Exploding the Empire*, 19.
39 Piketty, *Capital in the Twenty-First Century*, 746.

6

Death and the poet: *Suttree* and art that sustains

> There is a sustained belief, against all evidence, as the drama unfolds, that this woman will actually kill herself.
> (J. Howard Woolmer, letter to Cormac McCarthy, July 15, 1986)
>
> Learning to die is a practice of living, after all.
> (Stephanie LeMenager, 'Climate Change and the Struggle for Genre')[1]

In a folder containing early sketches for *Blood Meridian*, a page ends on a section McCarthy titled 'the godfire (chap head),' indicating that he was playing with the idea of making this a pivotal moment. What is 'the godfire'? It is unclear.[2] However, the brief passage that follows is one of the few descriptions of humans possessing a common soul in McCarthy's works, in contrast to nonhuman animals, which are frequently depicted as having access to a communal soul or common 'fire,' as the previous chapter demonstrated. The 'godfire' passage describes the kid and others members of Glanton's gang around a campfire at night: the men 'watched the fire which does contain within it something of the ~~soul of~~ man ^himself inasmuch as he is less without it, divided from his fathers and an exile. For each fire is all fires, the first fire and the last ever to be.'[3] This scene was excised, likely because the thematic force of *Blood Meridian* shears away from depicting the creative energy of humans. The published novel's version of the kid is about as far from any recognition of a common 'fire' as he can get and still maintain glimmers of pro-social ethics. Still, the language of the 'fire which does contain' some element of common human *being* recurs throughout McCarthy's fiction, suggesting that the 'godfire' stands for a deep knowledge of humanity, and narrative represents a vehicle by which this knowledge passes from individual to individual, linking them into a community.

The previous chapter examined nomads as human exemplars of a non-anthropocentric ethics, and nomadic economics as a system that values the wellbeing of complex adaptive systems over the wellbeing of individual species in that system. It also explored the way in which narrative codes the ineffable, expressing the meaningfulness of a being (its 'soul') in terms of time, event, and symbol. However, these foundational arguments about what a non-anthropocentric ethics might look like and the role of narrative in coding ethics leave an important question unexplored. Since nomadic ethics flourish in depopulated landscapes, can they be more broadly applied in an urban environment? This chapter, to answer that question, examines McCarthy's depictions of human communities and the 'fire' that connects them in *Suttree*.

Because *Suttree* is McCarthy's only novel to date with a primarily urban setting, it offers readers a sense of what a populated communitarian ethics might look like. Vereen Bell calls it a 'thickly populated novel—Dickensian in this respect,' and notes that 'both the novel's brisk pace and its cheerfully episodic and elliptical progress contribute to the illusion that the people in the book have taken command of its structure.'[4] The cityscape of Knoxville is described as a sort of hellscape, an '[e]ncampment of the damned,' but rather than denigrating its inhabitants, the novel aesthetically fuses the city's population with its narrative structure in a way that emphasizes the humanity of its filthy, Dickensian masses, offering images of healthy imagined communities subsisting at or below the poverty line yet characterized by solidarity and compassion (*S* 3). In one of the only examples we have of McCarthy explaining his own work, his Guggenheim Fellowship application includes this description of the manuscript that would become *Suttree*: 'The overall effect' of this novel-in-process, McCarthy writes, 'aims not at total knowledge of life in this city, but at an understanding of what life here would mean to a person who was totally aware. In a sense, then, the characters are the *embodiment of a single soul*.'[5]

Suttree also presents McCarthy's most direct representation of a character identified as an artist of the written word, albeit in the most generic sense, and for that reason, the novel offers the clearest argument for the role of art in affirming humans' sense of meaningful or 'right' orientation to their own place in the world and to others. Early drafts of the novel refer to the eponymous protagonist, Cornelius Suttree, as 'the poet,' suggesting that McCarthy envisioned identifying him explicitly as an artist.[6] Suttree's connection to poetry is less than obvious, however: at no point does Suttree write or identify himself as a writer. He is a poet in much the same way as is Stephen Dedalus; his narrative point of view represents the novel's arguments about the role of literature more than it represents the character's engagement in the profession. In much the same way as the novel might represent 'a single soul' through its myriad characters, Suttree might represent artistic endeavors writ large.

While McCarthy's nomadic wanderers offer insight into how he imagines an ethics of care enacted in the world, it is less easy to see the political and social applications of this embodied ethics of care. Suttree offers just such a vision. It is not only distinctive in McCarthy's corpus as an urban novel; it is also the most explicitly political, insofar as its depiction of the interconnections of economics, class, gender, and race illuminate both the alienating forces of capitalism and the regenerative forces of humans pushing back against that alienation. Louis Palmer argues that the rage and violence of class warfare simmers, barely contained, throughout Suttree, rendering it 'a chronicle of class war out of the Communist Manifesto, pitting a hapless proletarian underclass against a crass and rapacious owning class.'[7] McCarthy's works, in general, eschew calls for practical and political action, but they are nevertheless centered on the capacity for the artifact (in his case, narrative) to be a conduit for a radical reorientation of value, where the reader is tasked with restructuring their relationship to others in the world around them.[8] McCarthy's narratives focus more on men of action than on intellectuals, more on praxis than on artistic creation, but they nevertheless return, over and over, to the notion that the highest pursuit of human beings may be to learn to act in a creaturely way and to recognize the shared interdependence of natural systems. For an early screenplay version of *Cities of the*

Plain, McCarthy offers a sketch of a relatively minor character, a blind pianist 'whose blindness has bequeathed to him a humanity that his intellectual qualities might otherwise have smothered.'[9] The prophetic and humane role played by the blind pianist in that screenplay suggests McCarthy's use of art and suffering as twinned activities that focus attention on what meaningful engagement with others might look like, a way of life which 'intellectual' pursuits may be inadequate to teach. This chapter will attempt to unsmother that notion of humanity in McCarthy's most human-centric novel by examining *Suttree*'s structural and thematic calls for readers to practice a different way of seeing the world, a sight that is more prophetic than pragmatic.

One early draft sketch in *Suttree* suggests how the character of 'the poet' reflects the notion that art can be a vehicle for examining the 'common soul' of humanity and the ethics of communal wellbeing. In the published novel, this scene is where Suttree meets the 'Indian,' a 'stranger' who appears on the river during the early months of summer, 1952 (*S* 221). Suttree invites him over, the man gives Suttree bait, and they share a communal cup of coffee, the sharing of that beverage performed 'gravely' and representing the kind of hospitality that characterizes communal ethics throughout McCarthy's corpus (223). After that, the man disappears for a few days and, when he comes back, shares his real name—'Michael'—with Suttree as well as the story that he was jailed for 'vag' for those few days (224–225, 223). 'Vag,' as McCarthy defines it for a translator working on the book, is short for 'vagrancy—a catch-all sort of charge used for arresting people with no visible means of support.'[10] In an unpublished early sketch of this scene, Suttree sees the man after his absence and the man smiles at him. The narrator says of Suttree,

> Perhaps the poet even suspected that the radiance of Michael's smile and the warmth of his greeting in return hinged at least somewhat on the sound of his own name which he had not heard pronounced by another human being for almost seven years. He said: Hello Michael. And something happened in Michael that seemed to make him more whole.[11]

In the published novel, this kind of fulsome description of human warmth is tempered, but its thematic force still resonates. The protagonist's elliptical, reiterative quest is to find some deep connection with others that will grant his life purpose and meaning, or, short of that, to escape life altogether. What tethers him to life is human connection. Artistic creation is, fundamentally, an expression of desire for meaningful interaction or engagement with others. Through the character of 'the poet,' *Suttree* suggests that narrative can forge imaginative communities, and such an act may hold great power and significance. As this elided passage suggests, as is true for Michael, being truly *seen* by another may 'make [us] more whole.'

If *Suttree* is ultimately interested in those actions and attitudes that make us more whole and weave us into a complex living web, it is also interested in what rends us from each other. Palmer identifies the novel's thematic interweaving of order and chaos, community and disparate wanderings by individuals, as representing 'the fruits of an industrial civilization with its environment and human waste products, the rewards of class conformity and race and gender privilege against their terrible costs.'[12] The patriarchal order of industrial civilization, through the mouthpiece of Suttree's father, claims that the world is run by civically responsible, affluent people, and Suttree's community of dispossessed, unemployed, and lower-working-class folk is nothing 'but a dumbshow composed of the helpless and the impotent' (14). Suttree comes to believe that the 'common soul' is best represented through the 'helpless and the impotent,' but the novel does not present a facile optimism about human connection through the working-class masses. The very real vices of 1950s America—racism, sexism, and income inequality—wound racial and gender minorities and rend communities.

Consistent with the focus on injured bodies in the Border Trilogy, arguments for an embodied ethics are depicted through bodies in pain in *Suttree*. The novel is haunted by the act of suicide, the most extreme form of self-injury. Suicide enforces with finality the 'loneliness' of the individual—a loneliness that Suttree suggests is a common grief of all humans. The opening scene of the novel sees Suttree, literally adrift on his fishing boat, called to attention by the retrieval of a dead body being pulled out of the water. As the other fishermen and watchers gather, rumor suggests the body is of a suicide (10). Suttree, attempting to find information about this suicide, strikes up a conversation with an old man. He gives a catfish to the old man, apparently a common act, and they perform a ritual of refusal, where the old man objects to receiving the gift three times and then accepts it (12). Throughout the novel, the ritualization of caregiving, such as offering food, drink, or medical treatment, underscores its centrality to communal wellbeing. Plucking at the fabric of communal wellbeing are acts of injury and pain, which isolate the individual from the group, and the most extreme form of isolation, suicide, provides a through-line, drawing attention to the dire consequences of the unraveling of this delicate tapestry.

Suicide and moral choice in the Anthropocene

In *Anthropocene Reading: Literary History and Geologic Times* (2017), Tobias Menely and Jesse Oak Taylor suggest that literature about the Anthropocene offers critical insight into how we as a species are shaping our understanding of the epoch. 'The Anthropocene' is the term frequently used to codify that period of geological time defined by ineradicable anthropogenic changes in earth's stratigraphic signature, in sediments and ice and atmospheric shifts, changes from pesticides to plastics, from carbon dioxide concentrations in the atmosphere to fallout from nuclear bombs. The challenge with defining the Anthropocene lies not in identifying clearly marked boundaries of geological time affected by anthropogenic action, but rather in defining *who* the 'Anthropos' are. 'Responsibility and vulnerability are asymmetrically distributed' in this epoch, they point out.[13] Literature can provide a particularly resonant naming of the Anthropos: those who wound others, individually and corporately, and those made vulnerable in the wounding.

Stephanie LeMenager argues that 'climate fiction' or 'cli-fi' novels present climate-based catastrophe as the precipitating action that ultimately offers a radical invitation 'to white America and wealthy America … to learn to die.' Such fictions pose a need for white and wealthy Americans to recognize their own implication in the climate disaster toward which the planet careens. The call to 'learn to die,' she says, is a call to recognize oneself as 'nonsovereign and embodied.'[14] This call to die is often presented in McCarthy's fiction in the context of suicide, an act defended by several characters in different works as an ethical choice to remove oneself from the biome precisely because one recognizes one's own failure to behave in ways that heal rather than harm.[15] Characters openly contemplate the idea that humanity as a species may be so destructive that the planet would be better off without them. Because only white, privileged-class characters contemplate this question, McCarthy points to the particularly pernicious effects of one demographic on American ecosystems and human communities. Counter to these characters' contemplation of suicide are other characters who argue that humans may be adaptive and creative enough to find ways to heal their communities, if not the planet. This confliction plays out through *Suttree*'s thematic focus on suicide.

Despite the novel's opening in which Suttree watches from his skiff as the body of a suicide is dragged from the river, such deaths remain largely implicit through the rest of the novel. Wesley G. Morgan suggests that one other character may have committed suicide: a friend of Suttree's, 'Hoghead' Henry, who is referenced in only one sentence in the novel, appears to be based on a real-life acquaintance of McCarthy's, a boy who killed himself during a game of Russian roulette in his teenage years.[16] Suicide may be largely implicit, but critics nevertheless concur that it haunts the novel, an interpretative concurrence influenced by Frank W. Shelton's persuasive 1990 article 'Suttree and Suicide.'[17] Although Shelton focuses on the question of suicide as a metaphorical theme codifying Suttree's existential moral quandary about human meaningfulness, suicide in *Suttree* is a question of both material reality and existential philosophy. Obsessed with his dead twin and devastated by the death of his son, Suttree is haunted by the specter of death, his fear of it, and his anxiety about being worthy of the life that he currently has. He is a man in crisis, drinking to excess and engaging in risky behavior. Once, while wandering drunk and lost in a thunderstorm, he queries, 'Am I a monster, are there monsters in me?' (366) All of life is monstrous, and Knoxville is filled with the grotesque, the deformed, the abhorrent, and Suttree not least of all. Suttree is drawn to Joyce, a sex worker whom he calls 'the very witch of fuck,' at least in part because he feels a tragic communion with her that is due to the record of self-harm scarring her skin (393). He observes the 'light tracery of old razor scars on her inner wrists' and they engage in sensual and then sexual intimacy, and yet, even so, he questions, 'Why then this loneliness?' (404) It is an impossible quandary that Suttree returns to in his typhoid-induced dream vision at the end of the novel, when he claims that 'all souls are one and all souls lonely' (459). We are a species haunted by our desire for meaningfulness and for connection while simultaneously being chronically bad at both. Death, the only moment in which we are guaranteed to be utterly alone, is the isolating experience that we hold in common with every one of the billions of our species. Suttree's contrary poles of desire—to be 'unique' and to be un-lonely—reflect a fundamental tension at the heart of the human condition, but it is a tension that the novel embeds in descriptions of scars, vomit, dizziness, fever, physiological manifestations of hunger, cold, and fear, and physical expressions of psychological pain such as tears or self-harm. Existential questions about human meaningfulness can never be fully divorced from the ways our flesh encounters the world around us. Suicide is the most self-alienating act a human can take; in McCarthy's works, it is also an act always considered in the context of community: as a result of pain at having lost community; an act of love requiring a refusal to prolong the suffering of the community; or an attempt to reduce harm to the community by eliminating a damaging member of a predacious species.

David Kushner describes a conversation he overheard while he was at the Santa Fe Institute writing a profile of McCarthy. A group of biologists and evolutionary economists were discussing 'the relationship between animal behavior and marketlike forces,' and the subject of suicide emerged: 'the researchers dig into the idea that suicide attempts can be evaluated as a kind of expression of market forces—a threat to remove oneself as a source of benefits to others,' Kushner writes. Then, he says,

> The neuroscientist in the corner raises her hand and poses a question to the group: 'Does anyone know another animal besides humans who commit suicide?'
> Brains churn. Air conditioning whirs. For once, though, the scientists are stumped.
> Then the cowboy chimes in, as he often does, with the answer.
> 'Dolphins,' he says softly. 'Dolphins do.'[18]

While there is debate about whether it should be classified as suicide, there are accounts of dolphins' 'intentional failure to thrive' in captivity or isolated from their pods, where they refuse to breathe and suffocate. Dolphins and whales, too—as McCarthy shows in *Whales and Men*—are social species, and they exhibit vulnerability when affected by mass changes to group dynamics or isolation from their group.[19] Social species may be ill equipped to deal with the injury or loss of their members. Humans are no exception—except, perhaps, in their predilection for being the cause of their own isolation, injury, and death.

Applying the methodology of complexity science to suicide rates in developed nations, Rosalia Condorelli argues that a steep rise in suicide in the first two decades of the twentieth century and subsequent flattening of that rate in the late twentieth century suggests that Western society, a complex adaptive system, reacted negatively to the injurious isolation of modernization, and then began to adapt.[20] A complexity epistemological paradigm would hypothesize that humans would demonstrate negative or non-adaptive behavior in the face of rapid change but, over time, would adapt to the increased instability of their contexts: order arising from chaos. That premise seems to correlate with suicide patterns in Western nations, Condorelli notes. However, she does not address the more recent, troubling surge in rates of deaths of despair in the US in the early twenty-first century. A report for the Republican Joint Economic Committee made to the US Congress in 2019 found that 'failure to thrive' deaths (defined as deaths from suicide, drugs or alcohol, or alcohol-caused conditions such as cirrhosis) had risen worryingly. By 2013 deaths of despair had surpassed the previous record from 1907, and in 2019 they were higher than at any time previously recorded. The report explains that these data are partially accounted for by the opioid crisis, but even controlling for opioid-related causes, deaths of despair would still be higher than 'at any point in the past one hundred years,' indicating the profound impact of economic and social precarity in an age of unprecedented climate change, migration, and income inequality.[21]

In McCarthy's works, suicide is never depicted as selfish, egoistic, or weak. Instead, individuals contemplating suicide frame that choice in acknowledgments of fragmenting social cohesion and violence within human communities and expressed outward toward other species in their ecosystems. Suttree contemplates suicide but ultimately decides to 'flee' the lure of physical death by his own hand; he does so by leaving Knoxville and 'divesting' himself of his associations with his father, property ownership, and his biological family. Suttree diminishes the harm to his community that would be incurred by his suicide, recognizing it as a radical and absolute act of self-isolation. He practices instead a different form of death, a metaphysical 'dying into' the world. Suttree relinquishes his 'subtle obsession with uniqueness' and adopts in its place the humility to recognize the oneness of the 'souls' of all humans (113). His self-exile from Knoxville suggests a critical examination of the role of power brokers in urban environments, and the need for those born into strata that grant them the privileges of consumption, generational wealth accumulation, and freedom of movement to 'die' to those very structures. As Suttree quits Knoxville, a man driving a car stops to offer him a ride. The concluding scene, in which a solitary man on the road encounters the kindness of strangers, draws attention to a recurring theme in McCarthy's fiction: our alienation is as much a story we tell ourselves as is our radical connection to each other. In this conclusion, *Suttree* resolves the novel's quandary about how a privileged-class person might express moral responsibility in a world in which humans are largely responsible for the destructive forces at work in their world, but solely responsible for rectifying that harm.

Suttree's resolution to the problem of suicide is not unique for McCarthy. In a letter to J. Howard Woolmer dated July 15, 1986, McCarthy writes about a play he has recently seen and which affected him deeply, likely Marsha Norman's 1983 Pulitzer Prize-winning *'Night, Mother*. McCarthy describes his reaction to watching this play as a growing dread of its inevitable act. 'There is a sustained belief,' he writes, 'against all evidence, as the drama unfolds, that this woman will actually kill herself.'[22] McCarthy suggests a fascination with the use of suicide both as a literary device—an act that creates an existential threat to the subjects—and thematically, as a way to explore questions of human meaningfulness. His 2013 'novel in dramatic form,' *The Sunset Limited*, replicates the literary device of *'Night, Mother*: the play relies for its dramatic intensity on the audience's growing confidence that Black will fail to save White, and that White will commit suicide.[23] White's rationale for suicide is based on a cost–benefit analysis of continued existence. Given the accrual of '[t]orment, betrayal, loss, suffering, pain, age, indignity, and hideous lingering illness' that characterize human experience, he says, to what end does one persist? (*TSL* 137) White explains that '[b]ooks and music and art' assert meaningfulness in spite of suffering and indignity, but art has lost its ability to make an effective argument for meaningfulness in a post-Holocaust world (13). 'Western Civilization finally went up in smoke in the chimneys of Dachau,' he says (15). By implication, Western society's capacity for inhumanity trumps its capacity for generative creation. Not insignificantly, White is a white academic who has benefitted from a particular middle-class affluence. Black, who does not share White's evaluation of suicide as an ethical choice, is a working-class Black man in a high-poverty urban center. *The Sunset Limited* is, to date, McCarthy's most extended illustration of a sense of moral injury that is so profound as to create a viable philosophical defense of suicide. It also demonstrates the critical role of distinctions between people groups in terms of relative complicity and vulnerability. Because McCarthy's works tend to display a default narrative center—a white, masculine, and 'Western civilization' view of the US—that community's complicity in the world's unmaking takes center stage, but *The Sunset Limited* and *Suttree* suggest that any attempt to make the world again must look different when applied to this people who have so long dominated the 'narrative center' than it does when applied to historically economically and socially marginalized people.

 In McCarthy's works, characters who contemplate suicide express an existential pain that separates them from others and that is chronic in humanity, that engenders violence against the natural world, and that inflicts wounds both physical and emotional on human and nonhuman others. To cauterize the wound is, perhaps, to staunch the bleeding out of the life of the world itself, but against such rationality, the irrationality of hope persists. Without evidence that their actions make rational sense or have any hope of effectively 'making' what has been unmade, characters push back against the call to physically die with calls to live as nomads, street preachers, or their like. In *The Road*, for example, the man's wife tells him that living in this damaged world is impossible and to try is cruel, but that love gives us the illusion of a reason to try; the man in response looks at his boy and thinks, 'I have you' (46). The street preacher Black falls on his knees on an abandoned stage, swearing to find White and save him one more day, every day, for as long as it takes (*TSL* 142). *Suttree*, perhaps more than any of McCarthy's other works, presents arguments in favor of the evolutionarily justifiable notion of suicide in the context of urbanization and overpopulation that swept through 'first world' nations in the latter part of the twentieth century. Against its depiction of modern alienation, it makes a compelling case for the belief—however unjustifiable, however irrational—that we just might 'have' each other.

Suttree and an embodied ethics of care

Because it is an urban novel, the alternatives to alienation in *Suttree* are particularly interesting case studies for how McCarthy imagines an ethical value system might look in an industrialized landscape. However, it is important to note that extreme alienation—with suicide as its most dramatic instantiation—and radical connection are not pitted against each other but rather are aesthetically fused, suggesting that the fully aware person in modernity experiences both alienation and connection. The novel initially suggests social collapse through the use of bifurcating gnostic language applied to religious, political, and geographic images.[24] For example, Suttree remembers his dead twin and thinks that the dead twin is 'in the limbo of the Christless righteous, I in a terrestrial hell,' evoking the religious and locational aspects of gnosticism (14). Suttree concludes that he has more in common with whales and bats, 'life forms meant for other mediums than the earth,' a more ambiguous notion that suggests bifurcating evolutionary paths, where certain mammals remain sea creatures or airborne rather than earth-born like most of their mammalian kin (14). A political and geographic schism divides the 'netherworld' of the poor on the riverbanks from the 'upper' world of the fully employed citizens (e.g., 14).

Among these rifts, reciprocal and embodied acts of care emphasize the material body as the vehicle that, if it can receive injury, can also receive balm and succor. Acts of caregiving bind communities and individuals and form a counter-melody in this fugue-like narrative. For example, early in the novel, Suttree goes to a bar to hang out with his 'fellowship of the doomed'; throughout the rest of the novel, his peregrinations into the 'lower' world—the 'terrestrial hell' of Knoxville's McAnally flats—are movements into community characterized by kindness and mutual gestures of protection or comfort (13). As is characteristic in this death-haunted novel, Suttree is able to articulate the central argument at the heart of the text only when he finds the dead body of a ragpicker whom he has somewhat inconsistently looked out for. Suttree tells the dead ragpicker that he has no right to die alone. 'You have no right to represent people this way,' he tells the corpse. 'A man is all men' (422). Suttree's journey culminates in a gnostic dream-vision where the eternal judge charges him with a crime: '[Y]ou betook yourself to various low places within the shire of McAnally and there did squander several ensuing years in the company of thieves, derelicts, miscreants, pariahs, poltroons' (457). Even as he is being censured by the 'father/God' for his choice to live among thieves and derelicts, Suttree realizes that this community is one that breaks down the division between the lower and upper worlds; he imagines 'the archetypal patriarch' unlocking Hades, setting loose 'screaming fiends' who 'with their cloaks smoking carry the Logos itself from the tabernacle and bear it through the streets' (458). In the end, the destructive forces of this dark planet collide with the energy, resilience, hope, humility, and grace of the 'shabby' folk who live on it. In those moments when the literary grotesque emerges dominant, readers see most clearly the novel's claims about meaningful human existence. As Wolfgang Kayser argues, the grotesque in gothic fiction is 'revealed only by its confrontation with its opposite, the sublime.'[25] Gnostic imagery that suggests a division of the world thus gives way to the grotesque in images that fuse death, decay, and the divine, illuminating *Suttree*'s fundamental argument that a 'man is all men,' and the alienation we fear most is that which we must embrace in order to live an authentic life in modernity.

Stylistically, the novel's narrative structure reiterates its thematic focus on the double helix of humans' dual capacity and inclination for harm and healing, death-dealing and life-saving. The economics of harm and the ethics of healing are depicted through chiastic structures that emphasize the geographic divisions of race and class. Through symbolic transgressions of geographic boundaries, the narrator imagines ways in which people might stitch a divided human society together again. Chiastic structures, common in biblical and epic narratives, offer reiterative themes that double with inflections, much as in a musical fugue: theme A leads to theme B, with a returning theme A', followed by theme B', and so on. Scholars have previously noted chiastic structures in the novel, with perhaps the most thorough examination offered by Dianne C. Luce, who identifies 'metaphorical, geometrical patterns of escape and return, centrifugal pull, and spiraling descent.'[26] Through it all is the chiastic doubled-ness of human potentiality, symbolized by recurring emphasis on symbolic doubling. 'Nothing in the novel is undoubled,' Luce says. 'Suttree himself is doubled not only by his dead twin or by his "little buddy" Gene [Harrogate] or by Hooper the ragpicker (who stands for all mortals) but by all' (198). In addition to character doubling, the chiastic narrative structures suggest the capacity for inversion, from harm to healing and from healing to harm. They also suggest a critical dual reality: humans operate individually in terms of choice, yet their choices are ineradicably enmeshed in their communities. All souls may be lonely, but all bodies affect their ecosystems.

A chiastic narrative structure opens the novel, with a series of scenes in 'present day' 1952 forming the A theme. The thematic content of these initial scenes is reiterated in reverse sequence in the next section of the novel, a flashback to a year earlier (theme A'). The first scene introduces readers to Suttree on his houseboat; a suicide sparks his engagement with other fishers; he falls into a dream where he recalls his father's last letter, establishing his alienation from his paternal heritage; he dreams of his dead twin brother. His maternal uncle arrives the next day, and after Suttree insists that his father's classism drove Suttree from his family, he leaves to spend time with his working-class friends in a bar. In the next section of the novel, the narrative shifts into Gene Harrogate's perspective and reveals the events of the prior year, 1951: Suttree meeting Harrogate for the first time in jail; Suttree making his mother cry when she visits him in prison; being released; going to Market Street, whose 'piscean wares' suggest the twinned imagery latent in his decision to join the fishing community in Knoxville; meeting up with his working-class friends; and finally drinking himself to unconsciousness and nearly dying of exposure in a semi-accidental near-suicide. The chiastic structure looks like this:

  A (1952): a suicide (10)
    B: a ritual of food establishing connection with a lower-class friend (12)
      C: feelings of alienation (father's letter); rumination on his dead twin (14)
        D: angry rejection of his family (specifically, maternal uncle) (20)
          E: fellowship in a bar (23)
          E': one year ago (1951): fellowship in prison with Harrogate (41)
        D': violent rejection of his family (specifically, mother) (61)
      C': feelings of community on Market Street/piscean imagery (67)
    B': ritual of food at the diner with J-Bone, Boneyard, and Hoghead (77)
  A': first time Suttree almost dies of exposure while drunk (passive suicide) (78)

This chiastic narrative structure reiterates the major themes of the novel in fugue-like pairs (suicide, fellowship with the downcast, rejection of parents, and so forth) and is further emphasized by recurring symbolic imagery of doubledness: inverted twins (one dead, one living; one left-handed, one right-handed) and twinned communities (the poor Black and white districts in Knoxville; the river-based fishing community and the downtown city), illuminating the artificial alienation of human communities through economic and racial hierarchies.

    These alienating structures are critiqued through characters' broaching of the boundaries between their respective spaces. At one point, Harrogate, amorous of watermelons, expresses the narrative of white supremacy in the South that justified segregation by asserting essential and hierarchical racial differences.[27] Harrogate thinks that 'he'd not be put to living next door to niggers' and goes in search of a white neighborhood; the narrator mockingly subverts his racism: 'He'd come from the dwellingstreets of the whites to those of the blacks and no gray middle folk did he see' (101). Harrogate is too poor for the white community, yet refuses to see himself in common cause with the social rejection experienced by the Black community. In his stumbling and bumbling journey, he transgresses Black and white communities, unable to find a home in either because of his self-association with a racial hierarchy that makes him 'higher' than his Black neighbors.

Suttree's mental interrogations of race and class are more explicit than Harrogate's instinctive wanderings, but they replicate much of the thematic emphasis on the human predilection for violence toward its own species. Unlike Harrogate's, though, his wanderings tend to at least entertain glimpses of humans' capacity to regenerate or adapt in pro-social, communal ways. One such example occurs when Suttree trespasses in the abandoned remains of his ancestral home. He imagines the violence of his ancestors' heraldic tradition, and the narrator calls him the '[r]eprobate scion of doomed Saxon clans' (136). He leaves because 'he was only passing through' (136). Earlier, he has told his maternal uncle that his father 'married beneath him' and so considers his children beneath him. 'Blood will tell' was his father's favorite saying (19). Suttree genetically embodies two separate classes, the heraldic 'Saxon' of his father and the working class of his mother, and he metaphorically and literally 'passes through' the chandeliered halls of his ancestral home as well as the working-class neighborhoods his maternal uncle lives in. Like Harrogate, Suttree is meant to unlearn these artificial divisions, but, also like Harrogate, he usually fails to recognize the symbolic importance of his own transgression of these boundaries. For example, Suttree at one point wakes from a blackout drunk episode in the slums on the riverbank, a Black district that is 'a maze of shacks and coops, nameless constructions of tarpaper and tin' (81). He heads up, away from the riverbank, in search of a white neighborhood where he will know people; he 'cut down an alley and went past a row of warehouses.' In this working-class district, streets now have names, and train tracks divide them from the nameless maze below (82). Rather than its being a safe haven, however, a police car stops Suttree in this working-class neighborhood and arrests him for vagrancy (83). Later, a burial scene provides an ironic revision of Hamlet's Yorick scene, where Hamlet reflects on the artificiality of the division between nobility and peasants, as death makes equals of us all.[28] In this scene, Suttree's young son is being buried. Suttree hides during the funeral and afterward pays the gravediggers to let him fill his son's grave. The sheriff picks him up and, after calling Suttree a 'fourteen carat gold plated son of a bitch,' tells him, 'Everything's important. A man lives his life, he has to make it important' (156, 157). The sheriff voices the novel's insistence that readers find meaning in ordinary actions and practice an ethics of care that breaches the alienating divisions between humans and forges community out of isolation, because no one exists in isolation, and harm to any one harms all.

The multitude of characters in *Suttree* all experience and exemplify radical isolation from community. Some react with acts of violence or injury: Harrogate, alienated from Black communities by his belief in his own whiteness and from white neighborhoods by his vagrancy and poverty, plots mindless mayhem. He spends 'hot summer nights' in 'drunkenness and tales of violence,' ultimately attempting to blow up a bank and creating what feels like an earthquake in the city (264, 270). Joyce and Suttree attempt a romantic relationship, but his pain and hers are unbreachable; unable to heal each other, they find that the relationship founders and she leaves him (414–415). Other characters bridge that alienation, usually through a physical expression of care for another person. For example, a one-eyed Black woman with dwarfism serves as the unofficial medic to this frequently abused community of drunks; once, she puts ice on Suttree's head wound, 'a gesture both grave and gracious that acknowledged endless armies of the unbending pale' (229). Her connection with that mysterious sense of human interdependence is reiterated after Ab Jones dies. Suttree thinks that her blind eye is 'an eye for another kind of seeing like the pineal eye in atavistic reptiles watching through time, through conjugations of space and matter to that still center where the living and the dead are one.' As Suttree learns to pay attention to a deep knowledge of human interdependence, he too is able to see 'through conjugations of space and matter to that still center' (447).

In his notes on the novel, McCarthy suggests that he drew heavily for inspiration from Nathanael West's *Day of the Locust* (1939), a novel about a young artist who arrives in Hollywood to paint a studio set called 'the Burning of Los Angeles.' The painting becomes an allusion to the chaos that subsumes the city once its characters, the exploited laboring class in Hollywood, realize that the American Dream is a myth and revolt.[29] *Suttree* certainly conjures the rage of West's novel's poor, but in the end, Knoxville does not burn. This is not to suggest that McCarthy's novel mitigates the harm of industrialization, or of class and race implicated in the vicious stratification of America's urban centers. Instead, the rage and despair of the poor are countered by adaptation and by images of people who learn to live in the decay while making meaningful human connections: J. Bone and the rest of Suttree's under-employed, alcoholic crew; Ab Jones and the rest of the Black community in segregated Knoxville; Trippin Through the Dew, Joyce, and other socially marginalized sex workers. These characters experience a form of escape from alienating existence through mimetic nomadism: the Tennessee fishing communities may lack names on their streets or permanent housing, but they demonstrate that authentic and un-alienated life *is* possible in urban environments. If Suttree's internal journey is one aimed at dissolving the boundaries that isolate communities and individuals, the racially and wealth-segregated landscape of the novel suggests a radical repudiation of hierarchical economies. The novel suggests that human populations are as antagonistic to their own communal wellbeing as they are a detriment to natural systems. Against violence-coded power structures, acts of caregiving represent communitarian ethics.

Nor is it incidental that 'care' is embodied, given concretion in the image of a hand tending to a wound or offering a cup of water to a thirsty body. While McCarthy shies from explicitly political or activist-oriented narrative devices, his research notes and manuscript drafts show a consistent interest in the politics of care in the subject area of health and the human body. Such 'activism-oriented' moments can be found in *Whales and Men* and in the early screenplay version of *No Country for Old Men*. In *Whales and Men*, John returns to medical school and opens a clinic in a conflict zone as the physical manifestation of his internal transformation after witnessing the communal care of whales. In the screenplay *No Country for Old Men*, Sheriff Bell and Llewellen Moss manage to get the illicit drug money back from the hitmen, and Bell ensures that the local Texas community reaps the benefits of that cash in the form of 'Doc White' hiring thirty-two people to deposit $10,000 at a time (the maximum amount not flagged by the FBI for investigation) to form a 'corporation,' a shell entity that would evade taxation in order to build 'a clinic' for the community.[30] McCarthy's interest in the economic politics of healthcare provision in these early drafts suggests its thematic importance as representative of physical and metaphysical care for the corporate human body. Into such a context, the comforting hand a Black woman tending to white Suttree's wounds represents a form of care for an individual body that speaks to a larger recognition of care for others as the root of corporate health.

In one of the most memorable scenes of caregiving, as Suttree is preparing to leave Knoxville, his trans friend Trippin Through the Dew 'reached out sadly' and they 'stood there holding hands in the middle of the little street' (468). This image of connection is superimposed on a rift: Suttree is leaving, not to return, and even another hand holding him is not enough to actually hold him. Over and against images of care throughout McCarthy's fiction looms the ever-present specter of death as the ultimate separation. As Suttree rides away, the car passes the 'dead immured with the bones of friends and forebears,' and the dead represent the very body of Knoxville itself, the flesh and bone of its 'darker town' (471, 3). Death and the dead are not merely gothic horror, however; they represent what the modern world may wish to ignore but cannot: we are the dead, our bodies made of the very material stuff of others.

In this way, *Suttree* can be read as an *ars moriendi* for the modern age, a call for divestiture of the ego and of the accumulative 'stuff' of a privileged consumer class: only Suttree, of all his community, must divest himself of the 'amulets' of his father's class and status, taking 'for talisman the simple human heart within him' (468). His urban peregrinations stitch together the class- and race-divided purlieus of 'lower' Knoxville symbolically, but Suttree is no savior, literally or symbolically. In his only exemplary act, Suttree casts off every representation of his claims to status. The novel does not issue a call to *all* readers to remember their common end, but rather to *certain* readers to take responsibility for their role in the divisions of their communities, relinquish material claims to hierarchal status, and adopt in its place a non-self-centered humility. With that humility, readers may choose to live like McCarthy's wandering characters like Suttree when he heads out on the road, or the father and boy on their own ash-blighted path, or Billy Parham on horseback and on foot at the end of *Cities of the Plain*, in resilient, courageous, adaptive relationship to their bioregional homes. They may also choose to live like the rooted, working-class communities Suttree has left behind, perhaps alienated from capitalist 'success' but nevertheless 'carrying the fire,' along with their grief and pain, back into the 'common enterprise of men' (*TR* 238, *APH* 235).

Notes

1 Letter dated July 15, 1986, found in The Woolmer Collection of Cormac McCarthy, collection 92, box 1, folder 6; Stephanie LeMenager, 'Climate Change and the Struggle for Genre,' *Anthropocene Reading: Literary History in Geologic Times*, eds. Tobias Menely and Jesse Oak Taylor (Pennsylvania State University Press, 2017), 220–238: 346.
2 The *Oxford English Dictionary* notes that it appears to be a translation of 'Devangan,' a Brahman caste family named in the *Gazetteer of the Bombay Presidency* (1884) ('God-Fire, n.'). How McCarthy landed on this term is uncertain, although he is an avid reader of the *OED*.
3 The Cormac McCarthy Papers, collection 91, box 38, file 3, unpaginated.
4 Bell, *The Achievement of Cormac McCarthy*, 83.
5 The Albert Erskine Collection, box 29, italics mine.
6 The Cormac McCarthy Papers, collection 91, box 19, file 13; see, e.g., p. 372.
7 Louis H. Palmer III, '"Encampment of the damned": Ideology and Class in *Suttree*,' *The Cormac McCarthy Journal*, vol. 4, iss. 1 (2004), 183–209: 190.
8 Michael Lynn Crews demonstrates how a deep reading of McCarthy's allusions to other authors provides evidence of how this radical reorientation works. Crews traces a specific note on a draft of *Suttree*, 'Butterfly dream in Chuang Tzu (Communal soul) Abbey?,' to Edward

Abbey's *Desert Solitaire*. In *Desert Solitaire*, Abbey references the Taoist Chuang-tse in order to interrogate the 'real' and human interconnectedness with all creation. This concept is translated into *Suttree*'s dream-vision passage that leads Suttree to conclude, 'I know all souls are one and all souls lonely' (*S* 459). That single line in *Suttree* thematically recurs in *Blood Meridian* and in the epilogue to *Cites of the Plain*, both latter passages that reference ideas of a 'common soul' and humanity's inextricable connection to complex systems. The deep resonance of a single reference provides a glimpse into McCarthy's philosophy, his yearning for environmental justice, and his evolving aesthetic style, all at once. See Crews, *Books are Made out of Books*, 48; and The Cormac McCarthy Papers, collection 91, box 19, file 14, unpaginated.
9 The Cormac McCarthy Papers, collection 91, box 69, file 4.
10 The Cormac McCarthy Papers, collection 91, box 19, file 15.
11 The Cormac McCarthy Papers, collection 91, box 19, file 13, p. 372.
12 Palmer, '"Encampment of the damned,"' 186.
13 Menely and Taylor, 'Introduction,' 6, 8.
14 LeMenager, 'Climate Change and the Struggle for Genre,' 231, 230.
15 LeMenager criticizes McCarthy's *The Road* as a failure in this 'call to die' because the 'saviors' at the end of the novel, she claims, arrive first in the form of another white man. In fact there is no indication in the novel that the man is white, and it is the woman of the group who ultimately gives the boy the spiritual guidance that he needs in order to leave his father's dead body and continue on the road (*TR* 241). While Naomi Morgenstern and Nell Sullivan, respectively, offer more nuanced interpretations of the feminine masculinity at play in *The Road*, it is true that McCarthy's fiction as a whole fails to imagine *beyond* patriarchy. Yet what it does imagine, I argue, is precisely what LeMenager calls for in 'cli sci' fiction: a call aimed at the white audience consumer class that they 'learn to die.' See LeMenager, 'Climate Change and the Struggle for Genre,' 231. See also Nell Sullivan, 'The Good Guys: McCarthy's *The Road* as Post-9/11 Male Sentimental Novel,' *Genre*, vol. 46, iss. 1 (Spring 2013), 79–101; and Morgenstern, 'Postapocalyptic Responsibility'.
16 Wesley G. Morgan, 'Suttree's Dead Acquaintances and McCarthy's Dead Friends,' *Cormac McCarthy Journal*, vol. 11, iss. 1 (2013), 96–104: 98.
17 Frank W. Shelton, '*Suttree* and Suicide,' *Southern Quarterly*, vol. 29, iss. 1 (Fall 1990), 71–83.
18 Kushner, 'Cormac McCarthy's Apocalypse.'

19 See Brendan Borrell, 'Why Do Whales Beach Themselves?,' *Scientific American*, Sustainability, June 1, 2009.
20 The Durkheim Theory in sociology posits that the '*more* modernization levels and therefore weakening of social ties and social isolation increase ... *the more* social isolation, loss of identity and loss of the sense of life itself increase, and *the more* people commit suicide.' Suicide rates were measured taking into account marriage and divorce rates and other economic factors relative to suicide, which showed correlations suggesting that social alienation and economic vulnerability led to higher rates of suicide. Subsequently, Western Europe, the US, the United Kingdom, and Commonwealth nations saw those rates of suicide begin to flatten. See Rosalia Condorelli, 'Social Complexity, Modernity and Suicide: An Assessment of Durkheim's Suicide from the Perspective of a Non-Linear Analysis of Complex Social Systems,' *SpringerPlus*, vol. 5 (2016), 374–430: 375, 382, 385, italics hers.
21 'Long-Term Trends in Deaths of Despair,' Social Capital Project Report no. 4–19, Joint Economic Committee—Republicans, September 2019, 4, 9.
22 The Woolmer Collection of Cormac McCarthy, collection 92, box 1, file 6.
23 See my article '"A Howling void"' for a more thorough analysis of the role of suicide in this play.
24 In the novel, 'Gnostic workmen' in Knoxville tear down 'this shabby shapeshow that masks the higher world of form' (*S* 464). Petra Mundik recognizes that *Suttree* is the first of McCarthy's novels to explicitly name the influence of gnosticism, although she describes *Suttree*'s vision of the world as 'wholly dark, Southern Gothic' (*A Bloody and Barbarous God*, 5). As I have argued in '"The Sculptor's art": Mystery and the Material Body in *Suttree*,' the gothic world of Suttree is anything but 'wholly' dark. See Lydia R. Cooper, '"The Sculptor's art": Mystery and the Material Body in *Suttree*,' *You Would Not Believe What Watches: Suttree and Cormac McCarthy's Knoxville*, ed. Rick Wallach, Casebook Studies in Cormac McCarthy, vol. 1 (The Cormac McCarthy Society, 2012), 190–197.
25 Wolfgang Kayser, *The Grotesque in Art and Literature*, trans. Ulrich Weisstein (Peter Smith, 1968), 58. This argument builds on a more in-depth exploration of McCarthy's use of gothic and grotesque imagery to fuse death and life and in so doing to overcome the abjection of those depicted, in my article 'Cormac McCarthy, Tennessee, and the Southern Gothic.' I argue there that the 'medieval aesthetic' of the novel 'explains the problematically profaned sacred imagery in the

novel: *Suttree* is not interested in parsing the hideous from the holy, but rather in finding the holy within the hideous.' This chapter suggests a subtle distinction emerging in *Suttree* between more gnostic imagery used to describe the divisions of the worlds (above and below, limbo and hell) and the fusion of the abject with the subject, the gothic death-in-life as a reclaiming of this world's possibilities. See Cooper, 'Cormac McCarthy, Tennessee, and the Southern Gothic,' 53.

26 Luce, *Reading the World*, 197.

27 As the analysis of *The Gardener's Son* in Chapter 1 above suggests, Harrogate's representation of the intentionally created rifts between lower-class white and black communities in the post-war South is no accident.

28 The whole scene in *Hamlet* reflects this notion, with characteristic lines claiming, 'Imperious Caesar, dead and turn'd to clay,/Might stop a hole to keep the wind away.' William Shakespeare, *Hamlet*, The Riverside Shakespeare, 2nd edn (Houghton Mifflin, 1973), Act V, scene 1, lines 3541–3542.

29 On a page of handwritten notes, McCarthy writes 'CK West?' next to the line 'things became so burdened with meaning that their forms are dimmed' and also 'See West' (underlined twice) next to 'stars jostled on a black and seamless sea.' Not only does West's *Day of the Locust* seem to have provided some thematic resonance with McCarthy's project, but he seems here to be reminding himself to check for linguistic resonance as well. The Cormac McCarthy Papers, collection 91, box 19, file 13.

30 Stacey Peebles notes that these early drafts suggest McCarthy's interest in the politics of healthcare, along with his choice to avoid didacticism in revised manuscripts. Peebles, *Page, Stage, Screen*, 58, 64.

Epilogue

In a letter written to Albert Erskine on October 9, 1979, McCarthy mused on the distinctions between physics and literature. 'Physics is concerned with framing a description of reality and it can maintain a tradition, however esoteric, as long as there are people interested in it,' McCarthy writes.

> Literature, on the other hand, lacks this purity altogether, and as the rise of the masses makes itself felt on an ever increasing scale, those who pursue, or affect to pursue, excellence in letters are driven to higher ground where they scrabble about on the bones of the dead and cultish vogues that no longer have any rooting in the lives of people.

Then, self-consciously, McCarthy writes, 'Well great God who is this curmudgeon.'[1] Certainly, it seems curmudgeonly to mourn the rarity of 'excellence in letters' now, in an age so rich with vibrant literature, but McCarthy's more generalized anxiety about the relevance of literature resonates. In a world of climate crisis, disease, wealth inequality, and warfare, the relevance of science to daily life seems apparent in a way in which literary fiction may not. However necessary scientific and economic solutions to the systems that perpetuate and intensify inequality and environmental disaster are, though, they may not be sufficient to alleviate our alienation and loneliness. Where does the lonely person go to find the world, to reorient themselves to each other, to imaginatively reach out and hold on, for however long they can?

The first three chapters of this book examined the systems and particular communities named in the Anthropos, particularly those in the US, from the owners, operators, and profiteers in the American military and industrial complexes to those who profit from licit and illicit global capitalism at the expense of 'underclasses.' McCarthy's nomads, who wander in adaptive, creative small communities or as individuals who do not exceed the demands of their ecosystems, pose alternatives to pernicious images of aggressive, acquisitive men and exemplify how sovereign bodies might learn to 'die into' the world as non-sovereign bodies. In *Suttree*, McCarthy turns his attention to the corporate body in the urban center, and identifies those who profit from the 'patriarchy'—represented, helpfully, by the literal father in this tale—and those who subsist: the Black Knoxville community, sex workers, and itinerate day laborers. In all of his fiction, from rural Appalachia to the Sonoran desert and from San Francisco to Knoxville, complex biosystems require humans to recognize their non-sovereign status with responsibilities to other living beings. For McCarthy, answers to what makes a life meaningful or how to live in a creaturely way cannot be found solely in the natural and social sciences but must also be sought in language and literature. Food webs, economics, climate crisis, and imperialism collide with syntax and stylistics to create vibrant narrative tapestries.[2] Narrative is distinct from physics, however, as McCarthy's letter to Woolmer suggests. Artistic creation is always referential. The world may contain beings or natural systems that are beautiful without larger purpose than to be, but the artist creates an intentional and interpretive connection between the artifact and its audience. Furthermore, artistic creation operates much like scientific models of chaos: if chaos science studies the global nature of interrelated systems in order to explain unpredictability and irreducible complexity, art explores unpredictability and irreducible complexity in human experience that transcends temporal, social, and geographic divides.

McCarthy's as-yet unpublished novel currently titled *The Passenger* is rumored to be the culmination of his years at the Santa Fe Institute, weaving together his collaborative work on complexity science and narrative. Whether readers will have a chance to see the final, published version of this work is unclear. Equally unknown is whether that novel will offer its rumored meditations on 'madness, genius, and mathematical truth.'[3] Suicide, complexity mathematics, and complicated familial relationships appear to be the book's central themes, although, at the time I am writing this, perpetually delayed publication seems to be its most dominant theme. Regardless of whether or not *The Passenger* will ever exist in a McCarthy-authorized form, its rumored themes are not aberrations, nor are they new directions in his oeuvre. If there is one thing that I hope to have demonstrated through this book's non-chronological structure, it is that McCarthy has persistently paid attention to certain recurring themes: a human yearning for connection and meaningfulness; an awareness of the complex interdependence of ecological life; and a condemnation of human-caused destruction to the biosphere. His fiction has persistently issued calls for embodied ethics that take us out of comfort and into precarity, lives lived in recognition of and respect for complexity, contingency, and adaptation. Precarious lives are not, however, isolated ones; by turning attention to the margins of society in order to look for interventions in or solutions to the destructive tendencies of late modernity and capitalism, McCarthy wields narrative as a mechanism for imagining adaptive, resilient communities and individuals. Above all, McCarthy's approach to literature maps the methods of complexity science onto aesthetic narrative. His approach illustrates the complex interrelation of life, and, within that complexity, identifying the order that emerges. Through narrative, he 'maintains a tradition' of truth-seeking and truth-speaking that calls out pernicious legacies while invoking the best attributes of humanity at the same time.

As McCarthy's fiction from *The Orchard Keeper* through *The Road* illustrates so achingly, both chaos and order are true of human societies. We act out and experience both alienation and interconnection; we destroy and we heal. In the end, whether we acknowledge it or not, we belong to each other and we damage or mitigate damage to our world and to each other; we value or devalue human and nonhuman life. But in this messy tapestry of existence, storytelling is, like *The Crossing*'s image of God as a weaver, an act of ordering complexity. To commit suicide is to snip a thread. To tell each other our stories is to weave ourselves into our vast and colorful universe, and in so weaving our many stories, we hold onto each other, bridging the yawning dark until, like Scheherazade, we may one day wake into a more just dawn.

Notes

1. The Albert Erskine Collection, box 29.
2. Gleick, *Chaos*, 7, 5. In *The Counselor*, McCarthy offers insight into how he conceives of the deep connection between art and science when he has Westray offer the observation that time destroys every 'timeless creation' from 'art' to 'science' (*Co* 61–62). The link between art and science is their atemporality—their ability to evoke meaningfulness unbounded by the duration of a single human lifespan. We 'know' our world and ourselves through art as through science.
3. Jack Martinez, 'New Cormac McCarthy Book 'The Passenger' Unveiled,' *Newsweek*, Culture, August 15, 2015.

Bibliography

Archives

The Albert Erskine Collection, Special Collections of the University of Virginia Library, MSS 13497, Special Collections, University of Virginia Library, Charlottesville, VA.

The Cormac McCarthy Papers, The Wittliff Collections, Southwestern Writers Collection, Alkek Library, Texas State University-San Marcos.

The Guy Davenport Papers, box 133, correspondence, Harry Ransom Center. The University of Texas at Austin.

The Lyndhurst Foundation Records, 1970–2000, #04723, in the Southern Historical Collection.

The Louis Round Wilson Special Collections Library, The University of North Carolina at Chapel Hill.

The Woolmer Collection of Cormac McCarthy, The Wittliff Collections, Southwestern Writers Collection, Alkek Library, Texas State University-San Marcos.

Other materials

Agner, Jacob, 'Salvaging *The Counselor*: Watching Cormac McCarthy and Ridley Scott's Really Trashy Movie.' *The Cormac McCarthy Journal*, vol. 14, iss. 2 (2016), 204–226. 10.5325/cormmccaj.14.2.0204.

Amin, Samir, 'Exiting the Crisis of Capitalism or Capitalism in Crisis?' *Globalizations*, vol. 7, iss. 1–2 (March–June 2010), 261–273. 10.1080/14747731003593703.

Appadurai, Arjun, *Modernity at Large: Cultural Dimensions of Globalization* (University of Minnesota Press, 1996).

Arendt, Hannah, *The Human Condition* (University of Chicago Press, 1958).

Arnold, Edwin T., 'Cormac McCarthy's *The Stonemason*: The Unmaking of a Play.' *Southern Quarterly*, 33, iss. 2–3 (Winter–Spring 1995), 117–129.

Arnold, Edwin T. and Dianne C. Luce, 'Introduction.' *Perspectives on Cormac McCarthy*, rev. edn, eds. Edwin T. Arnold and Dianne C. Luce, Southern Quarterly Series (University Press of Mississippi, 1999), 1–16.

Aubry, Timothy, *Guilty Aesthetic Pleasures* (Harvard University Press, 2018).

Auerbach, Erich, *Mimesis: The Representation of Reality in Western Literature*, trans. Willard R. Trask (Princeton University Press, 2003).

Ballard, J. G., *A User's Guide to the Millennium: Essays and Reviews* (Picador, 1996).

Bannon, Brad, 'Divinations of Agency in Blood Meridian and No Country for Old Men.' *The Cormac McCarthy Journal*, vol. 14, iss. 1 (2016), 78–95. 10.5325/cormmccaj.14.1.0078.

Bannon, Brad, and John Vanderheide, eds., *Cormac McCarthy's Violent Destinies* (University of Tennessee Press, 2018).

Bell, Vereen M., *The Achievement of Cormac McCarthy* (Louisiana State University Press, 1988).

Bennett, Barbara, 'Celtic Influences on Cormac McCarthy's *No Country for Old Men* and *The Road*.' *Notes on Contemporary Literature*, vol. 38, iss. 5 (November 2008), 2–3.

Bentham, Jeremy, *An Introduction to the Principles of Morals and Legislation*. Dover Philosophical Classics (Dover Publications, 2007).

Bingham, Arthur, 'Syntactic Complexity and Iconicity in Cormac McCarthy's *Blood Meridian*.' *Language and Literature*, vol. 20 (1995), 19–133.

Biron, Rebecca, 'It's a Living: Hit Men in the Mexican Narco War.' *PMLA*, vol. 127, iss. 4 (2012), 820–834.

Blinman, Eric, '2000 Years of Cultural Adaptation to Climate Change in the Southwestern United States.' *Ambio*, Special Report no. 14. Royal Colloquium 'Past Climate Change: Human Survival Strategies' (November 2008), 489–497.

'*Blood Meridian* by Cormac McCarthy.' *Kirkus Reviews*, February 15, 1985. Accessed January 27, 2018. https://www.kirkusreviews.com/book-reviews/cormac-mccarthy/blood-meridian/.

Bloom, Harold, 'Introduction.' *Cormac McCarthy*, new edn, ed. Harold Bloom. Bloom's Literary Criticism (Chelsea House Publications, 2009), 1–8.

Blumenson, Eric, and Eva Nilson, 'Policing for Profit: The Drug War's Hidden Economic Agenda.' *The University of Chicago Law Review*, vol. 65, iss. 1 (Winter 1998), 35–114.

Borrell, Brendan, 'Why Do Whales Beach Themselves?' *Scientific American*, Sustainability, 1 June 2009. Accessed September 1, 2018. https://www.scientificamerican.com/article/why-do-whales-beach-themselves/.

Botticini, Maristella, 'A Tale of "Benevolent" Governments: Private Credit Markets, Public Finance, and the Role of Jewish Lenders in Medieval and Renaissance Italy.' *The Journal of Economic History*, vol. 60, iss. 1 (March 2000), 164–189.

Bowers, James, *Reading Cormac McCarthy's* Blood Meridian (Boise State University Press, 1999).

Bradshaw, Peter, 'The Counselor: Review.' *Guardian*, November 14, 2013. Accessed March 16, 2018. https://www.theguardian.com/film/2013/nov/14/the-counsellor-review.

Braidotti, Rosi, *Nomadic Subjects: Embodiment and Sexual Difference in Contemporary Feminist Theory* (Columbia University Press, 2011).

Brickman, Barbara, 'Imposition and Resistance in *The Orchard Keeper*.' *Myth, Legend, Dust: Critical Responses to Cormac McCarthy*, ed. Rick Wallach (Manchester University Press, 2000), 55–67.

Brinig, Margaret, 'Rings and Promises.' *Journal of Law, Economics, and Organization*, vol. 6, iss. 1 (Spring 1990), 203–215.

Brown, Fred, 'Cormac McCarthy: On the Trail of a Legend.' *Knoxville News Sentinel*, December 16,2007. Accessed June 22, 2018. http://archive.knoxnews.com/news/local/cormacmccarthy-on-the trail-of-a-legend-ep-412332474-360064991.html/.

'Burin, n.' *Oxford English Dictionary*, Oxford University Press, 2021. Accessed January 26, 2021. www.oed.com/view/Entry/24978.

Burton, Orville Vernon, *In My Father's House Are Many Mansions: Family and Community in Edgefield, South Carolina*, Fred W. Morrison Series in Southern Studies (University of North Carolina Press, 1987).

Butler, Judith, *Excitable Speech: A Politics of the Performative* (Routledge, 1997).

Button Pritchard, Rebecca, *Sensing the Spirit: The Holy Spirit in Feminist Perspective* (Chalice Press, 1999).

Cairns, David, and Shaun Richards, *Writing Ireland: Colonialism, Nationalism, and Culture* (St. Martin's Press, 1988).

Campbell, James R. '"Seeking Evidence of the Hand of God in the World": Transforming Destruction in *The Crossing*.' *Proceedings of the 2nd Annual International Conference on the Emerging Literature of the Southwest Culture*, privately distributed (University of Texas at El Paso, 1996), 13–17.

Campbell, Joseph, *The Hero with a Thousand Faces*, 3rd edn (New World Library, 2008).

Campbell, Lyle, and William J. Poser, *Language Classification: History and Method* (Cambridge University Press, 2008).

Charles, Ron, 'Apocalypse Now.' *Washington Post*, October 1, 2006. Accessed January 23, 2021.www.washingtonpost.com/wp-dyn/content/article/2006/09/28/AR2006092801460.html.

Chollier, Christine, '"I ain't come back rich, that's for sure," or the Questioning of Market Economies in Cormac McCarthy's Novels.'

Myth, Legend, Dust: Critical Responses to Cormac McCarthy, ed. Rick Wallach (Manchester University Press, 2000), 171–177.

Christie, James William, '"Days of begging, days of theft": The Philosophy of Work in *Blood Meridian*.' *The Cormac McCarthy Journal*, vol. 14, iss. 1 (2016), 55–77.

Clarke, Michael Tavel, 'The New Naturalism: Cormac McCarthy, Frank Norris, and the Question of Postmodernism.' *Studies in American Naturalism*, vol. 9, iss. 1 (2014), 52–78.

Condorelli, Rosalia, 'Social Complexity, Modernity and Suicide: An Assessment of Durkheim's Suicide from the Perspective of a Non-Linear Analysis of Complex Social Systems.' *SpringerPlus*, vol. 5 (2016), 374–430.

Cooper, Lydia R., 'Barracuda: Cars and Trucks in Cormac McCarthy's Fiction.' *Southwestern American Literature*, vol. 41, iss. 2 (Spring 2016), 7–18.

— 'Cormac McCarthy, Tennessee, and the Southern Gothic,' in *The Cambridge Companion to Cormac McCarthy*, ed. Steven Frye (Cambridge University Press, 2013), 41–53.

— '"A Howling void": Beckett's Influence in McCarthy's *The Sunset Limited*.' *The Cormac McCarthy Journal*, vol. 10, iss. 1 (2012), 1–15.

— 'Inside "La Periquera": Prisons and Power in *All the Pretty Horses*.' *Beyond Borders: Cormac McCarthy's* All the Pretty Horses, ed. Rick Wallach, Casebook Studies in Cormac McCarthy, vol. 3 (The Cormac McCarthy Society, 2014), 251–263.

— *Masculinities in Literature of the American West* (Palgrave Macmillan, 2016).

— *No More Heroes: Narrative Perspective and Morality in Cormac McCarthy* (Louisiana State University Press, 2011).

— '"The Sculptor's art": Mystery and the Material Body in *Suttree*.' *You Would Not Believe What Watches:* Suttree *and Cormac McCarthy's Knoxville*, ed. Rick Wallach, Casebook Studies in Cormac McCarthy, vol. 1 (The Cormac McCarthy Society, 2012), 190–197.

Connell, R. W., and James W. Messerschmidt, 'Hegemonic Masculinity: Rethinking the Concept.' *Gender & Society*, vol. 19, iss. 6 (December 2005), 829–859. 10.1177/0891243205278639.

Cornwall, Gareth, 'Ambivalent National Epic: Cormac McCarthy's *Blood Meridian*.' *Critique: Studies in Contemporary Fiction*, vol. 56, iss. 5 (2015), 531–554. 10.1080/00111619.2015.1019393/.

Corva, Dominic, 'Neoliberal Globalization and the War on Drugs: Transnationalizing Illiberal Governance in the Americas.' *Political Geography*, vol. 27 (2008), 176–193. 10.1016/j.polgeo.2007.07.008.

Crews, Michael Lynn, *Books are Made out of Books: A Guide to Cormac McCarthy's Literary Influences* (University of Texas Press, 2017).

Dai, Rongqing, 'Chaotic Order: A Consequence of Economic Relativity.' *Complexity in Economics: Cutting Edge Research*, eds. Marisa Faggini and Anna Parziale (Springer International Publishing, 2014), 117–135. 10.1088/1674-1056/19/11/110509.

Danta, Chris, '"The Cold illucid world": The Poetics of Gray in Cormac McCarthy's The Road.' *Styles of Extinction: Cormac McCarthy's The Road*, eds. Julian Murphet and Mark Steven (Continuum International, 2012), 9–26.

Dargis, Manohla, 'Wildlife is Tame; Not the Humans: "The Counselor," a Cormac McCarthy Tale of Mostly Evil.' *New York Times*, October 24, 2013. Accessed March 16, 2018. www.nytimes.com/2013/10/25/movies/the-counselor-a-cormac-mccarthy-tale-of-mostly-evil.html.

Daugherty, Leo, 'Gravers False and True: Blood Meridian as Gnostic Tragedy.' *Perspectives on Cormac McCarthy*, rev. edn, eds. Edwin T. Arnold and Dianne C. Luce (University Press of Mississippi, 1999), 159–174.

Deacon, David, '"Some Unholy Alloy": Neoliberalism, Digital Modernity, and the Mechanics of Globalized Capital in Cormac McCarthy's *The Counselor*.' *European Journal of American Studies*, vol. 12, iss. 3 (2017), 1–16. 10.4000/ejas/12364.

Dobson, Andy P., 'Yellowstone Wolves and the Forces that Structure Natural Systems.' *Plos Biology*, vol. 12, iss. 12 (December 2014), 1–4. 10.1371/journal.pbio.1002025.

Dominy, Jordan, 'Cannibalism, Consumerism, and Profanation: Cormac McCarthy's *The Road* and the End of Capitalism.' *The Cormac McCarthy Journal*, vol. 13, iss. 1 (2015), 143–158.

Donoghue, Denis, 'Teaching Literature: The Force of Form.' *New Literary History: A Journal of Theory and Interpretation*, vol. 30, iss. 1 (Winter 1999), 5–24.

Doumas, C., 'What did the Argonauts Seek in Colchis?' *Hermathena*, no. 150 (Summer 1991), 31–41.

Dudley, John, 'McCarthy's Heroes: Revisiting Masculinity.' *The Cambridge Companion to Cormac McCarthy*, ed. Steven Frye (Cambridge University Press, 2013), 175–187.

Eagleton, Terry, *Heathcliff and the Great Hunger*, Studies in Irish Culture (Verso, 1995).

'Early History of the San Francisco Fire Department.' *The Virtual Museum of the City of San Francisco*, Municipal Record, City and Council of San Francisco, 2017. Accessed January 22, 2018. www.sfmuseum.net/hist1/fire.html.

Eaton, Mark A., 'Dis(re)membered Bodies: Cormac McCarthy's Border Fiction.' *Modern Fiction Studies*, vol. 49, iss. 1 (Spring 2003), 155–179.

Edwards, Justin D., *Gothic Passages: Racial Ambiguity and the American Gothic* (University of Iowa Press, 2003).
Ellis, Jay, *No Place for Home: Spatial Constraint and Character Flight in the Novels of Cormac McCarthy* (Routledge, 2006).
Elmore, Jonathan, and Rick Elmore, 'Human Become Coin: Neoliberalism, Anthropology, and Human Possibilities in *No Country for Old Men*.' *The Cormac McCarthy Journal*, vol. 14, iss. 2 (2016), 168–185.
Elsner, Wolfram, 'Complexity Economics as Heterodoxy: Theory and Policy.' *Journal of Economic Issues*, vol. 51, iss. 4 (December 2017), 939–978. 10.1080/00213624.2017.1391570.
Fiedler, Leslie, *Love and Death in the American Novel* (Dalkey Archive Press, 1966).
Fisher, Mark. *Capitalist Realism: Is There No Alternative?* (Zero Books, 2009).
Fitzgerald, John, 'Illegal Drug Markets in Transitional Economies.' *Addiction Research and Theory*, vol. 13, iss. 6 (2005), 563–577.
Franklin, Seb, 'Virality, Informatics, and Critique: Or, Can There Be Such a Thing as Radical Computation?' *Women's Studies Quarterly*, vol. 40, iss.1–2 (Spring–Summer 2012), 153–170.
Frye, Steven, '*Blood Meridian* and the Poetics of Violence.' *The Cambridge Companion to Cormac McCarthy*, ed. Steven Frye (Cambridge University Press, 2013), 107–120.
— *Understanding Cormac McCarthy* (University of South Carolina Press, 2009).
— 'Yeats' "Sailing to Byzantium" and McCarthy's *No Country for Old Men*: Art and Artifice in the New Novel.' *The Cormac McCarthy Journal*, vol. 5, iss. 1 (2006), 27–41.
Gallagher, Catherine, 'The History of Literary Criticism.' *Daedalus*, vol. 126, iss. 1 (Winter 1997), 133–153.
Gell-Mann, Murray, *The Quark and the Jaguar: Adventures in the Simple and the Complex* (W. H. Freeman and Co., 1994).
Gell-Mann, Murray, and Merritt Ruhlen, 'The Origin and Evolution of Word Order.' *Proceedings of the National Academy of Sciences of the United States of America*, vol. 108, iss. 42 (2011), 17290–17295.
Giemza, Bryan, *Irish Catholic Writers and the Invention of the American South* (Louisiana State University Press, 2013).
Gleick, James, *Chaos: Making a New Science.* 20th Anniversary Edition (Penguin Books, 2008).
'God-Fire, n.' *Oxford English Dictionary*, Oxford University Press, 2018. Accessed June 8, 2018. www.oed.com/view/Entry/79625.
Gross, Louis S., *Redefining the American Gothic from* Wieland *to* Day of the Dead (University of Michigan Research Press, 1989).
Halberstam, Jack, *Female Masculinity* (Duke University Press, 1998).

Hansen, Tom, 'Frost's "Fire and Ice."' *The Explicator*, vol. 59, iss. 1 (2000), 27–30.

Haraway, Donna J., *When Species Meet* (University of Minnesota Press, 2008).

Hartigan-O'Connor, Ellen, 'Gender's Value in the History of Capitalism.' *Journal of the Early Republic*, vol. 36 (Winter 2016), 613–635.

Harvey, David, *The New Imperialism* (Oxford University Press, 2003).

Hawkins, Ty, *Cormac McCarthy's Philosophy*, American Literature Readings in the 21st Century (Palgrave Macmillan, 2017).

Hillier, Russell M., *Morality in Cormac McCarthy's Fiction: Souls at Hazard* (Palgrave Macmillan, 2016).

Hofmeester, Karin, 'Shifting Trajectories of Diamond Processing: From India to Europe and Back, from the Fifteenth Century to the Twentieth.' *Journal of Global History*, vol. 8, iss. 1 (2013), 25–49.

Holloway, David, *The Late Modernism of Cormac McCarthy* (Greenwood Press, 2002).

Hopkins, A. G., *American Empire: A Global History* (Princeton University Press, 2018).

Iser, Wolfgang, 'The Reading Process: A Phenomenological Approach.' *New Literary History*, vol. 3, iss. 2, *On Interpretation: I* (Winter 1992), 279–299. 10.2307/468316.

Jergenson, Casey, '"In what direction did lost men veer?" Late Capitalism and Utopia in *The Road*.' *The Cormac McCarthy Journal*, vol. 14, iss. 1 (2016), 117–132.

John Paul II, Pope, 'Easter Vigil: Homily of Pope John Paul II,' March 29, 1997. *Vatican*. Accessed March 30, 2018. http://w2.vatican.va/content/john-paul-ii/en/homilies/1997/documents/hf_jp-ii_hom_29031997.html.

Josyph, Peter, *Adventures in Reading Cormac McCarthy* (Scarecrow Press, 2010).

Jurgensen, John, 'Hollywood's Favorite Cowboy.' *Wall Street Journal*, Arts & Entertainment, November 20, 2009.

Kayser, Wolfgang, *The Grotesque in Art and Literature*, trans. Ulrich Weisstein (Peter Smith, 1968).

Keane, Patrick J., *Terrible Beauty: Yeats, Joyce, Ireland, and the Myth of the Devouring Female* (University of Missouri Press, 1988).

Kimmel, Michael S., 'Globalization and Its Mal(e)contents: The Gendered Moral and Political Economy of Terrorism.' *Handbook of Studies on Men and Masculinity*, eds. Michael S. Kimmel, Jeff Hearn, and R. W. Connell (Sage Publications, 2005), 414–431.

— *Manhood in America: A Cultural History*, 2nd edn (New York: Oxford University Press, 2006).

King, Edward, *The Southern State of North America: A Record of Journeys* (Blackie and Son, 1874).

King James Version Bible, 1611 version (Oxford University Press, 2010).
Knepper, Steven Edward, 'The Counselor and Tragic Recognition,' *The Cormac McCarthy Journal*, vol. 14, iss. 1 (2016), 37–54.
Kollin, Susan, '"Barren, Silent, Godless": Ecodisaster and the Post-Abundant Landscape in *The Road*.' *Cormac McCarthy: All the Pretty Horses, No Country for Old Men, The Road*, ed. Sara Spurgeon (Continuum, 2011), 157–171.
Kolodny, Annette, *The Lay of the Land: Metaphor as Experience and History in American Life and Letters* (University of North Carolina Press, 1975).
Kushner, David, 'Cormac McCarthy's Apocalypse.' *Rolling Stone*, December 27, 2007. Accessed July 1, 2009. http.//members.authorsguild.net/dkushner/work3.htm.
LeMenager, Stephanie, 'Climate Change and the Struggle for Genre.' *Anthropocene Reading: Literary History in Geologic Times*, eds. Tobias Menely and Jesse Oak Taylor (Pennsylvania State University Press, 2017), 220–238.
Leopold, Aldo, *Round River: From the Journals of Aldo Leopold*, ed. Luna P. Leopold, illustrated by Charles W. Schwartz (Oxford University Press, 1993, orig. 1953).
Levin, Carl, and Tom Coburn, 'Wall Street and the Financial Crisis: Anatomy of a Financial Collapse.' Majority and Minority Staff Report, Permanent Subcommittee on Investigations, US Senate, April 13, 2011.
Lincoln, Kenneth, *Cormac McCarthy: American Canticles* (Palgrave Macmillan, 2008).
'Long-Term Trends in Deaths of Despair.' Social Capital Project Report no. 4–19, Joint Economic Committee—Republicans, September 2019. Accessed January 23, 2021. https://www.jec.senate.gov/public/_cache/files/0f2d3dba-9fdc-41e5-9bd1-9c13f4204e35/jec-report-deaths-of-despair.pdf.
Lorde, Audre, *Sister Outsider: Essays and Speeches* (Crossing Press, 2007).
'Los Hermanos Penitentes: History of the Penitent Brothers.' *World History Online*, American History, August 11, 2017. Accessed September 1, 2018. https://worldhistory.us/american-history/los-hermanos-penitentes-history-of-the-penitent-brothers.php.
Luce, Dianne C., 'Beyond the *Border*: Cormac McCarthy in the New Millenium.' *The Cormac McCarthy Journal*, vol. 6, iss. 1 (2008), 6–12.
— 'Cormac McCarthy's First Screenplay: *The Gardener's Son*.' *Perspectives on Cormac McCarthy*, rev. edn, eds. Edwin T. Arnold and Dianne C. Luce (University Press of Mississippi, 1999), 71–96.
— 'Landscapes as Narrative Commentary in Cormac McCarthy's *Blood Meridian: Or, the Evening Redness in the West*.' *European Journal of American Studies*, vol. 12, iss. 3 (2017), 1–24. 10.4000/ejas.12259.

— *Reading the World: Cormac McCarthy's Tennessee Period*, University of South Carolina Press, 2009).
— 'The Road and the Matrix: The World as Tale in *The Crossing*.' *Perspectives on Cormac McCarthy*, rev. edn, eds. Edwin T. Arnold and Dianne C. Luce (University Press of Mississippi, 1999), 195–220.
Madsen, Deborah L., *American Exceptionalism* (University Press of Mississippi, 1998).
Malewitz, Raymond, '"Anything can be an Instrument": Misuse Value and Rugged Consumerism in Cormac McCarthy's *No Country for Old Men*.' *Contemporary Literature*, vol. 50, iss. 4 (Winter 2009), 721–741.
— 'Narrative Disruption as Animal Agency in Cormac McCarthy's *The Crossing*.' *Modern Fiction Studies*, vol. 60, iss. 3 (Fall 2014), 544–561.
— 'Regeneration through Misuse: Rugged Consumerism in Contemporary American Culture.' *PMLA*, vol. 127, iss. 3 (May 2012), 719–720.
Mandel, Ernest, *Late Capitalism*, trans. Joris De Bres, 2nd edn (New Left Books, 1975).
Martinez, Jack, 'New Cormac McCarthy Book 'The Passenger' Unveiled.' *Newsweek*, Culture, August 15, 2015. Accessed July 1, 2019. https://www.newsweek.com/cormac-mccarthy-new-book-363027.
Marx, Leo, *The Machine in the Garden: Technology and the Pastoral Ideal in America*, 2nd edn (New York: Oxford University Press, 2000).
McCarthy, Cormac, *All the Pretty Horses* (Vintage International, 1993, orig. 1992).
— *Blood Meridian: Or, the Evening Redness in the West* (Vintage International, 1992, orig. 1985).
— *Child of God* (Vintage International, 1993, orig. 1974).
— *Cities of the Plain* (Vintage International, 1999, orig. 1998).
— 'Cormac McCarthy Returns to the Kekulé Problem: Answers to Questions and Questions that Cannot be Answered.' *Nautilus*, November 30, 2017. Accessed January 23, 2021. http://nautil.us/issue/54/the-unspoken/cormac-mccarthy-returns-to-the-kekul-problem.
— *The Counselor: A Screenplay* (Vintage International, 2013).
— *The Crossing* (Vintage International, 1995, orig. 1994).
— *The Gardener's Son* (Ecco, 2015, orig. 1996).
— 'The Kekulé Problem: Where Did Language Come From?' *Nautilus*, March–April 2017. Accessed January 23, 2021. http://nautil.us/issue/47/consciousness/the-kekul-problem.
— *No Country for Old Men* (Alfred A. Knopf, 2005).
— *The Orchard Keeper* (Vintage International, 1993, orig. 1965).
— *Outer Dark* (Vintage International, 1993, orig. 1968).
— *The Road* (Alfred A. Knopf, 2006).
— *The Stonemason: A Play in Five Acts* (Vintage International, 1994).

— *The Sunset Limited: A Novel in Dramatic Form* (Vintage International, 2006).
— *Suttree* (Vintage International, 1992, orig. 1979).
— *Whales and Men*. Cormac McCarthy Collection, The Wittliff Collections, Texas State University, 91.97.5, n.d.
McLaurin, Melton Alonzo, *Paternalism and Protest: Southern Cotton Mill Workers and Organized Protest, 1875–1905* (Greenwood Publishing Co., 1971).
McNally, David, *Monsters of the Market: Zombies, Vampires and Global Capitalism* (Haymarket Books, 2011).
Menely, Tobias, and Jesse Oak Taylor, 'Introduction.' *Anthropocene Reading: Literary History in Geologic Times*, eds. Tobias Menely and Jesse Oak Taylor (Pennsylvania State University Press, 2017), 1–24.
Menely, Tobias, and Jesse Oak Taylor, eds., *Anthropocene Reading: Literary History in Geologic Times* (Pennsylvania State University Press, 2017).
Meyer, Stephen, 'Work, Play, and Power: Masculine Culture on the Automotive Shop Floor, 1930–1960.' *Boys and Their Toys? Masculinity, Class, and Technology in America*, ed. Roger Horowitz (Routledge, 2001), 13–32.
Miller, Tony, 'On the Road with Cormac McCarthy.' *Tony Miller BSC Director of Photography*. Accessed March 30, 2018. www.tonymillerdp.com/on-the-road-with-cormac-mccarthy/.
Mitchell, Lee Clark, *Mere Reading: The Poetics of Wonder in Modern American Novels* (Bloomsbury Academic, 2017).
Monbiot, George, 'Civilization Ends with a Shutdown of Human Concern: Are We There Already?' *Guardian*, Books: Opinion, October 29, 2007. Accessed March 30, 2018. https://www.theguardian.com/commentisfree/2007/oct/30/comment.books.
Monk, Nicholas, '"An Impulse to Action, an Undefined Want": Modernity, Flight, and Crisis in the Border Trilogy and *Blood Meridian*,' *Sacred Violence*, vol. 2, 2nd edn, eds. Wade Hall and Rick Wallach (Texas Western Press, 2002), 83–104.
— '"News from another world": Career and Critical Responses to Cormac McCarthy.' *Literature Compass*, vol. 10, iss. 2 (2013), 111–121.
Montague, Kate, 'Baroque Meridians: Between Myth and Actuality on the American Frontier.' *Cormac McCarthy's Borders and Landscapes*, ed. Louise Jillett (Bloomsbury Academic, 2016), 95–106.
Morgan, Wesley G., 'The Route and Roots of *The Road*.' Adapted from a paper presented at 'The Road Home: Cormac McCarthy's Imaginative Return to the South,' Knoxville, TN, April 26, 2007.
— 'Suttree's Dead Acquaintances and McCarthy's Dead Friends.' *Cormac McCarthy Journal*, vol. 11, iss. 1 (2013), 96–104.

Morgenstern, Naomi, 'Postapocalyptic Responsibility: Patriarchy at the End of the World in Cormac McCarthy's *The Road*.' *Differences*, vol. 25, iss. 2 (2014), 33–61. 10.1215/10407391-2773427.

Moynahan, Julian, *Anglo-Irish: The Literary Imagination in a Hyphenated Culture* (Princeton University Press, 1995).

Mundik, Petra, *A Bloody and Barbarous God: The Metaphysics of Cormac McCarthy* (University of New Mexico Press, 2016).

Nelson, Bryan, 'Humpback Whales around the Globe are Mysteriously Rescuing Animals from Orcas.' *Mother Nature Network*, July 30, 2016. Accessed January 27, 2018. https://www.mnn.com/earth-matters/animals/stories/humpback-whales-around-globe-are-mysteriously-rescuing-animals-orcas.

Nolan, Peter, *Capitalism and Freedom: The Contradictory Character of Globalisation* (Anthem Press, 2007).

Ó Tuathail, Gearóid (Gerard Toal), 'Problematizing Geopolitics: Survey, Statesmanship and Strategy.' *Transactions of the Institute of British Geographers*, vol. 19, iss. 3 (1994), 259–272. 10.2307/622322.

Palish, Alyssa, 'The Moment of Choice: Cormac McCarthy's "The Counselor."' *Los Angeles Review of Books*, November 2, 2013. Accessed January 23, 2021.https://lareviewofbooks.org/article/on-cormac-mccarthys-the-counselor/.

Palmer, Louis H. III., '"Encampment of the damned": Ideology and Class in *Suttree*.' *The Cormac McCarthy Journal*, vol. 4, iss. 1 (2004), 183–209.

Peebles, Stacey, *Page, Stage, Screen: Cormac McCarthy and Performance* (University of Texas Press, 2017).

Piketty, Thomas, *Capital in the Twenty-First Century*, trans. Arthur Goldhammer (Belknap Press of Harvard University Press, 2017).

Potts, James, 'McCarthy, Mac Airt, and Mythology: *Suttree* and the Irish High King.' *Mississippi Quarterly*, vol. 58, iss.1–2 (2004), 25–40.

Potts, Matthew, '"Their Ragged Biblical Forms": Materiality, Misogyny, and the Corporal Works of Mercy in *Suttree*.' *Religion and Literature*, vol. 47, iss. 2 (2015), 65–86.

Prescott, Orville, 'The Orchard Keeper.' *New York Times*, May 12, 1965. Accessed November 1, 2018. www.nytimes.com/1965/05/12/books/mccarthy-orchard.html.

Propp, Vladimir, *Theory and History of Folklore*, trans. Ariadna Y. Martin and Richard P. Martin, ed. Anatoly Liberman (University of Minnesota Press, 1984).

Quirk, William, '"Minimalist Tragedy": Nietzschean Thought in McCarthy's *The Sunset Limited*.' *The Cormac McCarthy Journal*, vol. 8, iss. 1 (2010), 29–46.

Ranney, Larry W., 'Colt 'Peacemakers' and '94 Winchesters: The Relationship to Climactic Narrative Rhythm and Character Delineation in the American Western.' *The Image of the Frontier in Literature, the Media, and Society: Selected Papers of the 1997 Conference of the Society for the Interdisciplinary Study of Social Imagery*, eds. Will Wright and Steven Kaplan (University of Southern Colorado, 1997), 129–133.

Richman, Barak D., 'Community Enforcement of Informal Contracts: Jewish Diamond Merchants in New York.' Harvard Law School, Discussion Paper no. 384 (September 2002), 1–57.

Robison, John Mark, 'The Authority of Currency in Cormac McCarthy's *Blood Meridian*.' *The Cormac McCarthy Journal*, vol. 15, iss. 1 (2017), 30–45.

Rocca, Alexander, '"I don't feel like a genius": David Foster Wallace, Trickle-Down Aesthetics, and the MacArthur Foundation.' *Arizona Quarterly*, vol. 73, iss. 1 (Spring 2017), 85–111. 10.1353/arq.2017.0003.

Ross, Robert J. S., and Kent C. Trachte, *Global Capitalism: The New Leviathan* (SUNY Press, 1990).

Roy, Arundhati, 'The New American Century.' *The Nation*, February 9, 2004, 11–14.

Sanborn, Wallis R., *Animals in the Fiction of Cormac McCarthy* (McFarland & Co., 2006).

Sandoval, Chela, *Methodology of the Oppressed*, Theory Out of Bounds, vol. 18 (University of Minnesota Press, 2000).

Santa Fe Institute, 2016. Accessed August 22, 2018. https://www.santafe.edu/.

Scarry, Elaine, *The Body in Pain: The Making and Unmaking of the World* (Oxford University Press, 1985).

— *On Beauty and Being Just* (Princeton University Press, 1999).

Schoonmaker, Sara, 'Globalization from Below: Free Software and Alternatives to Neoliberalism.' *Development & Change*, vol. 38, iss. 6 (November 2007), 999–1020. 10.1111/j.1467-7660.2007.00462.x.

Sepich, John Emil, 'The Dance of History in Cormac McCarthy's *Blood Meridian*.' *The Southern Literary Journal*, vol. 24, iss. 1 (1991), 16–31.

Shakespeare, William, *Hamlet*, The Riverside Shakespeare, 2nd edn (Houghton Mifflin, 1973).

Shaku, Soyen, *Sermans of a Buddhist Abbot: Addresses on Religious Subjects*, trans. Deisetz Teitaro Suzuki (Open Court Publishing, 1906).

Shaviro, Steven, '"The Very Life of the Darkness": A Reading of *Blood Meridian*.' *Perspectives on Cormac McCarthy*, eds. Edwin T. Arnold and Dianne C. Luce, Southern Quarterly Series (University Press of Mississippi, 1999), 145–158.

Shelton, Frank W., '*Suttree* and Suicide.' *Southern Quarterly*, vol. 29, iss. 1 (Fall 1990), 71–83.

Sinykin, Dan, 'Evening in America: *Blood Meridian* and the Origins and Ends of Imperial Capitalism.' *American Literary History*, vol. 28, iss. 2 (Summer 2016), 362–380. 10.1093/alh/ajw006.

Smith, Henry Nash, *Virgin Land: The American West as Symbol and Myth* (Harvard University Press, 1978).

Sombart, Werner, *The Jews and Modern Capitalism*, trans. M. Epstein (E. P. Dutton & Co., 1913).

Spurgeon, Sara, *Exploding the Empire: Myths of Empire on the Postmodern Frontier* (Texas A&M University Press, 2005).

Steinlight, Emily, *Populating the Novel: Literary Form and the Politics of Surplus Life*. Cornell University Press, 2018).

Sullivan, Nell, 'The Dead Girlfriend Motif in *Outer Dark* and *Child of God*.' *Myth, Legend, Dust: Critical Responses to Cormac McCarthy*, ed. Rick Wallach (Manchester University Press, 2000), 68–77.

— 'The Good Guys: McCarthy's *The Road* as Post-9/11 Male Sentimental Novel.' *Genre*, vol. 46, iss. 1 (Spring 2013), 79–101. 10.12 15/00166928-1907409.

Tatum, Stephen, '"Mercantile ethics": *No Country for Old Men* and the Narcocorrido,' *Cormac McCarthy: All the Pretty Horses, No Country for Old Men, The Road*, ed. Sara Spurgeon (Continuum, 2011), 77–93.

Taylor, Helen, 'The South and Britain,' *South to a New Place: Region, Literature, and Culture*, ed. Suzanne W. Jones and Sharon Monteith (Louisiana State University Press, 2002), 340–362.

Thiess, Derek, 'On *The Road* to Santa Fe: Complexity in Cormac McCarthy and Climate Change.' *Interdisciplinary Studies in Literature and the Environment*, vol. 20, iss. 3 (Summer 2013), 432–552.

Turner, Frederick Jackson, *The Frontier in American History* (Henry Holt and Co., 1962).

'Use It or Lose It: The Outside Effect of U.S. Consumption on the Environment.' '*Scientific American*, EarthTalk, 2016. Accessed January 23, 2021. https://www.scientificamerican.com/article/american-consumption-habits/.

Vanderheide, John, 'Varieties of Renunciation in the Works of Cormac McCarthy.' *The Cormac McCarthy Journal*, vol. 5, iss. 1 (2005), 30–35.

Wallach, Rick, 'Judge Holden, *Blood Meridian*'s Evil Archon.' *Sacred Violence*, vol. 2, 2nd edn, eds. Wade Hall and Rick Wallach (Texas Western Press, 2002), 1–14.

Warner, Alan, 'The Road to Hell.' *Guardian*, November 4, 2006. Accessed January 23, 2021. https://www.theguardian.com/books/2006/nov/04/featuresreviews.guardianreview4.

Watson, Patty Jo, Mary C. Kennedy, P. Willey, Louise M. Robbins, and Ronald C. Wilson, 'Prehistoric Footprints in Jaguar Cave,

Tennessee.' *Journal of Field Archeology*, vol. 30, iss. 1 (2005), 25–43. 10.1179/009346905791072440.

West, Nathanial, *Day of the Locust*, Penguin Classics (Penguin, 2000, orig. pub. Buccaneer, 1939).

'White Sands National Monument, New Mexico: History and Culture.' *National Park Service*, December 14, 2015. Accessed June 1, 2018. https://www.nps.gov/whsa/learn/historyculture/index.htm.

Williams, David, '*Blood Meridian* and Classical Greek Thought.' *Intertextual and Interdisciplinary Approaches to Cormac McCarthy: Borders and Crossings*, ed. Nicholas Monk (Routledge, 2012), 6–23.

Williams, Don, 'Annie DeLisle: Cormac McCarthy's ex-wife prefers to recall the romance.' *Knoxville News-Sentinel*, June 10, 1990, E1–E2. The Cormac McCarthy Papers, collection 92, box 5, file 1.

'William Anson.' *American Quarter Horse Association*, AQHA Hall of Fame. Accessed May 31, 2018. https://www.aqha.com/museum/hall-of-fame/people/a/william-anson/.

Winfrey, Oprah, 'The Exclusive Interview Begins.' Interview with Cormac McCarthy. *Oprah's Book Club*, July 2007. Accessed January 23, 2021. http://www2.oprah.com/obc_classic/obc_main.jhtml.

Witek, Terri, 'Reeds and Hides: Cormac McCarthy's Domestic Spaces.' *The Southern Review*, vol. 30, iss. 1 (Winter 1994), 136–42.

Wood, Ellen Meiksins, *The Origin of Capitalism* (Monthly Review Press, 1999).

Wood, James, 'Red Planet: The Sanguinary Sublime of Cormac McCarthy.' *New Yorker*, July 25, 2005. Accessed January 27, 2018. https://www.newyorker.com/magazine/2005/07/25/red-planet.

Woodson, Linda, 'Mapping "The Road" in Post-Postmodernism.' *The Cormac McCarthy Journal*, vol. 6, special issue on *The Road* (2008), 87–97.

— '"You are the battleground": Materiality, Moral Responsibility, and Determinism in *No Country for Old Men*.' *The Cormac McCarthy Journal*, vol. 5, iss. 1 (2005), 5–26.

Woodward, Richard B., 'Cormac McCarthy's Venomous Fiction.' *New York Times*, April 19, 1992.

Wyllie, Irvin G., *The Self-Made Man in America: The Myth of Rags to Riches* (Free Press, 1966).

Yousaf, Nahem, 'A Southern Sheriff's Revenge: Bertrand Tavernier's *Coup de Torchon*,' *Translatlantic Exchanges: The American South in Europe, Europe in the American South*, eds. Richard Gray and Waldemar Zacharasiewicz (Austrian Academy of Sciences, 2007), 221–238.

Index

agency 78, 87–96, 177
  lack of 111, 113, 114, 124, 126, 175
Agner, Jacob 116, 129n.28
alienation 30n.27, 54–61 *passim*, 118, 119, 139, 161, 172, 174, 186, 197–209 *passim*, 211n.20
  see also suicide
All the Pretty Horses (*APH*) 19, 58–60, 161, 166, 167, 169, 172–176, 182, 183
Anglo-Irish literature 135, 136, 137, 138, 152n.7, 154n.15, 155n.19, 155n.20
  see also gothic
animals 52–61 *passim*, 87–96 *passim*, 129n.28, 163, 164, 166, 169–182 *passim*, 185, 197, 198
  see also horses; whales; wolves
Anthropocene 195
  see also Capitalocene
anti-Semitism *see* Jewish communities
Appadurai, Arjun 125
archetypes 9, 10, 11, 12, 147
Arendt, Hannah 5, 20, 21, 31n.46, 31n.47, 127n.12, 133
argonaut *see* wanderer, argonaut
art 18–24, 192, 193, 194, 200, 213, 214, 216n.2

Aubry, Timothy 15, 16
Auerbach, Erich 69, 76, 78, 79, 81, 90

Bannon, Brad 109
Bell, Vereen M. 70, 191
Bennett, Barbara 137, 150
Bentham, Jeremy 160
biblical *see* narrative, biblical mode
'Big House' 137, 138, 139, 141, 154n.13, 155n.20
Bingham, Arthur 87, 88
Biron, Rebecca 100, 102, 112, 113
Blinman, Eric 188n.23
Blood Meridian (*BM*) 10, 69–99, 132, 163, 190, 210n.8
Bloom, Harold 6
Bowers, James 71
Bradshaw, Peter 106
Braidotti, Rosi 158, 167, 168
Brickman, Barbara 137
Butler, Judith 14

Cairns, David 143
Campbell, James R. 68n.46
Campbell, Joseph 9, 11, 29n.26
cannibalism 65n.9, 133, 134, 140
capitalism 7, 39, 56, 101–125 *passim*, 160, 184
  capitalist realism *see* myths, capitalist realism
  global capitalism 115–126, 126n.5

capitalism (*cont.*)
  human cost 20, 56, 59, 60, 63,
    65n.9, 101, 103, 105, 114,
    115–126 *passim*, 153n.8,
    168, 172, 173
  late capitalism 62, 101, 102, 103,
    104, 105, 116, 126n.5, 160
  wealth 35, 36, 44, 52, 63, 85, 86,
    101, 123
Capitalocene 132
Chollier, Christine 18, 19
Christie, James William 20, 31n.45,
    83, 84
Clarke, Michael Tavel 18, 19, 109,
    110
class 46, 49, 135, 137, 138, 143,
    144, 152n.7, 154n.9, 200,
    201–209 *passim*, 212n.27
  yeoman middle class 135, 136,
    152n.7, 155n.19
climate fiction 195
'coca-colonization' 140, 141,
    155n.22
colonialism 80, 133–135, 138, 143,
    144, 167, 183, 184
commodification 52, 58, 59, 73, 86,
    101, 122, 125, 140, 172, 175
community 125, 168, 182, 186, 191,
    195–209 *passim*
  animal 169–182, 185, 198
  see also alienation; Jewish
    communities
complex systems 9, 12, 13, 17, 158,
    178, 179, 180, 181, 192, 203
  chaos 12, 145, 146, 163
  complex adaptive systems (CAS)
    39, 70, 198
  complexity economics 8, 38, 39
  see also fractals
Condorelli, Rosalia 198, 211n.20
Connell, R. W. 43
consumption 72, 102, 116, 119, 123,
    129n.28, 131n.41, 132–141
    passim, 153n.8, 154n.9, 208
  see also cannibalism

Cooper, Lydia R. 127n.11, 128n.20,
    128n.24, 153n.9, 211n.24,
    211n.25
Cornwall, Gareth 77
corrida, novelistic 107
corrido 186
Corva, Dominic 120
Counselor, The (Co) 38, 43, 62, 63,
    100–107, 115–126, 129n.26,
    129n.28, 130n.29, 216n.2
craftsmanship *see* labor,
    craftsmanship
Crews, Michael Lynn 31n.46, 73,
    159, 163, 209n.8
criminal justice system 105, 120,
    121, 127n.11
Crossing, The (Cr) 23, 57, 58,
    68n.46, 159, 161, 163,
    168–171 *passim*, 176–180,
    185, 186, 188n.12, 215
currency 85, 86, 93, 112
  coins 84, 85, 101, 110, 111, 112,
    114
  diamonds 101, 115, 118, 123
  digital 103, 122, 123
  human 84, 85, 86, 101, 123, 125,
    126

Dai, Rongqing 39
Danta, Chris 134
Dargis, Manohla 106
Daugherty, Leo 77, 81, 83
Deacon, David 116
deep knowledge 11, 159, 161, 164,
    165, 168, 177, 191, 206
disaster (human-made and natural)
    8, 58, 89, 141, 142, 143,
    144, 156n.26, 161, 181, 184,
    195
Dobson, Andy P. 177, 178
Dominy, Jordan 20
Donoghue, Denis 26
drug trade 101, 102, 103, 107–108,
    112, 115, 120, 121, 129n.26
  see also markets

Index

Eagleton, Terry 135, 139, 143, 154n.15, 155n.20
Eaton, Mark A. 71, 83, 185
economies *see* markets
Ellis, Jay 20
Elmore, Jonathan and Rick Elmore 19
emotion *see* pathos
epic mode *see* narrative
ethics 50, 54, 56–61, 62, 72, 74, 76, 87, 115–126 *passim*, 151, 158, 159, 167, 195–201
   chance 110–114
   communal 108, 109, 124, 132, 163–164, 184–185, 187, 191, 193, 199
   companion species 163, 164, 169–170
   complex system 159, 164
   ethos of care 146, 148, 149
   embodied ethics of care 192, 195, 201–209
   land use 182–187
   non-anthropocentric 52, 133, 158, 159, 168, 169–182 *passim*
   utilitarian 59, 75, 159, 160, 168, 171, 172, 174, 182
   see also cannibalism; suffering; suicide; violence

fear 10, 11, 94, 136, 148, 171, 202
Fiedler, Leslie 135
fire 10–11, 89, 90, 93, 190
   carrying the fire 150, 151, 209
   godfire 190, 191, 209n.2
   see also soul
Fisher, Mark 26, 103, 104, 160
Fitzgerald, John 102, 103
fractals 141–146 *passim*
Frye, Steven 71, 134, 137

Gallagher, Catherine 15
Gardener's Son, The (*TGS*) 37, 45–50, 54, 67n.37, 106, 212n.27
Gell-Mann, Murray 13, 29n.22

Giemza, Bryan 137
Gleick, James 1, 12, 27n.1, 145, 216n.2
gnosticism 71, 72, 81, 108, 201, 202, 211n.24, 212n.25
God *see* sacred, God
gothic 134, 142, 146, 147, 196, 202, 211n.25
   American southern 134, 136, 137, 153n.9, 154n.13, 211n.24
   Anglo-Irish 135, 136, 137, 138, 139, 149, 151, 153n.9, 154n.13, 155n.19
grief *see* pathos
Gross, Louis S. 154n.13

Halberstam, Jack 45
Hansen, Tom 156n.26
Haraway, Donna J. 170
Harvey, David 115, 119
Hawkins, Ty 20
healthcare 166, 188n.19, 207, 208, 212n.30
Hillier, Russell M. 72, 73, 104, 127n.11
Holloway, David 18, 19, 20
Hopkins, A. G. 69, 82
horses 50, 58–59, 62, 67n37, 91, 92, 172, 173, 174, 175, 176, 183

imagination 103, 125, 133, 147, 148, 151, 158, 160, 164, 165, 186, 191, 202, 210n.15
   imaginative community 194
   social imaginary 125
imperialism 75, 82, 83, 136, 140, 141, 144, 149, 152n.7, 160, 183, 184
industrialization 24, 42, 46, 47, 73, 74, 135, 158

Jergenson, Casey 20
Jewish communities 71, 115–119
Jung, Carl 9, 147
Jurgensen, John 71, 140

Kimmel, Michael S. 42
King James Version Bible 77, 95
Knepper, Steven Edward 104
Kollin, Susan 19
Kolodny, Annette 64n.6
Kushner, David 29n.20, 143, 197

labor 5, 20–22, 31n.47, 46, 49, 83–86, 101, 102, 110–113, 119–122, 126, 127n.12, 167–172 *passim*, 184
  craftsmanship 7, 21, 22, 23, 24, 83, 84, 85
  professionalism 105, 107–115, 126
  techne 21, 84
  work 20–23, 31n.47, 83, 133, 172
landscape 35, 64n.6, 87–96 *passim*, 142, 148, 177, 183, 188n.23, 191
language 9, 11–14, 23, 72, 84, 144, 161–167 *passim*, 171–173, 186, 187, 201
  evolutionary linguistics 9, 10
  logos 150, 151, 202
  narrative 11, 161
LeMenager, Stephanie 190, 195, 210n.15
Leopold, Aldo 159, 163
Lincoln, Kenneth 41
Lorde, Audre 14
Luce, Dianne C. 8, 34, 54, 68, 94, 106, 153n.8, 161, 169, 176, 203

machines 38, 47, 50, 52, 56, 60
  cars and trucks 38–45, 50–64, 143
Madsen, Deborah L. 82
Malewitz, Raymond 19, 20, 84, 101, 107, 171, 177, 179
Mandel, Ernest 35, 36, 101, 102, 126n.5
Manifest Destiny 70, 78, 81, 82, 86, 100, 144
mapping 135, 139, 143, 144, 161, 162, 180, 186

markets 7, 8, 20, 38, 39, 44, 85, 101–105, 107–126 *passim*, 126n.5, 160, 173, 197
  see also drug trade; Jewish communities
marriage 137, 173, 175
Marx, Leo 34, 35
masculinity 7, 35, 36, 38–50, 51–53, 61–64, 194, 200
  hegemonic masculinity 43, 44, 45, 63
Messerschmidt, James W. 43
Miller, Tony 132
Mitchell, Lee Clark 15, 16
Monbiot, George 1
Monk, Nicholas 83
Morgan, Wesley G. 156n.23, 196
Morgenstern, Naomi 63, 210n.15
Mundik, Petra 72, 81, 128n.19, 211n.24
myths 9, 11, 29n.26, 185
  American exceptionalism 82, 84, 144
  capitalist realism 26, 104, 116, 160
  cowboy 183
  Greek 79, 80
  national myths 82, 134, 143, 144, 185
  self-made man 34, 35, 37, 44, 45–50, 52, 60, 61, 64

narrative 8–18, 57, 90, 107, 116, 120, 133, 158, 160–165, 186, 191, 192, 199
  biblical mode 76–78, 86, 87–96 *passim*
  chiastic structure 203, 204
  cinematic 101, 106, 107, 110, 113, 114, 116, 117, 120
  complex system 12, 17
  epic mode 76, 77, 78–87 *passim*, 90, 93
  erasure 101, 115–126 *passim*

Index

story-telling 133, 150, 151, 158, 186
tragedy 104
nationalism 86, 102, 103, 115, 135, 137, 185, 186
American identity 34, 40, 42, 43, 70, 77, 78, 185
'other' 83, 115, 131, 137, 144, 148, 149, 152, 163, 164, 171, 185, 200
No Country for Old Men (NCOM) 10, 38, 40, 61, 62, 100–115, 125, 127n11, 137, 207, 208
nomadism 23, 24, 32n.50, 48, 49, 153n.8, 167, 168, 169, 172, 182–187, 200
  adaptive 168
  intellectual nomadism 167, 168, 180
  mimetic nomadism 207
  nomadic economics 167, 171–172, 186
nostalgia 38, 139, 141, 142, 143, 155n.20, 167, 183

Orchard Keeper, The (TOK) 10, 33, 34, 37, 50–57, 106, 137, 153n.8, 166
Ó Tuathail, Gearóid (Gerard Toal) 144

Palish, Alyssa 124
Palmer, Louis H. III 192, 194
pastoral 34, 35, 47, 142, 183
  complex 34, 35, 36, 37
  sentimental 34
pathos 12, 30n.27, 52, 90, 91, 111, 125, 164–168 *passim*, 176, 179, 180, 181
Peebles, Stacey 4, 47, 104, 106, 131n.41, 169, 212n.30
performative indigeneity 144, 156n.29
poet *see* art
Prescott, Orville 34

professionalism *see* labor, professionalism
property 32n.50, 44, 59, 93, 117–119, 152n.7, 159, 167, 168, 182–186
prophesy 55, 76, 89, 133, 146–151, 193

race 46, 47, 49, 85, 92, 93, 95, 111, 154n.14, 156n.29, 204, 205
  see also Jewish communities; slavery
Road, The (TR) 38, 43, 63, 64, 71, 132–151, 152n.7, 153n.8, 154n.9, 155n.20, 156n.26, 186, 201, 210n.15
Robison, John Mark 19, 84, 85
Rocca, Alexander 5, 6, 7

sacred 22–24, 79, 85, 149, 175, 211n.25
God 22, 23, 49, 72, 85, 89, 129n.28, 150, 151, 163, 164, 177, 202
Sanborn, Wallis R. 169, 170, 176, 177, 179
Santa Fe Institute 6, 8, 9, 10, 13, 29n.20, 197, 214
Scarry, Elaine 15, 158, 162–166, 171, 186
Sepich, John Emil 72
settlers *see* colonialism; wanderer, argonaut
Shaviro, Steven 3, 77
Shelton, Frank W. 196
Sinykin, Dan 20, 83
slavery 31n.47, 46, 47, 75, 85, 86, 127n.12, 133–136, 140, 141, 152n.7, 154n.9, 186
soul 38, 52, 58, 62, 65n.10, 94, 110, 162, 164, 167, 169–182 *passim*, 190–201 *passim*, 202, 203, 209n.8
Spurgeon, Sara 183, 184, 185

Stonemason: A Play in Five Acts, The (TS) 7, 21–24, 108, 128n.19
suffering 103, 111, 147, 159, 162–167, 169–182 *passim*, 187, 188n.19, 193
  animals 90–93, 169–182 *passim*
  mutilation 71, 81, 180–181, 196–197
  torture 165–167, 171
  witnessing of 92, 159, 168, 169, 172, 173, 181–182
  see also suicide
suicide 147, 194, 195–201 *passim*, 203, 204, 211n.20
  call to die 195, 196, 199, 200, 209, 210n.15
  deaths of despair 197, 198
Sullivan, Nell 210n.15
Sunset Limited: A Novel in Dramatic Form, The (TSL) 65n.9, 199–201
Suttree (S) 65n.9, 67n.37, 137, 138, 190–209, 209n.8, 211n.24, 212n.25
syntactic style 87–96 *passim*, 107, 145, 146, 178, 212n.29

Tatum, Stephen 19, 107
Taylor, Helen 154n.14
techne see labor, *techne*
technology 47, 75, 82, 103, 122, 123
  see also machines
Thiess, Derek 142
'thing theory' 84, 111, 164, 171, 172, 177
trickle-down aesthetics 6, 7

urbanization 42, 191, 192, 201, 207, 214
use, reciprocal 163–164, 170–172
use value *see* value, material

value
  humans 59, 65n.9, 84–86, 101, 108–109, 112, 115, 123, 160, 168, 173, 184, 200
  immaterial 21, 38, 49, 52, 62, 84, 95, 108–109, 119, 123, 164, 167, 168–182
  material 21, 36, 49–52, 59, 65n.9, 84–86, 101, 111–115, 119, 121–126 *passim*, 171–175, 182, 184
Vanderheide, John 109
violence 75, 79, 166
  human-made 71, 72, 75, 76, 88, 91–96, 110–114, 147, 148, 163, 171
  war 72–77, 78–87, 163
  natural violence 75, 76, 88–90, 94–96
  see also suffering

Wallach, Rick 18, 71, 84
wanderer 60, 77, 78, 81, 89, 93, 96, 149, 168, 185
  argonaut 79, 80
  pilgrim 60, 80, 81, 162
  vagrancy 193, 206
wandering signifier 141
whales 94, 96, 169, 170, 171, 198, 208
Winfrey, Oprah 3–5
witness 78, 87–96 *passim*, 159, 168–173 *passim*, 181–182
wolves 57, 58, 95–96, 159, 169, 176–181
Wood, Ellen Meiksins 100
Wood, James 77
Woodson, Linda 64
Woodward, Richard B. 2–4, 26, 77, 138
Wyllie, Irvin G. 33, 35, 45

Yousaf, Nahem 127n.11

EU authorised representative for GPSR:
Easy Access System Europe, Mustamäe tee 50,
10621 Tallinn, Estonia
gpsr.requests@easproject.com

www.ingramcontent.com/pod-product-compliance
Lightning Source LLC
Chambersburg PA
CBHW070343240426
43671CB00013BA/2393